SECRECY
AND
DEMOCRACY

SECRECY AND DEMOCRACY

The CIA in Transition

Admiral Stansfield Turner

Former Director of Central Intelligence

Harper & Row, Publishers
New York, Cambridge, Philadelphia, San Francisco
London, Mexico City, São Paulo, Singapore, Sydney

A hardcover edition of this book is published by Houghton Mifflin Company. It is here reprinted by arrangement with Houghton Mifflin Company.

SECRECY AND DEMOCRACY. Copyright © 1985 by Stansfield Turner. All rights reserved. Printed in the United States of America. No part of this book may be used or reproduced in any manner whatsoever without written permission except in the case of brief quotations embodied in critical articles and reviews. For information address Houghton Mifflin Company, One Beacon Street, Boston, MA 02108. Published simultaneously in Canada by Fitzhenry & Whiteside Limited, Toronto.

First PERENNIAL LIBRARY edition published 1986.

Library of Congress Cataloging-in-Publication Data
Turner, Stansfield, 1923–
    Secrecy and democracy.

    Includes bibliographical reference and index.
    1. United States. Central Intelligence Agency.
I. Title
JK468.I6T87   1986   327.1'2'0973   85-45666
ISBN 0-06-097025-1 (pbk.)

86 87 88 89 90 MPC 10 9 8 7 6 5 4 3 2 1

Contents

Acknowledgments

IN LATE NOVEMBER 1982 my close friend and frequent collaborator in writing, George Thibault, told me it was time to get on with the book on intelligence that he and I had been discussing for some time. I agreed, set aside some of the projects I was then working on, and allocated the next four months to turning out a book about the lessons I had learned as Director of Central Intelligence. A little more than twenty-four months later I submitted the final manuscript to the publisher! In that interim, George Thibault's advice, editing assistance, regular encouragement, and memory of events that had occurred when we were in the world of intelligence together were the difference between getting here and not.

During the last year of my writing the patient and sound coaching of Houghton Mifflin's editor-in-chief, Nan Talese, was invaluable. My son, Geoffrey, then a lieutenant commander in Naval Intelligence, made a major substantive contribution by reviewing the book in its various stages. Bob Woodward of the *Washington Post* was kind enough to read several drafts and to provide advice on the art of writing books.

Numerous other friends and associates read and commented most helpfully, and I am indeed indebted to them: John Koehler, John Waller, Rusty Williams, George Kalaris, Herb Hetu, David

Schoenbaum, Brian Thompson, John Keeley, Walt Elder, and Bill Brink. Bill Adler counseled me wisely, and patiently nurtured this book from its inception. Frances Apt edited the manuscript with wonderful skill and understanding and in the process gave me a marvelous lesson in grammar. My wife, Karin, provided invaluable advice and encouragement and helped in every aspect of writing this book from research to filing to typing to editing.

Anthony Lapham generously counseled on dealing with the CIA in obtaining the necessary security review of the book. That review stemmed from the agreement that CIA employees execute to submit their writings for security clearance. I estimate that between 10 and 15 percent of the time it took me to complete the book was spent in arranging with the CIA for its clearance. And Tony spent an inordinate amount of his time helping to argue my case. It was all most unreasonable and unnecessary.

SECRECY
AND
DEMOCRACY

Introduction

1985 has been called by some the "Year of the Spy." It was, indeed, a year in which there was an amazing number of exposures of intelligence operations, both in the United States and abroad. Some thirteen Americans were uncovered as spies for other countries, including two active and one former CIA official, the first FBI agent ever to be charged with espionage, one person charged with spying for China and another for Israel (not just the Soviet Union), and an extensive ring of individuals spying from inside the U.S. Navy. On the other side, three Soviet intelligence officers defected to the West, with one of those redefecting in bizarre circumstances. There was also a rash of West Germans defecting or attempting to defect to East Germany because of fear that their spying for the East had been revealed. And French intelligence bungled a "covert action" intended to deter peace activists from interfering with French nuclear testing in the South Pacific.

The immense amount of public attention devoted to these and other cases reinforces a key point of this book—that our intelligence activities cannot be put back under the cloak of near-total secrecy that existed in the thirty years immediately following World War II. The principal reason I wrote this book was to inform the American people about those aspects of our intelligence activities that can safely be opened to the public. Without public support for our sizable intelligence organization, we run the risk of more debilitating public criticism, such as that encountered by American intelligence in 1975–76. And we must recognize that intelligence is a risk-taking business. There will be mistakes and failures that open it to criticism.

The area where more mistakes have been made in the past than anywhere else is in counterintelligence, or in uncovering the kind of spies that we found so frequently in 1985. The considerable discussion in this book of how we conduct counterintelligence is particularly relevant in today's circumstances. We as a nation are understandably distraught that our counterintelligence was not good enough to detect many of the traitors caught in 1985 any earlier than it did. Back in 1975–76, though, we were distraught at the revelations of excesses of intrusions into our private lives carried out in the first thirty years after World War II in the name of counterintelligence.

It is my hope that the chapters on counterintelligence will help readers better understand the delicate balance between too little and too much counterintelligence. Our democratic society will always prefer less intrusion into its citizens' lives than that prevalent in totalitarian societies. We will, thus, always be at some disadvantage in preventing spying against us.

Another lesson, though, of the spying events of 1985 is that the Soviets are vulnerable, too. Any American chief of intelligence would have shaken the CIA to its core if even two—let alone three—relatively senior CIA officers had defected to the East in 1985. In my view, these defections from Soviet intelligence agencies reinforce the conclusion I reach in the last chapter: that American intelligence is better than that of the Soviet Union. One of the reasons I conclude that is that the Soviets, because they are more cavalier about intruding into their citizens' lives in the name of counterintelligence, alienate many of their own people. In short, the very advantage they have in detecting spies turns out to be one of the reasons their own people defect.

The problems which the West Germans and the French encountered in 1985 highlight another key point in *Secrecy and Democracy*—namely, that in democracies there is a clear need for external oversight of intelligence activities. In both the German and French experiences, their political authorities were caught off guard by the way their intelligence was being conducted. In both cases because the ingrained attitudes and habits of the intelligence professionals were not tempered by broader political considerations, the state was embarrassed. Providing the requisite political control is by no means an easy proposition, as desirable as it may be, and how that can be achieved is a major theme of this book.

Precisely because we have made substantial progress in achieving political oversight of intelligence activities while retaining the requisite secrecy, our intelligence system today is unlike any other. This book attempts to describe how we arrived at this approach to an art as old

as recorded history. It is not a memoir or a chronicle of my steward-
ship as the Director of Central Intelligence. Above all, it is not an
apology for errors I may have made. It is also not intended to titillate
the curious with accounts of spying and intrigue. I'll leave that to the
novelists. I hope it is a book that accurately and honestly discusses the
problems which are inevitable when an open and democratic society
tries to carry out secret intelligence operations, and indicates how
complex it is to reconcile such a society and such activities. I am writing for those who want to understand these complexities and can accept the fact that simple solutions, even when possible, are seldom
useful. Those who criticize our intelligence as a threat to our society's
values and those who would condone any kind of intrusion into our
personal privacy for the sake of the nation's security are both wrong.
Between those outlooks is the mature appreciation that there is a need
for good intelligence capabilities, but the need cannot justify abuse of
the secrecy that must surround intelligence activities.

To understand this inevitable tension, we must review the significant changes that have taken place in American intelligence in recent years, especially two that were virtual revolutions.

The first was the imposition of external oversight by the Congress
and the White House over all secret intelligence activities. Of the
world's democracies, only the United States has gone so far to ensure
that even this, the most secret arm of government, is responsive to
the will of the people.

The second was the growth of technological methods of information-gathering. American ingenuity has applied satellites, computers, and other products of innovative technology to the collection
of intelligence data, with superlative results. Only the United States
has the scientific base and the wealth to develop technology for intelligence purposes to such an extent.

American intelligence also recently crossed several other important thresholds. In the mid-to-late 1970s, thirty years after the end of
World War II and the establishment of the Central Intelligence
Agency, the first generation of intelligence professionals—many of
them veterans of the Office of Strategic Services (OSS)—reached retirement age. Leadership passed to people whose experiences, view
of the world, and values reflected the post–World War II generation.

In those same thirty years the public's attitude toward intelligence
changed. In the 1950s and 1960s, in the spirit of the cold war, we
trusted the government to do what had to be done. In the 1970s, we

suddenly realized that we did not always agree with what had been done, and we wanted to be more involved in the decisions. For intelligence agencies, the shift in attitude meant a profound reassessment of the way they did business.

Finally, as America's interest in developments overseas expanded from the military strength of a few communist countries to the political, economic, and military developments in most of the more than 150 nations of the world, intelligence requirements increased measurably.

In early 1977, as these major developments were reshaping American intelligence, I was unexpectedly thrust into its center as its chief, the Director of Central Intelligence, or DCI. Although as a naval officer I had worked closely with intelligence organizations, I was in fact an outsider to the intelligence profession. As such, I viewed the changes differently from the way the professionals did, and I reacted differently. On the one hand, I was not intimately familiar with the mechanics of the system—certainly a disadvantage, since I could not easily appreciate at first how the professionals felt the changes would affect their ability to do the job. On the other, I had no institutional bias or resistance to change—an advantage when arguments against change are based heavily on tradition rather than on logic.

This book, then, is about my experiences from 1977 to 1981 guiding American intelligence through change and, more important, trying to establish more effective intelligence practices for the long term. What emerged in that period was an American model of intelligence that, in my view, is an improvement over the traditional European model, which we originally copied. It fits our needs and our national character better and it is more in harmony with our democratic form of government. I believe, as well, that it ensures better intelligence work.

The first revolution, that of oversight, was a major factor in the shaping of the new model. Secret agencies within democratic governments are anachronisms, because popular controls break down when citizens cannot know everything their government is doing. Secret, unaccountable power is subject to misuse, ranging from deliberate, improper diversion of resources to just plain carelessness in the making of decisions. In 1975–76, three major investigative commissions probed deeply into allegations of past intelligence abuses. They found that intelligence agencies had taken advantage of the privilege of secrecy by intruding unduly into the lives and privacy of Americans. The findings were followed by considerable criticism in the media. Some of it was well deserved, some irresponsibly exaggerated, and some simply incorrect. Nonetheless, it created a public demand for more control over intelligence activities. That led to two new systems by which the Congress and the Executive now act as surrogates for the people in overseeing intelligence agencies.

In February 1976, President Gerald Ford issued the first Executive Order on Intelligence. That summer the Senate established its Select Committee on Intelligence. The House of Representatives followed a year later. These actions answered the call for oversight, but the intelligence professionals questioned whether the new oversight process would undermine the secrecy that is essential to intelligence. There was no doubt that the intelligence agencies were forced to crack open their doors far wider than ever before. The question was, "How far?" How much does a congressional committee need to know to be sure nothing illegal or immoral is being done? Can it know that much without exposing sensitive and necessary operations? How much detail can a conscientious intelligence professional reveal if he fears it may jeopardize the life of an agent helping us overseas? There is no easy way to balance the need for sufficient oversight by the Congress in order to ensure a degree of accountability with the intelligence agencies' need to gather and protect the information they require to perform their function.

The second revolutionary change, based on vastly expanded technical capabilities, forced many adjustments in the collecting of intelligence. In this case, misunderstanding was as great inside intelligence circles as outside. Many older professionals viewed the turn toward technology as the beginning of the end of the traditional craft of spying, and they fought it, ignoring the potential it gave us to use agents more adroitly and expose them less often to risk. We would, for instance, no longer think of sending an agent to risk his life for information we could obtain from a satellite photograph. Espionage carried out by human beings can focus on those areas where there is no substitution for man's observations—for example, in finding out what other people have in mind and intend to do in the future. How to satisfactorily integrate traditional intelligence collection by people with new technical methods has become a real issue. Old habits do not die easily.

Our expanded technical capability has also emphasized the importance of close teamwork among the half-dozen different agencies that operate the technical systems. The data produced by one system are often the very clues the next system needs to pick up the scent and carry on. But it is easier to acknowledge the desirability of teamwork than to achieve it. Each agency is semiautonomous and has its own ideas about where to concentrate its collection efforts. Improved technical capability, then, has led to a persisting struggle between those who seek stronger central authority over intelligence and those who would either yield their autonomy to a central authority or who genuinely fear the effect of powerful central control over any secret apparatus.

In 1977, then, American intelligence was nervous as it confronted these two revolutions. On top of that, it was threatened by the loss of public support. Since no public institution can survive in our democracy without public support, the restoration of that confidence was essential. The widespread criticism had not only affected morale, it had also made the professionals less willing to take risks, to undertake efforts that might fail and lead to further criticism. All significant intelligence collection involves taking risks. Encouraging risk-taking while installing an oversight process to make intelligence more accountable was to prove an interesting challenge for me.

The American model of intelligence that evolved is by no means the last word. Intelligence is a dynamic profession and the point of this book is not to extol, or even describe, the particular model that evolved. Rather, it is to explain how we got where we did and to anticipate where we may be going. Having steered our intelligence activities from 1977 to 1981, I want to record the reasoning behind the changes that were put into effect. "Those who do not remember the past are condemned to repeat it," said the philosopher George Santayana. It is my hope that the history of how and why the new model of American intelligence evolved may benefit those who will make future changes. I also hope it will assist the public in understanding the conflicting pressures on the intelligence profession, for that profession needs both the support and the scrutiny of the American public.

I conclude with some suggestions for further improving our intelligence under the conflicting demands of secrecy, oversight, and technical progress. I do so realizing my vision has its own limits, as do the views of others. I cannot escape that. But I do want to share the special quality of the period during which I was privileged to serve as the Director of Central Intelligence.

PART ONE

THE CHALLENGE

ONE

The Phone Call

THE PHONE CALL came on February 2, 1977, in Naples, Italy. I had been Commander of the Southern Flank of NATO for eighteen months. The perquisites of the job included a huge marble villa with a view that swept from Mt. Vesuvius on the east across the Bay of Naples to the Isle of Capri in the south, a motor yacht, a twin-engine aircraft, a cavernous office constructed in the era of Mussolini, a constant, sometimes interesting social life, and the opportunity to travel around Europe. I had the nominal prestige of command in time of war of all the armies, navies, and air forces of Greece, Turkey, and Italy in addition to the navies of the United States and Great Britain when they were deployed in the Mediterranean Sea. It was a pleasant job, but I was bored professionally.

For all intents and purposes, I was out of the U.S. Navy — even out of the United States military. Although I reported to an American general, Alexander Haig, the Supreme Allied Commander in Europe, I worked only for NATO. NATO is almost all politics. Preparations for war are made by the commanders of national forces. It was peacetime, and I commanded virtually none.

The Navy had assigned me to Naples in 1975, out of Washington and out of the Navy's mainstream. I was considered dangerous by those of my more conservative colleagues who felt threatened by unconventional ideas. I had been a strong supporter of Admiral Elmo (Bud) Zumwalt, a surprise appointment as chief of the Navy in 1970. He was the youngest man ever to hold that job, the most intelligent and dynamic Chief of Naval Operations since Admiral Chester Nimitz, and the most open to change where it seemed needed. He attempted several major shifts in the Navy that put him head to head against old-line Navy men. One of his ideas was to loosen the Navy's fixation on large aircraft carriers. Every experienced naval leader, including Zumwalt and me, appreciates the importance of the carrier and the vital role it has played and will continue to play for many years. There is a split in opinion, though, on whether the day of the supercarrier is passing and whether we need to begin broadening our naval capabilities. Zumwalt also tried to make the Navy more appealing to the young men and women on whom it depended for its future. Not enough high-quality sailors were enlisting and re-enlisting to keep the Navy strong. Zumwalt made a number of changes to reflect what was taking place outside the Navy and to reduce the gaping and growing differences between civilian and military life. Among the most publicized were his approval of beards and somewhat longer hair and the modernization of uniforms. Many of the ideas came from his freewheeling discussions with junior officers and senior petty officers on bases and ships all around the country. I applauded and supported his efforts to move the concerns of people higher on the Navy's list of priorities.

Zumwalt had accelerated my advancement. I was a rear admiral when he became CNO. Since it was important for a new admiral to get a good sea assignment as early as possible, Zumwalt arranged a very good one for me in command of an aircraft carrier task group in the Mediterranean. After I had spent just a short time there, he pulled me back to the Pentagon to take charge of the Navy's Office of Systems Analysis, an office he had founded a few years before. He called me his "resident s.o.b.," his devil's advocate. I was there only a year, though, before he arranged my promotion to vice admiral and assigned me to be President of the Naval War College in Newport, Rhode Island. He gave me free rein to do what I felt was needed to make study there a truly rigorous educational experience for the senior officer stu dents. I changed the curriculum from a passive program, where students were lectured to most of the time, to one where they were actively involved in serious reading, writing, and critical analyses of ideas. This upset many students, who longed for the more leisurely pace of the past, but in the years since then, I haven't heard of many graduates who didn't feel they grew intellectually at Newport — and that was the whole point. When Zumwalt's four-year term as CNO was expiring in 1974, I was assigned to one of the best jobs at sea for a vice admiral — command of the Second Fleet, in the Atlantic. Almost as soon as Zumwalt left, though, the Navy began to turn back the clock. Zumwalt's men were pushed aside, and in 1975, although I was given the fourth star of full admiral, I was "sent away" to Naples.

By the summer of 1976 I was beginning to think about turning in my uniform. I thought I saw the handwriting on the wall; I was unlikely to get back into the influential areas of the military again. I felt if I were going to try my hand in the business world, I should do so soon. I was fifty-two years old and had been in the Navy ever since entering the Naval Academy in 1943. At just this time, however, an Annapolis classmate, Jimmy Carter, became the Democratic Party's nominee for President. From what little I knew of Jimmy Carter, I thought him a man with a keen mind and an interest in taking a fresh look at defense issues. If he became President, we in the military might again be challenged to think through questions more critically and inventively. There might be more opportunity for iconoclasts to influence decisions on defense matters. I decided it was worth waiting to see whether he was elected.

Now, on February 2, 1977, President Carter was at the helm in Washington. At four-thirty in the afternoon my aide, Lieutenant Commander Walter (Butch) Williams, bounded into my office.

"Admiral, there is a 'secure' call coming through for you from Washington."

The call was from the Secretary of Defense on a special phone with a scrambler. Since I worked for NATO and not for the U.S. Department of Defense, I assumed he was not calling about my job as Commander of the Southern Flank. While I waited for the proper connection, I thought about the new secretary. Because of my hope that Jimmy Carter was going to take a truly fresh look at defense, I had greeted Harold Brown's appointment with reservations. He had been both an Assistant Secretary of Defense and the Secretary of the Air Force in the Kennedy and Johnson administrations and was one of a group who had been making defense policy for years. Still, my reservations were not strong, because I did not know the man.

"Admiral Turner," said the Secretary of Defense, "the President would like to see you in Washington tomorrow. Can you get here?"

I said I could. Then, trying to smoke out what this was all about, I asked if there was anything I could prepare for. That didn't elicit any hint.

The entire conversation took only a couple of minutes. Butch set to work lining up transportation, and I called my wife, Patricia, and asked her to pack a bag for me. Then we speculated on what this might mean. Perhaps there was to be a discussion about military affairs, such as one I had had with then-Governor Carter in Atlanta two years earlier. Or perhaps it meant a new assignment. We quickly worked out a code for some possible assignments so that I could double-talk any secret news to her from Washington. "Say a prayer for me," I concluded and hung up, eager to get on with my preparations.

Next, I wanted to get whatever advice I could before I left. I pushed the intercom on my desk and asked my executive assistant, Navy Commander Bernard F. McMahon, to get three other top aides to drop what they were doing and come into my office for a skull session. I had chosen Bernie McMahon for his position because he was a brilliant thinker and a superb leader of men. He had served in Washington only once, but that was enough for him to know all the ropes. Of the three people he summoned, one was U.S. Army Lieutenant General Robert C. McAlister, number two in the command. McAlister and I had graduated just one year apart, he from West Point and I from Annapolis. We had worked comfortably together for the past year and a half, and I respected his judgment. He was a low-key, steady person who complemented my high-tempo style perfectly and was the only one in headquarters who had personal insight into the upper reaches of the military. He walked through the doorway connecting his office and mine.

Commander George E. Thibault, Jr., was in the midst of a

game of handball on a court next door to the headquarters. A Marine orderly summoned him to break off the game, and he arrived just after McAlister. George had worked as my special assistant at the Naval War College and the Second Fleet and had come with me to Naples. I depended on him as a source of ideas, as a sounding board, and as a talented craftsman of speeches and articles on military strategy.

The third person was another Navy commander, Roberta L. Hazard. Bobbie Hazard and George Thibault worked side by side on special projects. Bobbie, who had been in Zumwalt's front office, had a good feel for Pentagon politics, knew the cast of characters in Washington, and was as bright as they come.

McAlister's reaction was "Well, finally." He had clearly expected that, as a classmate of the President's, I might be sent to a more demanding assignment. Mac was immediately convinced that the President planned to make me Chairman of the Joint Chiefs of Staff. I thought that was just wishful thinking; the President probably was taking soundings from his four-star officers, soliciting opinions. That would be a perfectly normal procedure before he selected one of them for any top job. In any event, I felt I needed to be ready for a wide array of questions, so I asked the four of them to play President and try me out.

"What's wrong in the Defense Department and what are your ideas for change?"

"What are the first three things you would do if you were Chairman of the Joint Chiefs of Staff? Or Chief of Naval Operations?"

"Should we buy the B-1 bomber? More nuclear-powered aircraft carriers?"

"Is the state of readiness of our military forces satisfactory?"

"Can we continue without the draft?"

Then someone mentioned that Ted Sorensen, the President's choice for the CIA, had withdrawn his name. The President had said he would submit another within a week. That was the only appointment he was currently under pressure to make. Could he be interested in me for the post? We discussed it briefly but thought it unlikely.

"Stan," Mac said, "the President is your classmate and friend; he wouldn't do that to you."

We moved back to military issues.

Just then Butch rushed in to say that there was a chance we could catch the Concorde out of Paris that evening at eight o'clock. By six, Butch and I were airborne in a Navy jet. An hour and a half later we landed in Paris. When we reached the counter for the Concorde, the attendant said, "You must be Admiral Turner." We were the last passengers to check in.

In a few minutes we were over the Atlantic and the pilot announced that he was about to go supersonic. Even Butch, who had flown over four hundred combat missions in Vietnam, was thrilled to watch the meter on the forward bulkhead of the cabin notch upward to almost twice the speed of sound. As I settled back and tried to relax, answers to potential questions from the President on the military issues of the day raced through my head. The real question on my mind, though, was "What kind of a fellow is Jimmy Carter?" And, more important, "How do I deal with him?"

I had no memory of Carter as a fellow midshipman among the 820 in our class. We did not live in the same part of the four-thousand-man dormitory, Bancroft Hall. Our paths must have crossed, but I couldn't recall any conversations. My first remembered contact came in 1971, at our twenty-fifth class reunion. What I recalled so well was how warmly he had complimented me. "We're proud of you, Stan; you've accomplished a lot," he said. I was flattered but knew he deserved praise much more than I. In Navy terms I had done well, but he, a governor, was by far the more successful.

Meeting him at that reunion led me, three years later, when I was President of the Naval War College, to invite him to address the students on the role of a governor. Once again I was impressed by his warmth and sincerity. As he departed, he invited me to stay with him in the governor's mansion if I ever came to Atlanta.

Six months later, I did go to Atlanta on Second Fleet business and arranged a thirty-minute call on him. I was barely seated when he shot his first question at me about the state of the U.S. military. What were its strengths and weaknesses? What were the merits and liabilities of the way we made defense decisions? Who were the best thinkers on defense matters? The questions continued — tough, intelligent, relentless. I felt mentally drained when, precisely half an hour later, the meeting ended.

I also remembered well that, as I walked out of his office,

Jimmy Carter patted me on the shoulder and said, "By the way, Stan, the day after tomorrow I am going to announce my candidacy for the presidency."

"Good luck, Jimmy," I said. But when I turned to leave, I couldn't help feeling inwardly amused by the implausibility of this classmate and obscure Southern governor becoming President of the United States.

The Concorde touched down at Dulles International Airport outside Washington three hours and fifty-five minutes after leaving Paris, not quite nine hours after Harold Brown's call. Butch had performed a miracle.

A few minutes after eleven the next morning Rear Admiral M. Staser Holcomb, executive assistant to Secretary Brown and one of my closest friends, showed me into Harold Brown's office and introduced us. When Staser left, Brown and I sat down on a couch and an easy chair at one end of his very long office. The fact that I was scheduled to talk with him for only ten minutes suggested to me that I was not going to get a new military assignment. No Secretary of Defense would want to give a top job to an admiral he had never met without having a good discussion with him. Brown was polite and friendly, but terse and all business. In just a moment he shifted from pleasantries to the topic I wanted to hear about. All he said, though, was "The President has something he wants you to do. He'll tell you about it when you see him." The meeting had lasted, in fact, three minutes.

Now, as I was being driven to the White House, I knew that I had to face it: I was going to a civilian post, most probably the CIA. Trying to think how to respond if that was what the President suggested, I found it extremely difficult to face up to the possibility. We turned down Pennsylvania Avenue and went through the West Gate to the White House. A guard checked me off on his list.

The wait in the reception room of the West Lobby seemed interminable. About 11:35, remembering how extremely punctual Mr. Carter had been in Atlanta, I wondered whether the receptionist had told his office I was there. But finally I was escorted to the reception room off the Oval Office. Accustomed to the palatial, mirrored, wood-paneled, two-story anterooms of the kings, presidents, and prime ministers I had called on in Europe, I was astounded. The outer office of the President of the United States was small and cramped, with just enough room for a receptionist's desk, a two-seat couch, and two armchairs. From there I was ushered directly into the Oval Office and was told to sit in one of the two wingback chairs in front of the fireplace. Anticipating the arrival of the President, I hardly felt like sitting down. When I did, I tried to take in my surroundings carefully so that I could tell Patricia what it was like. Harry Truman's THE BUCK STOPS HERE sign was on the President's large, immaculate desk at the other end of the room, and George Washington peered down at me from over the fireplace. Then a door I hadn't noticed, because it blended into the curving wall, opened, and the President, with his broad, warm smile and loping gait, came over to shake my hand.

"It's nice to see you, Stan. Thanks for coming. How did you get here?" A photographer appeared from nowhere. "Let's go into my private office. I want you to meet the Vice President."

We went through the same curved door and down a short, narrow hallway to a tiny, cozy office. There was a window and a French door behind and on either side of the desk and a small couch to one side. A portrait of Rosalynn Carter hung over the fireplace. Vice President Walter Mondale shook my hand, and he and I sat down on the couch.

With the same warmth and sincerity as at our class reunion in 1971, the President praised my record of service to the Navy and the country, referring specifically to assignments I'd had; he'd done his homework. He commended my sense of integrity and dedication, and I felt embarrassed. Then came the punch line.

"Stan, I'm considering you for Director of Central Intelligence." (Years later I heard a story for which I cannot vouch. My name as a possible choice, it was said, came to the President after he had gone to bed one night. He rose and jotted it on a pad at his bedside. In the morning, Rosalynn saw the scrawl and asked, "Why do you have Stan Turner's name written down?" The drowsy Carter thought a minute and replied, "I don't remember.")

The President went on, "I have two candidates in mind; you are one."[1] He stressed that being Director of Central Intelligence

1. The other choice was General Bernard W. Rogers, then Chief of Staff of the Army and, by coincidence, a Rhodes Scholar at the same time I was one.

involved not only running the CIA, but managing the entire community of intelligence agencies throughout the government.

"What do you think, Stan?"

All that I had worked toward in the military would go out the window if I said, "Yes, I'm interested," and the President selected me. There was so much I felt needed to be done in the military. Zumwalt had been able to make only a dent, and even that was being obliterated. What I did not stop to think was that the Director of Central Intelligence reported directly to the President and had an even more important opportunity to make a contribution. I fell back on the brief discussion of the CIA I had had with my advisers in Naples. I told the President that if I had the qualities he so generously ascribed to me, I believed he needed those qualities badly in the military. The military was facing lots of problems, and I would prefer to help him solve them.

And then I decided that this meeting was an opportunity of a lifetime. I would go for broke. On the Concorde I had thought that perhaps the President would ask me what I would like to do next. He didn't, but I volunteered.

"Mr. President, I would really like to be the Vice Chief of the Navy. Then, a year and a half from now, when the present CNO's statutory term expires, I would like to move up, if that suited you."

To me it would have been ideal to serve a year and a half as number two before taking over as the CNO. I could study all the issues, place the right people in the right places, and be ready to get off to a flying start for the brief four years the law permits anyone to head one of our military services. That was the best hope I had for breaking the resistance to change that was holding the Navy back.

The President made short shrift of the idea.

"Stan, being Director of Intelligence would be much better preparation for going on and being Chief of the Navy or anything else in the military. The law provides that you can stay in uniform while serving as Director of Central Intelligence, and I think you should." He then brought the Vice President into the conversation for the first time.

"Fritz, you've checked on this. There's no reason Stan couldn't go back to another military assignment, is there?"

The Vice President assured me not only that I could go back to the military, but that Harold Brown would give me a memorandum to that effect. I realized this was no promise of another military assignment, just an assurance there could be one. I responded that I didn't think a return to the military would be practical. The next big change of leadership in the military, both the chairman's job and the CNO, would come in just a year and a half. I couldn't possibly tackle what needed to be done at the CIA and leave after that short a time. After we had discussed that for a few minutes, the President said, "Fritz, I have just narrowed the field from two candidates to one."

Mondale nodded assent. I felt suddenly numb at the realization that my thirty-year military career was over. "Mr. President, I'll do my best." I added that when I was finished with this job I would not worry about another military assignment. I was looking forward to trying the business world.

I could see that the President was becoming impatient to bring our meeting to a close. Yet I had a sense of incompletion. I knew that when, in the future, I needed any support from the President to do my job, I would come into his office as a supplicant. In the minute or so I had now before leaving that office, I still had a modicum of bargaining power and should use it to gain something I would need to be an effective Director of Central Intelligence.

"Mr. President," I ventured, "you said that I am to run the entire Intelligence Community. I don't believe the Director of Central Intelligence has enough authority to do that."

The President seemed taken aback. "The director controls the budget of all of the intelligence agencies," he said, and the Vice President explained, "You are chairman of the committee that constructs the budgets for everybody."

"Being chairman of a committee like that in Washington gets you nowhere," I replied.

"If that proves to be the case, I will change the rules," the President said, winding up the meeting.

He then instructed the Vice President to get me the forms to fill out for my security clearance with the FBI and to be sure Harold Brown wrote that memorandum for me right away. I began to wonder what Fritz Mondale's role as Vice President was going to

be. Throughout the meeting he had been silent except when
called on. I was concentrating on the President and his reactions
so much that I had only a slight impression of the Vice President,
as a quiet, reserved man who was definitely playing the role of
number two.

Now I was in his hands as we left by the side door and went
down the corridor to his office. It seemed a little awkward for both
of us that the Vice President of the United States was in charge of
getting me some forms and a memo. After a few minutes he called
Hamilton Jordan and asked him to join us. Jordan, a warm and
outgoing man, was not in blue jeans, as the media led one to anticipate, but in shirtsleeves and tie. He seemed very much "in
charge" of the White House and had a larger and nicer office
than did the Vice President. He was quite willing to make decisions and give orders. I was astounded when he told the President's counsel, Robert Lipshutz, to give the FBI only two days to
complete its investigation of me. This was Thursday; he wanted
to be ready to go public with the nomination on Monday. He told
me emphatically to keep secret all that was going on.

As soon as I could find a phone, I called Patricia. Our code
didn't include the CIA job, so I had to think one up. "Darling,
we're going to the bush leagues." It didn't take her a moment to
remember that the last Director of Central Intelligence was
George Bush. I asked her to join me in Washington as soon as she
could get a flight; I wanted her to share the new experiences. I
didn't need a code with my son, Geoffrey, a naval lieutenant. Two
years before, he had advised me that he was transferring to the
intelligence branch of the Navy as a specialist. I suggested that he
could go into intelligence later on, but that if he transferred now
he could never change his mind and return to the line. To drive
home my prejudice, I told him most intelligence was just "bean-
counting."

"Geoff, I've just left the Oval Office. I'm going to be the Chief
Bean Counter!"

I felt sorry for him. I suspected that he had left the line of the
Navy in part so as not to have to follow his dad around; I was
Commander, U.S. Second Fleet, and he was assigned to a ship in
that fleet at the time he decided to move to intelligence. Now I
was going to be his boss again.

By the weekend more than my family knew; *Time* magazine printed a rumor that I was the new nominee. Hamilton Jordan all but admitted to me that he had leaked the story as a trial balloon. The rest of the media picked it up quickly. TV cameramen soon hovered in the lobby of my hotel, and reporters tried to phone in. My life was changing precipitately.

TWO

"Best Job in Washington"

ON SUNDAY AFTERNOON the Vice President phoned. Because of mounting press interest, it was important, he felt, for me to get up to Capitol Hill on Monday to meet the senators who would be key to my confirmation. He asked me to come over to his house and talk strategy.

I drove to the big white Victorian home on the Naval Observatory grounds on Massachusetts Avenue that, until three years before, had been the residence of the Chief of Naval Operations. The Vice President, a White House legislative aide, and I discussed which senators I knew and which senators would be most influential in ensuring the confirmation. Eventually we worked out a list of those I should see; the aide was to start making appointments the next morning. Then the Vice President phoned Henry (Hank) Knoche at the CIA. Knoche, a CIA professional, had been acting as the Director of Central Intelligence since George Bush left with the change of administration two and a half weeks previously. Mondale asked him to meet me at CIA Headquarters in an hour to advise me on how to approach the senators.

I drove to the CIA's tightly guarded compound just across the Potomac River in Langley, Virginia. There, I was directed by a guard to the underground parking garage; another guard whisked me to the top floor in the director's elevator. I was taken to Knoche's office, where he and an old Navy friend, Admiral Daniel J. Murphy, were waiting. Dan and I were contemporaries in the Navy and leapfrogging rivals. We had been promoted to rear admiral at the same time, but under Zumwalt's tutelage I became a vice admiral a year ahead of him. Zumwalt had promised that in another year I would move on to command of the Sixth Fleet in the Mediterranean, possibly the best job in the Navy. Dan, however, was executive assistant to Secretary of Defense Melvin Laird, and when the time came to send a new commander to the Sixth Fleet, Laird, who outranked Zumwalt, sent his man instead.

I ended up with second choice, the Second Fleet. A year later, though, I got my fourth star ahead of Murphy with my Naples assignment. Then, a few months before I was called back from Naples, the job of Deputy to the Director of Central Intelligence for Intelligence Community Affairs was upgraded to four stars or the civilian equivalent. With a push from former Secretary Laird, Dan Murphy was given that assignment and his fourth star. Now if I were confirmed, he would be my deputy for the Intelligence Community.

It could have been awkward for Dan to serve as my deputy, given our service rivalry, but he had generously phoned the day before to say he would like to stay on and would be pleased to work for me. I respected Dan as a very bright, politically attuned person who had obviously done a superb job for Laird, and I had every confidence that he would have worked for me loyally. Yet I was from the Zumwalt, surface-ship, analytic side of the Navy, and he was from the traditional, aviation, political side. We looked at the world quite differently. My inclination was to have someone with a specifically analytic bent in this deputy's job. Also, I wondered whether it would look proper to have active duty naval officers in two of the top three jobs in American intelligence. (The third is the Deputy Director of Central Intelligence, or DDCI, who is the DCI's alter ego.)

I neither knew nor had heard of Hank Knoche. He had been a career CIA analyst until George Bush appointed him DDCI in the summer of 1976. As soon as we met, Hank, a man of large frame and warm, friendly manner, thoughtfully asked if I would like to see the office I would occupy as director. He led me through a door from his office to an office I had been in just once before, when I had called on the then-director, William Colby. That was in the course of getting a CIA briefing before undertaking my assignment in Naples in 1975. I didn't remember that the office was so long and narrow. I now noticed that it was wood-paneled except for one side, which had floor-to-ceiling windows with a view of lovely green trees as far as you could see. The office itself was not elegant, and its narrowness I thought awkward.

The meeting with Knoche was akin to the familiar experience of going aboard a new ship as captain and meeting your executive officer. Now, though, I sensed a different sort of tension. We talked about my forthcoming congressional calls and about particular senators who might have strong views on one or another aspect of intelligence. When I told him the Vice President wanted him to accompany me on the calls, Hank sat speechless for a long time. Finally he said, "I don't think that's a good idea."

"Hank, he was very explicit," I pressed.

He stammered a bit, then sat in silence. I found it difficult to believe anyone could refuse instructions from the Vice President of the United States, but it was clear he just wasn't going to do it. I concluded that he may have been thinking that should I not be confirmed, he'd be asked to step up to the position. My reaction was that if Hank could not shift his loyalty to a new superior, something that is quite normal in the military as seniors come and go, he was going to have an uphill battle to hold his job as my deputy. Loyalty has always meant a lot to me in the selection of associates. I hoped Hank's attitude would change once I was actually on the job.

Over the next few days the CIA delivered to me a series of briefing books, each prepared by a major branch of the Agency as well as by the legal office, the legislative liaison office, and others, to help me prepare for my confirmation hearings. I found them too long and detailed to be useful. The technical branch's note-book, for instance, was two inches thick and filled with technical minutiae that I was not likely to use. The books seemed to be collections of briefing papers picked off the shelf, rather than something tailored to my needs. Worse, they gave only the Agency's side of controversial issues, which would hardly help me appreciate the pros and cons of major questions or guard against the minefields that might lie in my cross-examination by the Senate.

Hank Knoche also generously organized a series of dinner meetings at the CIA with the top people. They all tried to be helpful, but I found them difficult to understand. There was the specialized terminology, which was new to me and hard to follow, but that was not the most serious problem. I found a disturbing lack of specificity and clarity in response to my questions. I wondered whether the problems were so great or the secrets so deep that the staff didn't want to share them until I was confirmed, or if they simply weren't accustomed to being incisive and direct. After the second dinner, I canceled the others. I was physically exhausted each day from running back and forth on Capitol Hill, and the long dinner discussions were just not productive enough to make them worthwhile. Overall, then, my first encounters with the CIA did not convey either a feeling of warm welcome or a sense of great competence.

This was, indeed, a surprise and disappointment to me. Over the years I had come to hold the CIA and its intelligence product in high regard. The briefing I had requested and received from the CIA before going to Naples was far more useful than the one I received from the Navy. Once in Naples, I arranged to receive weekly packages of CIA intelligence materials. I found these an important supplement to the military intelligence reports I received.

There were other preconfirmation meetings, including separate ones with the leaders of all the other agencies of the Intelligence Community. Lieutenant General Lew Allen, Director of the National Security Agency (NSA), particularly impressed me with a firm statement that the NSA took its direction on what information to collect from the Director of Central Intelligence. All I needed, he said, was to tell him what I wanted. If that was true, it was reassuring, and I had no reason to believe he was not being forthright. I also met with the four most recent CIA directors. Richard Helms was under investigation for possible perjury before a congressional committee in 1973 and was very defensive. George Bush exuded enthusiasm and admiration for the CIA. "It's the best job in Washington," he said. He expressed no concerns about the recent exposures of abuses and did not talk about how to control them. Bill Colby was low key and warm, and inspired confidence. I knew James Schlesinger well enough that he had measurably helped my military career when he was Secretary of Defense. We had a long, substantive discussion.

In 1973, before becoming Defense Secretary, Jim had been Director of Central Intelligence for only five months. But even in that brief time he had taken dramatic action to reduce the size of the CIA. Now, four years later, he told me that the CIA was still overstaffed from Vietnam days and that management procedures were very poor. He then threw out an odd line: "I suspect that [James] Angleton secretly still has an office out there at Langley." He cryptically explained that Bill Colby had fired Angleton and that I'd hear plenty about him in time.

My calls on Capitol Hill turned out to be extremely useful. From ten short meetings in the first two days alone — most of them only ten or fifteen minutes long — I learned more about intelligence issues of national interest than from anything else I did. Senator Jacob Javits of New York was tops. He urged me to try to dispel the mystique that surrounds intelligence. He believed that there was much misinformed opinion in both Congress and the public about the intelligence apparatus, and that that gave rise to considerable mistrust. He suggested the CIA tell the country more of the true story of how intelligence works, how dedicated its people are, and how valuable its product is. He also argued that we should understand our opponent better and suggested the CIA tell the public how badly off the Russian people are under Marxism. He felt that we do not understand that, although the Soviet Union is a major military power, its standard of living is appallingly low compared with ours.

Senator Henry (Scoop) Jackson of Washington made the valuable point that letting people know what intelligence did not know was sometimes almost as important as saying what it did know. Senators Walter Huddleston of Kentucky and Birch Bayh of Indiana, both of whom had served on the Senate committee that conducted one of the investigations of intelligence in 1975–1976, were concerned about whether a legislative charter for intelligence activities was needed. My impression was that liberals and conservatives alike sensed that the congressional investigations had harmed our capabilities. Now everyone was hoping for a responsible performance by the new special committees on intelligence in both houses to restore balance and confidence.

At 10:04 A.M. on February 22 in Room 235 of the Russell Senate Office Building, my confirmation hearing opened. The room was full of spectators. There were no indications of any opposition to my nomination. Yet, in this unfamiliar and somewhat forbidding atmosphere, I was relieved by the presence of Senator John H. Chafee of Rhode Island. In 1969 and 1970 as a Navy captain I had been his naval aide and executive assistant during his first year and a half as Secretary of the Navy. We became close friends. He's a warm, upstanding man, and I admire him greatly. It was a happy coincidence that he, a new senator, was a member of the committee that would oversee my work.

Another helpful happenstance was that through John Chafee I had some acquaintance with Senator Barry Goldwater, the ranking minority member of the committee. Several years earlier, Barry Goldwater had come along on a trip John Chafee made to inspect the Navy's activities at the South Pole. I spent three nights across the hall from the senator in a Quonset hut on the Antarctic ice. It was fun to see this legend close up and to hear his straightforward "give 'em hell" rhetoric. Now, after the chairman of the committee, Senator Daniel Inouye of Hawaii, opened the hearing with brief remarks about the responsibilities of the job of Director of Central Intelligence, Barry Goldwater quipped about being willing to go to the South Pole with me if I ever decided to do that again.

In my opening statement I stressed three goals I had set for myself: objectivity — all reporting and analysis coming from the Intelligence Community must be scrupulously free of bias, either conscious or unconscious; legality — intelligence agencies, like all arms of government, must reflect the mores of the nation and abide by its laws; and restored reputation — neither the CIA nor the other American intelligence agencies deserved to be tarred as they had been, and their reputation for trustworthiness and professional competence must be restored.

Then the questioning began. One by one the senators, alternately by party and in order of seniority, were allowed ten minutes each by the chairman. To me what followed was a fascinating exercise in constitutional government. I was grateful that that was one of the subjects I had studied in my postgraduate work at Oxford University. What was taking place was a jousting over the division of authority and responsibility between the Executive and Legislative branches. Over and over these senators, Republican and Democratic, probed to see how I viewed my responsibilities to them, not just to the President. Because their committee was less than a year old, precedents and procedures had yet to be established. They were concerned with the relationship between the Executive and Legislative Branches on intelligence.

Chairman Inouye opened: "My first question is related to whether you will honor our requests for information."

What he wanted to know was how much power I was going to let Congress have, since information is often equated with power, especially in intelligence, where secrecy abounds.

Senator Charles McC. Mathias, Jr., of Maryland put it even more bluntly in asking whether the committee would have "full access to knowledge."

In my preparatory work I had come to understand that we were in a delicate period of determining just how much the Congress needed to know about intelligence. I was convinced that it was necessary and desirable to present enough to let the legislators make sound judgments on the value of intelligence activities, but not so much as to risk an operation's success or to give away the President's authority.

I hedged my answer: "I believe that deliberations on policy decisions within the Executive Branch are not necessarily suitable for transmittal to the Congress [and] there are some very delicate details of covert intelligence operations which the committee may not want to hear."

Mathias pounced. "Well, I would say to the admiral that that phrase 'may not want to hear' is a bit of a sore phrase around here."

I recalled that such congressional oversight as there had been before the establishment of this committee was ineffective because of a feeling in Congress that it was best not to hear what intelligence was doing.

Chairman Inouye asked if I would, without a request, advise the committee "as to information which you feel we should know about."

There was a feeling on Capitol Hill that the CIA answered

questions satisfactorily, but only if Congress knew what questions to ask. I believed that I could assure him on that one and did.

The impact of Watergate and President Nixon's efforts to misuse the CIA was evident. I was asked what would I do if I had serious differences with the President as to what intelligence agencies should and should not do. Senator Bayh, for instance, wanted to know whether I would consider "reporting those significant differences to this committee."

Here my military sense of loyalty to the chain of command forced me to balk. I replied, "I do not believe that I would report such differences to this committee. I believe that as long as I am employed in the Executive Branch of the government, my loyalty is to the President of the United States. I believe that if every member of the Executive Branch who disagreed with the President went to the press or to the Congress independently, we would have anarchy."

Birch Bayh wouldn't let up. "Admiral, if you will excuse me, we . . . are talking about a President who is embarking on something that is clearly illegal, clearly unconstitutional. Don't you have a responsibility . . . to go to one of those committees that might be in a position to change that policy or say, 'Wait a minute, Mr. President, let's rethink this'?"

I answered, "I would come to you, sir, but after having resigned my office."

Senator Inouye wanted to be sure that U.S. intelligence would be independent of military control, even though I was going to remain on active duty. Senator Richard Lugar of Indiana wondered if I might have difficulty making "unpopular decisions with regard to colleagues who might be in command over you when you resume your career." And others worried about my ambitions to go on in my military career.

Senator Joseph Biden of Delaware put it bluntly: "Are you in a position to indicate to this committee that it is not your intention to seek the chairmanship of the Joint Chiefs of Staff or the Chief of Naval Operations?"

"Yes, sir," I responded. That was what I had told the President the first day. I was retaining my active duty status partly because that was what the President had indicated he wanted, but also because being in uniform was almost like having a security blanket to hold as a new world swirled around me.

Another line of questioning brought back reminders of a different facet of my initial meeting with the President. Barry Goldwater asked, "How can the director of the entire Intelligence
Community operate effectively when someone else controls most
of the money?"

Senator Huddleston echoed the same thought: "Is there any
way to really manage the Intelligence Community without having authority over the purse?"

And Joe Biden: "The director needs greater control over the
entire Intelligence Community, including the purse strings, particularly that aspect which is part of the Department of Defense."

I felt I could not let on that I had already raised the issue of
control of the budget with the President. He had not had time to
move on it yet. On the broader issue of control over the Community, I said, "The principal problem that concerns me, from the
preliminary view I have had of the Intelligence Community, is
ensuring that all of the shreds of intelligence which are available,
whether they are in Treasury, FBI, Defense Intelligence [Agency],
or anywhere else, are brought together."

At a little after noon the hearing recessed for lunch. Patricia,
my mother and father, my roommate from Oxford days, and a
number of other friends went the short distance to the Navy Yard
for lunch together.

My baptism on the Hill was about over. The afternoon session
was an anticlimax. The most interesting line of questioning was
about whether Congress needed to enact any legislation to sort
out the complicated maze of U.S. intelligence activities.

Senator Mathias explained that "it has been a subject of concern in the Congress that we should develop statutory charters for
the different elements of the Community that are not governed by
charters at this time." He then asked, "Do you have any problem
in working with the Congress in the development of that kind of
statutory base?"

I responded, "No, sir ... I am certainly open-minded and
would look on the interest of the Congress in better definition of
the responsibilities of each of these agencies as something that
could be a big help to the Director of Central Intelligence."

Chairman Inouye had promised me that the hearing would last
only one day. I planned to fly back to Naples that evening to close
out my military command. He ended my part of the hearing by

saying, "We appreciate your forthrightness and your responses to our questions, and although this may sound rather premature, and maybe uncalled for, I don't see any problems tomorrow at three o'clock in the afternoon [when the committee was to vote on my confirmation]. So if you have an assignment in Naples, I would say to you bon voyage, and you can go ahead, knowing that you will be confirmed, sir."

Dan Inouye is a gentleman through and through. Even though I was not worried, that assurance meant a lot as Patricia and I boarded a plane just an hour later. I was paying my farewell calls in NATO when, on February 24, the Senate confirmed my appointment as Director of Central Intelligence. All uncertainty was behind me. In five days I would turn over my NATO command and within the hour head back to Washington and a new career.

THREE

The Curtain Rises

CIA HEADQUARTERS is an uncomplicated, modern, white seven-story building in a pastoral setting of lawns and woods. It is anything but sinister. As you approach the main building's entrance, you see to the right and in front a dome-shaped auditorium known as the Bubble. It appears to stand alone, though it is connected to the Headquarters by an underground tunnel. This physical separation from the Headquarters building permits people who do not have security clearances to participate in ceremonies or meetings without the risk of their seeing those CIA employees who can never acknowledge that they work for the CIA. Strangers are never permitted to walk around the halls of the Headquarters even under escort; years of diligent effort to conceal an undercover CIA person's identity could go out the window.

It was in the Bubble on March 9, 1977, that Associate Justice of the Supreme Court Byron White swore me in as the twelfth Director of Central Intelligence. I had not known Justice White previously, but when I'd been asked whom I would like to have swear me in, I had instantly requested "Whizzer" White, a boyhood idol as an All-American football player and Rhodes Scholar. He was gracious in responding to my request.

The composition of the audience reflected the three distinct roles of the Director of Central Intelligence: (1) intelligence adviser to the President, (2) coordinator of the activities of all of the agencies of the United States Intelligence Community, and (3) head of one of those agencies, the CIA.

President Carter's presence symbolized the first of those responsibilities. Arriving early, at my request, he and I met in the CIA conference room on the seventh floor with the heads of all the agencies of the Intelligence Community. He expressed his strong support for us and engaged in a short discussion. When the chief of Army intelligence referred to me as the "titular head" of the Intelligence Community, Carter shot back, "He's not the titular head, but *the* head!" A bit later, when the President and I lingered in my office while the others went ahead to the auditorium, he said, "Stan, when you come up with your plan to reshape the Intelligence Community, be bold."

By law the DCI is not at the Cabinet level, but his role as intelligence adviser gives him direct access to the President. That access is important, because it means the President will hear from him whenever intelligence matters arise. Many people will, quite properly, offer their opinions to the President on issues of intelligence. But if I could keep the President's confidence, he would want to hear from me. I had every reason to believe President Carter did have confidence in me, though our personal contacts had been few and we had not worked closely together. The role of presidential adviser gave me the opening; now I was going to have to earn continued access to him.

Also present were Secretary of State Cyrus Vance, Secretary of Defense Harold Brown, Secretary of Energy James Schlesinger, Attorney General Griffin Bell, Director of the FBI Clarence Kelley, Assistant to the President for National Security Affairs Zbigniew Brzezinski, Director of the Office of Management and Budget Bert Lance, representatives of the Secretary of the Treasury, and the Director of the Drug Enforcement Agency. Their presence symbolized my second role, that of head of the Intelligence Community of the United States. The term indicates that more elements of our government than just the CIA collect information abroad and evaluate it. Some, like the Defense Department, have many more people engaged in intelligence than does the CIA; others, like State and Treasury, collect very useful intelligence just through the normal activities of their representatives overseas. Those involved in these various efforts are under the control of their primary leaders, the Secretaries of Defense, State, Treasury, Energy, Commerce, and so on. Yet some coordination of all the undertakings is needed to avoid duplication and even conflict. The DCI is charged by law with coordinating these "community" efforts.

The bulk of the audience at my swearing-in ceremony was the top leadership of the CIA in Washington, typifying my third role, head of the Central Intelligence Agency. Under this title, I was responsible for the full management and operation of the best-known element of the Intelligence Community.

The triple role of the DCI is unique. One or two countries have imitated the CIA. None has established a position comparable to the DCI; that is, no country has a single point of contact at the top of national intelligence, except for small nations with only military intelligence agencies.

I was soon to discover one of the disadvantages of this system. A few months after the swearing-in, one of my staff told me that a foreign intelligence officer was to pay a courtesy call on me the next day. I couldn't help exploding, "That's the fourth intelligence official from that country who has called on me in the past three months! How many must I take time to see?" My staff member pointed out that each of these four was indeed my counterpart. Each represented one of my multiple responsibilities. When you multiply four or five counterparts by several dozen friendly countries, you find it difficult to do more than see visitors.

Our single DCI system stems, in part, from our national tendency to seek tidy organizational solutions to problems. It also derives from a lack that became apparent on December 7, 1941. What we knew about Japanese plans to attack Pearl Harbor was not fully shared among the intelligence organizations. That failure led to our putting one person in charge and to seeing that all intelligence information was funneled into and interpreted by one agency.

We can see that our system is unique when we compare it with the systems of other democratic countries. Take, for example, Great Britain. Its counterintelligence work, preventing the spying by other countries, is done by MI-5. Its electronic surveillance is handled by the uninformatively named GCHQ, or Government Communications Headquarters. All analytic work is done by a small organization known as the Joint Intelligence Committee. The research for developing new technical means for data collection, like satellites, is carried out by several groups. And still other organizations perform other intelligence functions. (During World War II, a British organization named MI-6 did espionage and covert action work similar to that done by the CIA.)

Theoretically the British must coordinate four separate agencies that report to four different Cabinet officers, plus military intelligence; the CIA performs all of these roles and reports only to the President, through the National Security Council.

Of course, it is not all that simple in our scheme either. The CIA's espionage role is duplicated to a small extent by the military. The CIA handles counterintelligence abroad only; the FBI is responsible for it in the United States. That means there must be close coordination between the two agencies in monitoring the movements of enemy spies in and out of the United States. The CIA's electronic surveillance is only a small part of a much larger effort centered in the military's National Security Agency. The CIA's analytic work deliberately competes with that of the Defense Intelligence Agency, the State Department's Bureau of Intelligence and Research, and a number of other analytic entities.

The DCI coordinates these overlapping, competing elements to ensure both good teamwork and a full sharing of information. It is a neat arrangement laid down in a combination of statutes, presidential Executive Orders, and established practices. The British system, in contrast, is loosely structured and requires much informal coordination. It is not an unreasonable arrangement for them, because their operations are smaller than ours and because informal cooperation has long been part of British governmental practice. Interestingly, though, despite the formal structure and lines of authority in our system, it takes a great deal of informal cooperation to make it work. In part that's because the system is large and cumbersome, but in part it is owing to our penchant for bureaucratic competition in government.

I shouldered the three responsibilities of the DCI when Justice White had me take the oath of office. Patricia was holding the Bible. I kissed her and proceeded to the podium to introduce President Carter. His remarks included a description of American intelligence as

> a community that has been investigated and perhaps damaged by revelation of past mistakes, a community that inherently is divided but which shares a common responsibility and a common purpose, a community that must face the most difficult possible conflicts between openness and frankness and public scrutiny inherent in the principles of a democracy, with the mandatory requirements for confidentiality in the collection of crucial intelligence information in relationship with our allies and friends throughout the world.

He stressed his commitment to the legality and propriety of intelligence activities, saying he wanted to know immediately if mistakes were made, because their concealment followed by revelation could deal our intelligence "a devastating additional blow."

I followed the President off the podium, down the main aisle of the auditorium, and out to his waiting limousine, flanked by the Secret Service. In another few minutes I had said goodbye to my family, who had all come in from across the country, and to my guests. It was a short ride in the elevator up to the seventh floor. The in basket was full.

PART TWO

GETTING TO WORK

FOUR

The Haunting Past

ONE OF MY FIRST and most urgent concerns was to put the CIA's much criticized past behind us. Neither the CIA nor I wanted to push problems under the rug, so I resolved to address them directly, make whatever changes were needed to prevent a recurrence, and move on to the work we were being paid to do. But it wasn't easy.

Starting in late 1974, the American and foreign press and television were full of stories of intelligence misdeeds. The CIA, though only one of the alleged offenders, took the brunt of the criticism. The complaints were manifold. Some 300,000 Americans considered to be potentially dangerous to our national security were indexed in a CIA computer, and separate files were created on approximately 7200. Millions of private telegrams were obtained by the National Security Agency between 1947 and 1975. Countless "dangerous" citizens were placed under surveillance, with bugs on their telephones, microphones in their bedrooms, or warrantless break-ins of their homes. There was extensive use of fellow citizens as informants. Tax returns were obtained from the IRS and scanned for information about citizens. Army intelligence infiltrated domestic dissident groups, collected information on prominent citizens sympathetic with such groups, and created an estimated 100,000 files on Americans between the mid 1960s and 1971. Several plots were hatched — but never carried out — to assassinate foreign political leaders who were irritants to the United States government.

James Schlesinger, several years earlier, when he was in the Office of Management and Budget, had conducted a study of the CIA, so he knew something about its workings when, in February 1973, he became DCI. Dismayed by articles he began seeing in the press, he tried to uncover all the skeletons in the CIA's closet before the newsmen did. He asked every CIA employee to inform him of any instance of improper activity he or she knew of or had heard about. He compiled a list that ran to 683 pages and came to be known as "the Family Jewels." When Schlesinger left the CIA, it fell to Bill Colby, the CIA professional who succeeded him, to decide what to do with the Family Jewels.

Colby took a considerable number of corrective actions, but the revelations continued. Finally on December 22, 1974, the floodgates opened when Seymour Hersh of the *New York Times* broke the first comprehensive story of past CIA abuses. Hersh focused on the CIA's spying on Americans in the name of counterintelligence. The fat was in the fire. In-house course corrections would no longer satisfy critics. Demands mounted for a full-scale investigation.

In January 1975 President Ford appointed Vice President Nelson Rockefeller to head a blue ribbon task force to investigate allegations that the CIA had spied on Americans. The Senate followed with a special committee chaired by Senator Frank Church of Idaho and the House with one under Representative Otis Pike of New York. In the course of the next fifteen months these three groups called witness after witness and gradually extracted document after document from the Intelligence Community. The involvement of the CIA, NSA, the FBI, and Army intelligence in domestic spying was reported extensively in the media. The facts themselves were damning, but hype made it worse. The impact on the intelligence agencies was devastating.

Much the same thing had happened to the U.S. military toward the end of the Vietnam War. Exposures of the My Lai massacre, the secret bombing of Cambodia, and the Phoenix project all rightfully outraged the public, which then, unfortunately, condemned everything military. The good was thrown out with the bad. Junior officers began changing out of uniform on base or ship to avoid attracting attention en route to and from their homes. Senior officers gritted their teeth and waited for the storm to blow over. I hoped it would pass more quickly for the CIA than it had for the military.

Only five months after I became DCI, though, we were back on the front pages in a story that reported an unpleasant exchange at a hearing before the Senate Select Committee on Intelligence sitting with a subcommittee of the Senate Committee on Human Resources.

> SENATOR KENNEDY: With regard to the activities that took place in these safe houses, as I understand it from the records, two-way mirrors were used. Is that your understanding?
>
> ADMIRAL TURNER: Yes, sir. We have records that construction was done to put in two-way mirrors.
>
> SENATOR KENNEDY: And they were placed in the bedroom, as I understand. And rather elaborate decorations were added, at least to the one in San Francisco — French cancan dancers, floral pictures, drapery, including installation of bedroom mirrors, three framed Toulouse-Lautrec posters with black silk mats, and bedroom curtains and recording equipment . . . Other documents would suggest that your principal agent out there called the operation "Midnight and Climax" . . . Do you draw any kind of conclusion about what might have been going on out there in these safe houses?
>
> ADMIRAL TURNER: No, sir.
>
> [There was general laughter from the spectators.]
>
> SENATOR KENNEDY: There is a light side to it, but there is also an enormously serious side.

The serious side the senator referred to concerned drug-testing by the CIA. Back in the 1950s the use of hallucinogenic drugs like LSD had gained popularity in the United States, and there were ominous reports of communist countries using drugs to extract information, modify behavior, and otherwise tamper with mental processes. The CIA, fearful that these largely untested drugs might be used on American intelligence officers, set out to learn exactly what their effects were. Although the purpose was reasonable, many of the CIA's methods for learning about the effects of drugs were deplorable. Some of the experimentation took place in

CIA-owned houses in New York and San Francisco, where, as the senator had noted, there were elaborate decorations and two-way mirrors. Some of the testing was done by inducing an individual to leave a bar and come to one of the houses. The drugs were then administered without the individual's knowledge, and his or her reactions observed, sometimes through the two-way mirrors.

This unethical procedure had been unearthed by the Church Committee in 1975. When the committee asked the CIA for the appropriate documents to study the activity, the CIA could not produce everything that was requested. Then, in the summer of 1977, well after the Church Committee had disbanded, I was told that we had found in a remote archive some of the documents the committee had requested. Of course, it looked as if the CIA had deliberately held back the documents when the committee most needed them. In fact, unearthing them was an instance of good work by a diligent CIA employee, Frank Laubinger. While researching a request under the Freedom of Information Act on this subject, he searched financial records, rather than simply going through operational files, as had been done previously. Sure enough, he found many data about the funding for the drug program.

I immediately sent the information to Senator Dan Inouye, Chairman of the Senate Committee on Intelligence, and asked to appear in person to explain what we had found. Volunteering didn't make life any more pleasant when I did testify, because though these activities had been conducted twenty to thirty years earlier and had long since been stopped, they put the CIA on the front pages again.

Even with these new data, we had an incomplete picture. I reported to the Congress that we knew that in six of 149 cases, the subject had not been aware that he'd been given drugs. Of the remainder, there were some cases where it was clear that the testing was voluntary; in others, we just could not tell. This program had been conceived by a CIA middle-level manager, Dr. Sidney Gottlieb. His unit had such autonomy that few in the CIA knew the testing was going on, and though the tests yielded no useful information, they continued for twelve years. In all professions it is easy to get so close to your work that you fail to realize you are not using good judgment. To prevent that, you need someone with a detached viewpoint to take an occasional look at where you are going. The CIA, with its natural emphasis on secrecy, had no internal system to provide an objective, critical review. Consequently, for an ill-conceived project involving relatively few people, the entire CIA was condemned.

Exactly one year after these hearings on drug experimentation, the CIA was back in the press for another error of the past. This time it was the prolonged incarceration of a Soviet defector, Yuri Nosenko, who came to the United States in 1964, a few months after the assassination of President John F. Kennedy. Nosenko came to public attention in 1978, when a special committee was set up in the House of Representatives to study the assassination again. Nosenko had been a KGB officer during the time that Kennedy's assassin, Lee Harvey Oswald, had lived in the Soviet Union, from 1959 to 1962. When Nosenko first arrived in the United States, he was extensively debriefed by the intelligence agencies. He was especially interrogated about any connection between Oswald and the KGB. He contended that the KGB had paid no attention to Oswald. Now, in 1978, this special House committee wanted to review Nosenko's testimony on that issue. This led to an airing of the disgraceful way the CIA had attempted to determine whether Nosenko was telling the truth.

It was the job of the counterintelligence branch under James Jesus Angleton (whom Schlesinger had mentioned to me warily) to check on whether a defector was truly defecting or pretending to defect in order to spy on the United States. Angleton concluded that since Oswald had worked on the U-2 spy plane when he was in the U.S. Marine Corps, it was unlikely that the KGB would have overlooked him entirely when he was in the Soviet Union. There was, then, cause to be suspicious of Nosenko's story about Oswald. It appeared to Angleton that the Soviets might have sent Nosenko to plant a story that would absolve them of any complicity with Oswald in the Kennedy assassination. Angleton's suspicions were heightened by an earlier Soviet defector, Anatoli Golitsyn, who claimed he knew Nosenko was a double agent. In Nosenko's favor, if he were a genuine defector, was that his knowledge of Soviet intelligence operations would have been more current than Golitsyn's, making him more valuable to us than Golitsyn. Clearly there was cause for Golitsyn to want to discredit Nosenko. It was also on Nosenko's side that he gave us some valuable information about Soviet intelligence operations. He led us to uncover an audio-surveillance system the Soviets had installed in the U.S. embassy in Moscow (fifty-two microphones in the embassy's most sensitive areas), and he directed us to a very high level Soviet spy inside a Western European government. However, when Angleton balanced the pros against the cons, he decided that Nosenko was a double agent, and set out to force him to confess.

But Nosenko was not a man who could easily be bullied. He proved to be so tough and obstinate that when he would not give in to normal interrogation, Angleton's counterintelligence team set out to break the man psychologically. A small prison was built, expressly for him, on a secret base near Washington. He was kept there in solitary confinement for three and a half years. Ostensibly this was to isolate him so that the interrogation would be more effective. In fact, on only 292 of his 1277 days in that prison was he questioned at all. When he was interrogated, sometimes it was for twenty-four hours without any break. When he wasn't being questioned, he was under twenty-four-hour visual observation by guards, who were forbidden to talk to him. He had no contact with the outside world, no TV, radio, or newspapers during the entire time. For over two years he was given nothing to read. When he constructed a makeshift calendar out of threads, it was taken from him. His diet was regular but meager. In his own words, "I was hungry, and this was the most difficult for me because how I tried not to think about food. I was thinking about food because all the time I want to eat. I was receiving very small amount, and very poor food."[1] His prison cell was concrete, about eight feet square, with no windows, only an opening with steel bars in the top half of the door. A single steel bed with a mattress but no pillow or sheets and an occasional blanket were the only furnishings. From time to time he was allowed to go outside into a small compound surrounded by walls so high that he could see only the sky. His clothing was inadequate for the Virginia winters. He was denied toothpaste and a toothbrush and was permitted to shave and shower only once a week. During the entire

1. Testimony before the House Select Committee on Assassinations, August 7, 1978, p. 525.

period he was administered one or more of four drugs on seventeen occasions. Doctors periodically also pressured him psychologically.

In 1976 the CIA assigned an officer, John Hart, to do a thorough, objective study of how Nosenko was handled. Hart reported, "His accommodations were . . . absolutely unacceptable, in my personal opinion, from any civilized point of view."[2] Despite all this, Nosenko never changed his story. The whole procedure was a travesty of the rights of the individual under the law. There was no conceivable excuse for treating Yuri Nosenko in this manner. The nation's security was not at stake. Even if he had been a double agent, he was no threat. We did not have to believe what he told us about the Soviet Union. We didn't even have to listen to him. What may have driven Angleton was that had Nosenko been a double agent and confessed, he could have given us even more useful information about Soviet intelligence operations than he did. But this hardly justified the inhumane treatment. It was all unnecessary. Fortunately, and I suppose surprisingly, the story has a happy ending. Nosenko recovered from his ordeal. He has become a remarkably well adjusted U.S. citizen and has done nothing to cause us to believe he was not a genuine defector.

After reading the Hart study on Nosenko and after studying thoroughly the CIA's involvement in drug-testing, I realized how far dedicated but unsupervised people could go wrong in the name of doing good intelligence work. I saw the pressing need to do more than ride out the mistakes of the CIA's past. Something was inherently wrong when a Gottlieb or an Angleton had so much freedom to do so much harm — and all to no advantage to the United States. The more I probed, the more I blamed these and other abuses on a practice that in the jargon of intelligence is called "compartmentation."

Secrets in the CIA are generally more sensitive than in almost any other area of government. The truly important ones are the identities of the people who risk their lives spying on hostile countries for us and those which reveal the technical means we use to spy. The lives of agents and our continued ability to acquire good information depend on those secrets being kept. In contrast, ex-

2. Testimony before the House Select Committee on Assassinations, September 11, 12, 13, 14, and 15, 1978, p. 517.

cept in wartime, military secrets generally pertain to what we know about the enemy and what the characteristics of our weapons are, not how we got that information or who got it for us, and on whom we will continue to depend for future information. Although it is difficult to say one secret is more important than another, the sources and methods by which the CIA works do relate more directly, even in peacetime, to lives and to our ability not to be surprised by an enemy. These concerns have spawned reliance on compartmentation. Under such a system, secrets are divided into discrete segments, or compartments. An individual is allowed to know only those details of a secret operation with which he must deal directly. Others know only their portions. In this way, if there is a leak or defection, the chance of an entire operation being exposed is reduced.

For instance, when we need information in a foreign country someone specifies exactly what is needed, though he doesn't know what capability we have of getting that information; someone else may know all of the spies we have available in that country and will select the one most suited to this task; still another will develop the plan for the selected spy to get the information and transmit it back to us, even though he doesn't know the spy's identity; and, finally, someone overseas will contact the spy to transmit the instructions and receive the information that is collected. Only a few people at the top will know all parts of the operation. Just as parts of an operation are kept separate, so is one operation from another. Those who know all about one operation probably will know nothing of another operation.

I found the system of compartmentation eminently sensible. I couldn't help wondering, though, if it had been used deliberately to keep people from knowing what they properly needed to know to supervise the Gottliebs and Angletons. I found it difficult to believe, for instance, that DCI Dick Helms knew what was being done to Nosenko when he continued to approve his prolonged incarceration. As the pieces fell into place, I could see that Angleton had manipulated the system by constructing elaborate barriers around sensitive information. He had built a powerful empire within the CIA. If anyone challenged him, he could say or imply that there was other information the challenger did not have that justified his actions. He acquired such autonomy that even his superiors sometimes could not find out what he was doing and in many cases were intimidated by him. Angleton's barony was not the only one built in the CIA by controlled access to knowledge, but it was the most harmful.

I doubted the CIA could survive another round of damaging criticism and publicity such as that of 1975–1976. I could appreciate that compartmentation was necessary, but checks on the Angletons had to be established. The solution was neither simple nor obvious. To find it, I had to learn how each of the key elements of the spy business was then operating: espionage, counterintelligence, covert action, technical spying, some less obvious forms of intelligence-gathering, analysis, and the marketing of the final product. In the next seven chapters, I discuss what I found, as well as some problems that had eluded the investigators and the press.

FIVE

Espionage:
The Dark Science

IN THE WORLD of espionage, there are two kinds of spies. They both risk exposure, arrest, and sometimes their lives in the clandestine search for information to forewarn the United States. They are called case officers and agents. The case officer is always a CIA person, usually an American, usually overseas. He is the contact between CIA Headquarters and the agents who do the actual spying. Agents generally are foreigners who are willing to spy for the United States. Some do so for money, some because they prefer our ideology to that of their own countries, some because they carry a grudge against their government, some for adventure, and some because of a personal friendship with the case officer who recruits them. CIA psychologists appraise the reliability and truthfulness of the agents. Some of the psychologists are overseas, where they can interview agents. More often they are at Headquarters and use descriptions furnished by the case officer or interviews with people who know the agent or reports on the agent's personal characteristics, like handwriting.

Citizens of the country are the best agents. They have better access, can move more easily in their country, and have a legitimate network of friends and associates on whom they can rely for help. Spy movies and novels to the contrary, it is not easy for an outsider to gain access to significant classified information inside another country, at least not in hostile countries or those with efficient counterintelligence services. If, for example, you want to know what decisions the Cabinet in some country is taking, you need someone who sits in on Cabinet meetings or types the minutes of those meetings or can get into the Cabinet room to plant a microphone. Most Americans could not do that. Language alone is a major barrier.

The risks of espionage begin with the process of persuading someone to be our agent. In many societies any contact with a foreigner may subject a citizen to special surveillance. Since it frequently takes a number of meetings for a case officer and a potential agent to reach agreement on what the agent will or will not do, those contacts may tip off local security services and lead to the prospective agent's arrest. Although it's not always possible, all intelligence services would prefer to avoid this risk by recruiting the agent outside his country, where surveillance is less likely.

Once an agent agrees to help us, there is a risk in establishing regular communications with him. The case officer must first communicate to the agent what information we need. Even this is not always simple. Language differences are very important when precision is vital. Sometimes the request concerns technical information that neither the case officer nor the agent fully understands. Because no agent wants to risk his life for the wrong information, more communication may be needed to clarify the mission.[1] The CIA's technical specialists invent all manner of clever devices to permit case officers and agents to communicate without having to meet face to face. But everything from secret writing to electronic wizardry sooner or later can be detected, so the quest for newer methods is never ending.

The major risk to the agent usually comes in the course of gathering the information. If he asks a secretary to pass him copies of Cabinet minutes, he is vulnerable should the secretary be unable to conceal their relationship. If he goes into a Cabinet room to plant a microphone, he may be discovered.

When the agent attempts to transmit his findings to the case officer, there is a risk similar to the one posed when he received his instructions.

1. "His" is used throughout in a general sense. Both men and women act as case officers and agents for most intelligence services.

Exposure and arrest sometimes become a cat-and-mouse game. In July 1977, the Soviets arrested and expelled Martha Peterson, a U.S. embassy officer in Moscow. They accused her of spying. This was an unusual deviation from the normal practice of giving little or no publicity to the expulsion of persons protected by diplomatic immunity, who were caught spying or allegedly spying. *Izvestia,* a government newspaper, played this up as a sensational spy case; Ms. Peterson was supposed to have been caught in the act of stocking a "dead drop" with cameras, gold, Russian currency, instructions, and ampules of poison for one of her operatives.[2] *Izvestia* used the apprehension of Ms. Peterson to support its most sensational charge: that she earlier had been an accessory to the murder of a Soviet citizen who had stood in the way of CIA-backed espionage operations. The newspaper said she had supplied ampules of poison to an unidentified male accomplice, who used them to eliminate an innocent Soviet citizen. The Soviets photographed Ms. Peterson sitting at a table alongside what it said was her espionage paraphernalia. The United States did not acknowledge guilt in the Peterson case.

There are times when the Soviets harass Americans without any justification, just to make the CIA look ineffective and to discourage their citizens from working with us, to keep us off balance. Often this starts a round of expulsions of diplomats from both countries, whether they are known to be spies or not. In this case we elected not to risk a "spy war" by retaliating in kind. It was only a few months later, though, that the Soviets took the offensive again. This time they arrested a Soviet citizen in Moscow on charges of working for the CIA. They gave his trial a lot of publicity and sentenced him to death.

They got their due eight months later, in May 1978, when the FBI arrested three Soviet spies in Woodbridge, New Jersey. They had been set up by a U.S. naval officer who pretended to be spying for them but was working for the FBI. Two of the Soviets, Rudolf P. Chernyayev and Vladik A. Enger, though ostensibly working at the United Nations, did not have diplomatic status. That meant we could take them to court, something the Soviets were not able to do with Ms. Peterson, who did hold diplomatic

2. A "dead drop" is something left at a prearranged spot to be recovered later by the person for whom it's intended.

status. The Soviets had simply expelled her from their country, but we had the opportunity to put Enger and Chernyayev in jail. That started a fierce debate within the administration.

Griffin Bell, the Attorney General, insisted that lawbreakers should be prosecuted whenever possible. Secretary of State Cy Vance and I opposed prosecuting in this case. Vance felt we had more to lose by antagonizing the Soviets than we would gain by putting a couple of spies in jail. A summit meeting between Carter and Leonid Brezhnev was coming up the following month, and the negotiations on SALT II were also in a delicate stage. I argued against prosecuting because I believed that the Soviets would retaliate. When the President sided with Bell and we took the men to court, the Soviets did just that.

First they arrested an American businessman on charges of dealing on the black market. He was tried, convicted, held in custody for few weeks, and released. Then, for the first time, the Soviets publicly disclosed the Martha Peterson case, by that time almost a year old.

We persisted in prosecution despite these pressures. The two Soviets were convicted, and each was sentenced to fifty years in prison. While the sentences were under appeal we traded them for five Russian dissidents who wanted to leave the Soviet Union. Attorney General Bell was satisfied that the "criminals" had been tried. The country gained more satisfaction, though, in obtaining the freedom of the dissidents than in placing the two spies behind bars.

Bell and the President were right in going ahead with the prosecution of the Russians, since nothing untoward happened as a result. The spy war became nothing more than the ripples over Martha Peterson and the businessman. There was no interruption of the SALT II or summit meetings. I had argued against prosecuting largely because of the strong concern of the CIA's espionage branch that retaliatory actions might get out of control.

One of the major tenets of intelligence is that all intelligence services work very hard to protect their case officers and agents and to rescue them if they get caught. The most daring exploit I witnessed in my four years as DCI was a successful effort by the Agency to protect the life of an agent who thought he was about to be arrested. In part this is a moral obligation; in part, it is a pragmatic matter, because it assures future agents that they will be taken care of if at all possible. But it is also an expression of the rapport that develops between a case officer and his agents. Usually the relationship is very personal and close. The agent works on a one-to-one basis, seeing only one case officer during any given period. (Case officers do rotate stations every few years.) A case officer and a handful of his superiors are the only ones who know who the agent is. The sense of responsibility of those few individuals for an agent is very strong. There was, then, a reluctance to see outsiders like the President and the Attorney General becoming involved in decisions that could possibly affect the ability of the intelligence professionals to protect their people. Their concern was understandable, but because we could hardly admit that those were our grounds, we lost.

Ironically, though the professionals worried too much about outside interference when case officers or agents were caught, they didn't worry enough inside the Agency about what had gone wrong. Sometimes when a Martha Peterson was accused or a Soviet citizen brought to trial, we were innocent, but sometimes we weren't. In the latter circumstances, I noted a reluctance on the part of the espionage branch to conduct thorough appraisals of what went wrong. This is the most glamorous arm of the CIA, and I sensed that its members' unwillingness was largely a matter of pride; they did not want to air mistakes before a new director. I therefore had to insist on examining how our people in the field and those in the Headquarters had performed. Fortunately, there were not many compromises to be investigated. When there were, we started by looking not only at the actual espionage action, but also at the way we normally went about business at the particular CIA overseas station. Could it be that our communications to the station were being deciphered? Were we dividing up our messages and sending different parts through different communications channels? Could someone have planted bugs? We employ many foreigners in U.S. facilities around the world. All highly secret conversations at a CIA station are supposed to take place in protected rooms that are specially constructed to prevent anyone's planting microphones in them. Were we confining discussions about agent operations to such rooms? Were they as secure as we thought? Was it even possible that our Headquarters in Langley had been penetrated by a Soviet mole?

After checking these general sources of compromise, we reviewed both the case officer's and the agent's methods of operation. It's always possible that the agent doesn't follow good procedures and thus compromises himself. Agents sometimes become overconfident, taking chances that are unwise and unnecessary. Occasionally an agent will be so indiscreet and daring that we suspect he may be a double agent and is, in fact, taking no risk at all. Sometimes agents simply become philosophical about what fate may have in store for them and get careless. That's why we go first to the psychologists to ask whether they see this agent as someone who may throw caution to the wind, and next to the counterintelligence experts to scrutinize every indicator of inconsistency in the agent's reporting that may show he has been deceiving us all along. Hard evidence is usually lacking. Most often, the best we can do is arrive at a subjective estimate. We had one case of a very important agent who supposedly committed suicide after being caught by his country's security police. I'll always wonder whether he may not still be alive and working for that security service.

Another possibility, of course, is that the error may be the case officer's. He may be negligent when contacting the agent, not taking elaborate precautions to ensure that he is not being followed to a rendezvous or when making a "dead drop." It's always difficult to tell if the case officer follows procedures carefully. In the end we must rely on their training and judgment.

Because so much depends on the individual case officers, I decided early on to find out who they were and how we were training them. An extensive recruiting system exists in the United States, including many clearly marked offices that are listed in telephone books. CIA recruiters participate openly in job fairs on a large number of college campuses; they advertise in national newspapers and magazines and use other normal techniques of any business or government agency in recruiting. The CIA looks for college graduates who have excelled academically and who work well with people. There is a strong preference for men and women with three or four years of experience in business or the military after college. They have more maturity and experience than the average graduate fresh from college. The CIA wants them to have thought about their life goals, tried a job or two, and be ready to make an informed and ultimately stable decision about the future. Once these people are out in the field, they are very much on their own and must be able to make critical decisions quickly and with confidence. There's usually no one to turn to in a risky situation with an agent in a hostile country.

I visited the training facility where newly recruited case officers are sent for six months of "tradecraft" training. Some of the training was in the classroom; some in the field, doing things like practicing secret communications or following someone without being detected by that person or being followed by someone else. In my first exchange with a group of recruits in 1977, I found that they wanted assurance, after all of the public criticism, that they were entering an honorable profession, one the country wanted and would support. I assured them of what I truly believed — that they were indispensable to our national security. I told them that their lives would not be easy nor their careers filled with public reward, but, instead, that their reward would come in knowing how substantially they were contributing to their countrymen's freedom and to the preservation of our way of life. Theirs was indeed an honorable profession, with values and standards that reflected the nation's. I subsequently encouraged the inclusion in recruit training of forthright discussions of the ethical dilemmas and moral standards of intelligence work and of the process we were going through of ensuring that those standards were met by introducing external oversight into the system. My hope was to help these young men and women anticipate the complex ethical issues they would face in the field. With some deliberate forethought and reflection they might make better judgments. It wasn't easy to open up these kinds of discussions at first. Such issues had not been part of the agenda when the instructors went through their own training, and few of them believed that espionage, ethics, and oversight were all compatible. The importance of the discussions sold itself over time.

It was more difficult to figure out what to do about those few case officers who deliberately used their training and experience for their own gain, a rare occurrence but one that had to be guarded against. There are special temptations for someone engaged in espionage, because there are so few checks on what he is doing. A case officer may sometimes work with people who offer him a bribe or a deal. The secrecy that shrouds his work from his superiors and his family makes it easier for him than for a man in another walk of life to give in to these temptations.

On April 12, 1977, just five weeks after I became DCI, Bob Woodward of Watergate fame published a story in the *Washington Post* that immediately caught my attention. It alleged that a former CIA officer, Edmund P. Wilson, had been involved in procuring the timing pencils used in September 1976 to detonate the bomb that killed the former Chilean ambassador to the United States, Orlando Letelier, in Washington. The story said that Wilson was also involved in plotting assassinations on behalf of President Muammar Qaddafi of Libya. What especially caught my eye, though, was the following: "There is some evidence that Wilson may have had contact with one or more current CIA employees who have access to supplies of timing pencils." Did we have some disloyal or dishonest people inside the CIA? When would Woodward write his next story, with more details?

I had met Woodward briefly in 1966 when he was a junior officer in the Navy and again, a few weeks before this, on a TV talk show. He seemed a reasonable and friendly person, so I asked the public affairs officer, Herbert E. Hetu, to see whether he could get Woodward to hold any more stories until I looked thoroughly into this charge. Herb told Woodward that I did not know whether his allegation about Wilson's getting assistance from inside the CIA was true or not and that I wanted to get to the bottom of the matter. He pointed out that, as a new man in the Agency, I had nothing to hide and every reason to want to know if this kind of thing was going on. He promised that if Woodward let me have a few days to sort it out, I would give him an exclusive story on what I found. Woodward apparently thought that the prospect of a scoop was worth his holding back for a bit. Or perhaps he didn't have any more details on our people. For whatever reason, he agreed.

I quickly found that the CIA was well aware of the points Woodward had made. Another former CIA employee, Kevin Mulcahy, had come to the CIA and to the FBI in September 1976 to volunteer information about Wilson's activities. Mulcahy had worked for Wilson until he became convinced that many of Wilson's business activities were either illegal or improper. He reported this to the number two man in espionage, Theodore (Ted)

Shackley, and to an officer on the staff of the CIA's inspector general. Mulcahy's story had led to the uncovering of the two current Agency employees to whom Woodward had referred. I will call them Hilliard and Lowell. All this, in turn, led to a full investigation of these two employees by the CIA and an investigation by the FBI of Wilson and others who were no longer under CIA jurisdiction.

Lowell was a middle-level case officer in the espionage branch. He admitted that while on an overseas assignment he had done work for Wilson on the side. He had gone so far as to have a calling card printed, showing that he worked for Wilson's firm. Moonlighting is not illegal for most government employees, but CIA regulations permit it only when the person has the express approval of the Agency, because it often makes it more difficult for him to maintain his cover, his false identity. By working for Wilson, Lowell had attracted attention to himself and could easily have compromised his covert status with the CIA. It is difficult enough to play one cover role at a time; it is almost impossible to play several. Of even more serious concern was that he might have given people who knew he worked for the CIA the impression that Wilson's activities were being carried out on behalf of the CIA. There was also the question of whether his work for Wilson was illegal. Mulcahy's accusation that Wilson was supplying arms to Libya indicated that it might be, though the evidence was not conclusive.

Hilliard was not a case officer; he was a support person who arranged for the various supplies that case officers require. He had interceded on Wilson's behalf with a manufacturer of timing pencils. In so doing, he had given the impression that the order to be delivered to Wilson was actually for the CIA. Once the bill came to the CIA, however, Hilliard's improper dealings were uncovered. When I talked to him, he professed that he was simply doing a favor for an old friend by putting him in touch with the manufacturer. He did not intend, he said, to give the CIA's stamp of approval to Wilson's purchase. The CIA's investigator had accepted Hilliard's claim that he had been duped by Wilson and had not been an accomplice. His case had already been settled with a mild reprimand. Lowell's had not.

In both cases one additional fact bore heavily on my views.

Hilliard and Lowell had each broken CIA regulations previously and been officially reprimanded. There was no suggestion that either earlier infraction was related to Edmund P. Wilson, but it was clear that both men had shown a disregard for the rules of the Agency.

I soon found that almost no one agreed with me on the handling of these cases. Not one CIA professional concurred with my instant reaction to fire the two men. Hank Knoche, the men's supervisors, the inspector general, and all the others I consulted were in favor of some lesser punishment. Only Robert (Rusty) Williams, a man I brought into the CIA as a special assistant, joined me in favoring dismissal. Because I did not yet understand the culture of the CIA, I found it very difficult to go against all this counsel. I was also concerned that my ignoring the advice of the top leadership might make it more difficult to establish my authority with them and elicit their future cooperation. I had been there only six weeks, so they were still taking my measure. Was I going to be on their team, or was I someone to resist? I wanted badly to curb the adverse publicity the Agency was still receiving, because it was forcing the professionals to spend too much time explaining the past rather than looking ahead. Being firm with Lowell and Hilliard might lessen the effect of Woodward's next story, but was it fair even to consider the impact on my role in the Agency or the publicity we would probably receive when I determined the men's fate? Was my military background prejudicing my view?

After considerable agonizing, I found that my aversion to retaining men of questionable standards in the organization was too strong for me to do anything other than dismiss them. They were jeopardizing my ability to keep the Agency under control. They were second offenders, so it was clear that they disdained the rules. I fired Lowell and Hilliard. Time was to prove me right with respect to Lowell. He turned up not long after in Libya, working for Wilson. That was good enough evidence to me that he was quite willing to skirt not just the rules of the CIA, but the law, as Wilson did. To my knowledge, Hilliard has not been identified with Wilson since his firing.

I met Bob Woodward and gave him the facts. On April 27 he ran a story that was accurate and straightforward; he wrote that I had fired two CIA employees who had provided unauthorized assistance to Wilson and that this signaled a new era of strict compliance with the rules. He added that my willingness to publicize their firing ran "counter to a long CIA tradition of handling such matters quietly." It did, but it also brought to an abrupt end the media's attention to the story. The next mention of it was years later, when Wilson was heading for jail; then the firings were mentioned as a commendable response by the CIA to Wilson.

The publicity was behind us, but we were still faced with the question of how much deeper into the organization Wilson's influence went. During my inquiries on Lowell and Hilliard, I found out about two very senior officers who were in touch with Wilson. One was Ted Shackley. When I asked him about his relationship with Wilson, he assured me that it was purely social, mainly ties between their wives. He went to Wilson's farm on weekends, but fully understood that there was to be no connection between the CIA and Wilson. Here, again, I was in a dilemma. I had no evidence of any wrongdoing on Shackley's part, yet I could not understand how he could associate with someone like Wilson. I expected a higher sense of integrity in a man who held a position as sensitive as his. If I had known then as much about Wilson as I know today, I probably would have asked Shackley to retire. I would have done so not on the grounds that he had done anything improper, but that he was associating with a man of very questionable character. At the least, he was giving others in the CIA the impression that Wilson was still on good terms with us. It may have been just that which drew Hilliard into supporting him by ordering detonators. Still, it was difficult at the time for me to do anything so drastic as to force out such a senior person as Shackley on the basis of only tentative information. (Wilson is now serving a fifty-two-year prison term for conspiring to smuggle guns to Libya, for conspiring to ship forty tons of high explosives to the same country, and for conspiring to murder two U.S. prosecutors and six other people.)

The other senior officer who was suspect was Thomas Clines. Clines had been seen with Wilson and Lowell in a restaurant at a time when we knew Wilson was trying to get various forbidden materials to ship illegally to Libya. He claimed it was a chance meeting. That seemed unlikely to us, but no hard evidence turned up, even after an investigation by the inspector general. Clines voluntarily retired a year later and borrowed money from Wilson to start a business. In early 1984, Clines pleaded guilty on behalf of his company to charges of filing false invoices that masked illegal profits from transporting U.S. arms to Egypt from 1979 to 1981.

I still had to worry about Wilson's creating the impression that he was working on assignments for the CIA under contract. He obviously had been quite successful in getting people outside the CIA, as well as inside, to make this assumption and to do things for him. It is difficult to counter such an impression. Some people are gullible and tend to believe all manner of stories about what the CIA may be doing. A Naval Academy classmate whom I barely remembered wrote me a congratulatory letter when I became DCI. I sent a polite reply. He wrote again, asking a question, and I replied once more. A few years later I was asked to testify in court, because this man had used my correspondence to represent himself as working for the CIA. He bilked a number of patriotic citizens out of several hundred thousand dollars to fund his supposed endeavors for the Agency!

The best I could do to counteract the impression Wilson was creating was to make it clear to the entire Agency that there was no connection between us and him. I called a meeting in the Bubble and stated unequivocally that there was to be no association between the Agency and Wilson. I also had a message sent to all the CIA stations in the field. I am told that Wilson believes that message was the beginning of his downfall. He no longer could masquerade as being an associate of ours, and any CIA person who supported him knew he was doing so at the risk of losing his job.

In Woodward's story about my decision to fire Hilliard and Lowell, he quoted me as saying that I found it "the most difficult decision I have made in thirty years of military service." Looking back, I believe that was an exaggeration on my part. But it seemed extremely difficult at the time because none of the professionals in the Agency supported me.

Happily, there was also a positive aspect to my early contacts with our espionage work, some marvelous successes in the field. One was the very risky planting of a sensing device to monitor a secret activity in a hostile country. The case officer had to do the placement himself, escaping surveillance and proceeding undetected to a location so unusual that had he been found, he undoubtedly would have paid with his life. Contrary to popular spy novels, CIA case officers are seldom exposed to life-threatening circumstances, but in this instance I asked to be awakened in the middle of the night when the case officer reported back safely at base.

There's no objective way to measure how good CIA espionage is, but it is true that no matter how much we rely on technology, there will always be a need for human spies. The Soviets know this and have a much larger espionage effort than ours, but larger does not necessarily mean better. We have seen some pretty clumsy Soviet attempts at espionage; the Enger and Chernyayev case was one. It is my belief, though I cannot state it with absolute certainty, that the product of our smaller human intelligence effort meets our needs as well as the larger Soviet effort meets theirs.

SIX

Counterintelligence:
Is There a Mole in Our Midst?

WE ATTEMPT to recruit foreigners to spy for us; foreign powers attempt to recruit Americans to spy on us. The job of counterintelligence is to find those Americans who do become agents of a foreign power. Sometimes an American becomes a spy unwittingly; that is, he is inveigled into loose talk or braggadocio and lets secrets out of the bag. What is more dangerous is an American who becomes a recruited agent and gives away secrets deliberately.

The most threatening recruitment is that of one of our seemingly loyal intelligence officers. If he becomes a mole, not only can he pass on what he knows in the course of his normal business, but he can burrow around for the specific information desired by the country he is working for. He may, for instance, try to find and pass on the identity of our agents in a foreign country, compromising our intelligence-gathering there for many years. He may try to find out the characteristics of sophisticated technical spying systems so that our enemies can find ways to counter them.

Another type of mole we worry about is the phony defector, as Nosenko was thought to be. Such a person will initially share with us some enticing secrets he has been given to use as bait. Eventually, he hopes, we will share some secrets with him. We are often tempted to do just that to verify information we have uncovered in his country. In time, he may learn much about how effective American intelligence is and how it operates. He will concentrate on one kind of information on which his country places great value: who is spying for us in that country. The Soviets are very patient in this sort of operation. They are willing to plant such a man and leave him for years before expecting any substantial return.

The use of moles is a longstanding tradition in intelligence. Back in biblical days the King of Syria asked whether there was a spy inside his own camp when Elisha, using spiritual insight, was predicting his moves to the King of Israel. Moles, those who spy against their own country, like agents, have diverse motivations. Often it's money; perhaps it is an ideological sympathy with the other country's way of life and disdain of one's own. Our British and German allies have had a rash of apparently ideologically motivated moles since World War II. Several, who defected to Moscow when they became suspect, were especially damaging because they had operated at high levels for prolonged periods. Although our record is better, it is not perfect. William H. Martin and Bernon F. Mitchell were employees of the National Security Agency who became moles for the Soviets. They fled to the Soviet Union when they came under suspicion in 1960. We surmise by their willingness to flee that they were ideologically committed to spying for the Soviets. Other moles who we knew operated from inside were two U.S. Army sergeants also assigned to the National Security Agency. They committed suicide in the mid 1960s just before being arrested for spying. Whether their motivation was ideology or, more likely, simply money is not clear.

There have been two well-publicized cases of CIA officers defecting, though both had left the Agency before doing so. Philip Agee had such personal and financial problems that he was having difficulty playing his CIA undercover role adequately and resigned from the CIA in 1968. In his letter of resignation, Agee expressed his admiration for the CIA and his regret at having to leave. He even hoped he might be able to come back some day. But, deeper in debt and with other emotional problems, he ended up in Cuba. We assume that he was brainwashed. By 1975 Agee had published a revealing and derogatory book on the CIA and begun lashing out at his former employer, primarily by making public the names of those fellow case officers whom he could remember. We believe he also passed on to the Cubans whatever other secrets he recalled. This seems to be a case of the Cubans' taking advantage of Agee's financial and emotional vulnerabilities. Both they and the Soviets have exploited him fully. Whether he was won over ideologically or was simply taken in by the flattery of becoming a well-known figure is difficult to assess. He has skirted the fringes of existing U.S. espionage law, and because that law is antiquated, whether Agee could actually be convicted is unclear. He remains abroad so as not to bring that to a test.

Another CIA traitor was David H. Barnett, who resigned from the CIA in 1970 after twelve years of service. When he was arrested in 1980, he confessed to having spied for the Soviets since 1976. He had identified CIA personnel and divulged how the CIA tracked Soviet shipments of armaments to Indonesia. Such deliberate passing of secrets is punishable under law, and Barnett was jailed for ten years. Money appeared to be his motive. Fortunately, there is no evidence that he was a mole while on active service, when he could have done even more harm.

There are others who have given away classified information, some of it very damaging, but they were not actually moles, because they were not recruited while inside our intelligence apparatus. Also, most were low-level employees. During my years as DCI, we had two major cases of spying by Americans. One was that of two young men in California, Christopher Boyce and Daulton Lee.

Both Boyce and Lee had been raised in upper-class, privileged surroundings near Los Angeles. Boyce had dropped out of one college after another and found his way into a clerk's job with the TRW Corporation in Redondo Beach. TRW was doing some contract work for the CIA. Boyce's life was unsatisfying, and he was disillusioned with the United States in the wake of Vietnam. Lee was deeply into drugs and debt. In early 1975, they began plotting for Boyce to purloin secret documents from TRW and for Lee to take them to Mexico City, where he would sell them to the Soviets. In April of 1975, Lee made his first trip, followed by numerous others. Then the Mexicans noted that some of his actions around the Soviet embassy were unusual. He was arrested in January of 1977.

I had to decide how much information the CIA would release so that these two obvious traitors could be prosecuted. In this instance we would have to produce in court at least some of the documents that had been stolen and explain what they were. Only then could a jury evaluate the extent of the damage to national security. Even though the Soviets had the documents, we did not want to expose them further in public. Other nations did not have the information, and if it got into the U.S. press, it might help persevering reporters deduce and expose other secrets that had not reached the Soviets. Day by day, as the trial progressed, I found the Agency's general counsel, Anthony Lapham, at my door with one difficult issue after another requiring decision. I quickly developed full confidence in Tony, a forty-one-year-old graduate of Yale and of Georgetown University Law School. George Bush had recruited him from private practice. He is a large, hulking man with a quick, keen mind and a sense of humor that shows clearly how much he enjoys life. Although he was an outsider to the Agency, he had won the confidence of the professionals because he worked well with them. On a case like that of Boyce and Lee, he first had to determine how far the professionals thought we could go; then he went over the ground with me, and we reached a decision on just what we would say in court.

In this instance we authorized Leslie C. Dirks, chief of the Agency's technical branch, to testify in considerable detail about Project Pyramider, the system that had been compromised.

> Project Pyramider is a system to provide a means for communicating with CIA agents, foreign agents, emplaced sensors, and provide backup communications for overseas facilities. The key distinction is covert communications as opposed to standard, routine satellite communications. It also has to do with communications with what we call emplaced sensors — these are pieces of equipment left behind in various parts of the world which collect data remotely and later relay that data back to stations that we man. One example would be a seismic sensor. There are seismic sensors all over the world for the purpose of detecting earthquakes and also for the purpose of detecting underground nuclear explosions.[1]

1. Transcript of Leslie C. Dirks's testimony in the trial of Christopher Boyce, pp. 966-1014.

Each time we authorized a statement like that, it was likely to lead to a demand by the defense or the court for further details that might well go beyond what we believed we could afford to say. Fortunately, we never reached the point where we had to ask the Attorney General to halt the prosecution because we could not disclose what was requested. We did get a conviction. Boyce was sentenced to forty years in jail and Lee to life.[2] Robert Lindsey, who has written two books on the Boyce-Lee affair, reached the interesting conclusion that Boyce "betrayed his country for excitement."[3]

William Kampiles may have been similarly motivated. Kampiles came to work at the CIA in March of 1977. He was assigned to a twenty-four-hour watch center that monitors intelligence around the world. Never knowing what might come up next, the people at the watch center keep a lot of reference materials on hand. Among them was a manual that described a photographic satellite system called the KH-11, which Kampiles read in the course of his duties. After a time he began to express dissatisfaction with standing unglamorous watches at all hours of the day and night. He pleaded that he had always wanted to be a case officer in the espionage branch. His record in the watch center was not sufficiently impressive to persuade the espionage branch to accept him. He was repeatedly turned down for a transfer, his performance on watch deteriorated, and consequently any chance of a future transfer vanished. In November 1977, after only eight months in the CIA, marked by considerable acrimony between him and his supervisors, he resigned. When he left he took with him a copy of the KH-11 manual. He claimed later that he planned to sell the manual to the Soviets, become their agent, and then return to the CIA and offer to be a double agent for us. In that way he would gain entry to the espionage branch after all. Even if true, it was a crazy scheme. As it was, an extremely valuable set of secrets went to the Soviets for only $3000. We caught on, and Kampiles was arrested and sent to jail for forty years.

There were many errors and lessons in this case. The CIA's security procedures were surprisingly lax. Each copy of the KH-11

2. Boyce escaped from jail after a little more than two years, but was apprehended after seventeen months.
3. *New York Times Magazine*, October 2, 1983.

manual was serially numbered, but not regularly inventoried. When we learned that one was missing, we also found we could not account for thirteen others! What was even more disconcerting was that, despite all the criticism of Kampiles' performance in the watch center and the denial of his applications for transfer, his supervisors rang no alarm bells about the reliability of a very new, young, and discontented employee who had access to highly sensitive information. Kampiles may well have been entertaining a James Bond view of what life in the CIA should be and, like Boyce, was searching for greater excitement.

The Kampiles case also posed some knotty legal problems when it came to trial. We had to produce a copy of the KH-11 manual that Kampiles had sold, yet the CIA and the Defense Department both wanted to avoid making this highly classified document public for much the same reason that the Pyramider document in the Boyce-Lee trial needed protection. In an arrangement worked out with the judge, only the attorneys, jury, expert witnesses, and the judge were allowed to read the manual; it was not entered as part of the record of the judicial proceedings. That worked quite satisfactorily.

There was also the matter of explaining how we had caught on to what Kampiles had done without risking the future usefulness of the technique we had employed. As the case progressed, both Tony Lapham and I found that we had developed enough confidence in the judge to tell him the true story. We did so by placing a 150-page explanatory document in our safe in his chambers. Thus, our representative was present whenever the safe was opened, ensuring that only the judge read what was in it.[4]

Wayward intelligence officers becoming moles are not the only counterintelligence problem we worry about. The Soviets attempt to recruit Americans who have access to secrets from organizations outside the Intelligence Community as well as within. The greatest number of such recruitments have been in the Departments of Defense and State, where much intelligence and security

4. A safe, or rather two safes, figured prominently in another CIA court case. We again proposed putting some secret evidence in a safe in the judge's chambers, but this judge evidently feared the CIA might go into the safe in his absence and alter the evidence. He suggested that we put our safe inside his safe! When Tony Lapham told me of the judge's proposal I said, "Let's do it," and the scheme worked very well.

information is handled. In 1977 we uncovered an American in the State Department, Ronald L. Humphrey, who was giving classified documents on Far Eastern matters to Truong Dinh Hung, known as David Truong, a representative of the North Vietnamese government. Here another difficult legal question arose. Truong was sending the documents he obtained from Humphrey by courier to representatives of the North Vietnamese government in Paris. What Truong did not know was that his courier, Mrs. Dung Krall, was working for the CIA. She was a Vietnamese married to an American naval officer. When all the evidence was in, it was clear that we had a case against Truong and Humphrey. We could not, though, prosecute and still live up to a promise the CIA had made to Mrs. Krall that she would not have to appear at a public trial and disclose her role in assisting us. Of Vietnamese origin, she had a genuine concern for relatives who remained in Vietnam. I was adamant that we would not violate our agreement with her. Moreover, thanks to Mrs. Krall we had stopped the flow of secret documents to Vietnam. That's what we had enlisted her to help us do, not to see the case through to jail sentences for Truong and Humphrey.

Attorney General Griffin Bell's people treated the CIA's arrangement with Mrs. Krall lightly. They persisted in believing that we were telling her not to testify so that we could continue using her as an agent. That was of secondary importance to us, and it was, in fact, uncertain that she could be brought into any future operation. What was very important was our moral commitment to Mrs. Krall. The Justice Department tried to take over responsibility for Mrs. Krall and pressure her into testifying. There was considerable tension between the organizations. The CIA managed to work out an arrangement whereby she could testify with minimal risk to her relatives. She did, and Truong and Humphrey were each sent to jail for fifteen years.

A similar case occurred in August 1979, when a Navy yeoman, Lee Madsen, who worked in intelligence in the Pentagon, was caught in a bar attempting to pass secret documents to a Soviet case officer. He, too, is in jail.

How do counterintelligence people find a Boyce, Lee, Kampiles, Humphrey, Truong, or Madsen? One technique is to recruit our own moles inside hostile intelligence services. Former DCI

John McCone stated in 1963, "Experience has shown penetrations [of foreign intelligence services] to be the most effective response to Soviet and Bloc" efforts to plant moles with us.[5] That is why recruitment of Soviet intelligence officers has always had a very high priority with the CIA. The next best thing to an active mole working for us inside a foreign intelligence organization is a recent and genuine defector from its intelligence service. He will bring with him his memory of his country's espionage network in our country.

Another technique is to check on Americans we have good grounds to suspect. An individual's supervisors or coworkers may become suspicious of an unusual or changing behavior pattern, such as indebtedness, alcoholism, drug addiction, or extravagant spending. As I've noted, William Kampiles' prolonged dissatisfaction with his job should have made his superiors wary of retaining him in his sensitive position. Boyce grew marijuana plants in the TRW safe; the practice was not in itself remarkable, but the site was a bit unusual. Simple observation of his behavior should have prompted a second look by his supervisor. In almost all of the British cases, the high-level moles displayed abnormal patterns of activity that should have alerted someone.

More difficult is the government employee who has retired or resigned, taking with him a good deal of classified information. There are no supervisors to keep an eye on him, and intelligence agencies cannot pry into his private life. Only when there are grounds for reasonable suspicion that a law has been broken can the FBI conduct surveillance. That may not come until many secrets have been lost. We pay a price for respecting the rights of our citizens, and therefore must accept that our counterintelligence efforts will never be as effective as the KGB's.

Sometimes the initial clues we need for a counterintelligence investigation may just fall into our lap — serendipity. An agent may be working on some matter of foreign intelligence when he chances on something that alerts him. For instance, we may ask an agent to photograph some documents in a foreign ministry. One of those may certify that the information is authentic because it came from an agent inside the U.S. government. Just

5. McCone memorandum to President's Foreign Intelligence Advisory Board, October 8, 1963.

knowing that an American with access to that particular piece of information gave it away would be a good starting point for the painstaking work of picking up one clue here and one there and piecing them together. Sometimes we're not the ones who pick up the odd clue; it may be a friendly intelligence service that shares it with us.

The most important specific tool of counterintelligence is the polygraph, a controversial instrument that stirs strong feelings in both its advocates and its opponents. The latter, in part, have an emotional reaction against the unpleasantness of the experience of being tested. I volunteered for testing twice and each time found it repugnant just to have my honor implicitly questioned. And the sensation of being wired to a machine and not having any idea what it is registering created a sense of tension. Civil libertarians loathe the polygraph because of the potential for injustice. After a good deal of observation of the results of polygraph tests, I believe that potential definitely exists. It is low, but polygraph tests are subject to the attitude of the person doing the testing and his interpretation of the readings. I have seen a number of questionable results, and I would not count on a polygraph test as the only evidence against an individual. I view the polygraph only as a supplementary counterintelligence device when used on our own personnel.

There are two situations in which such use is called for: the screening of new applicants for employment (the CIA and the National Security Agency both use this) and the periodic, unscheduled retesting of employees. What I found extremely helpful was the confessions that were elicited during the retesting. We learned of people taking classified documents home to work on them, of staff having unauthorized discussions with newsmen, and of personal habits that raise questions of reliability. In addition, the fact that every CIA and NSA employee knows that he or she may be subject to a surprise polygraph test in itself inhibits loose security practices.

Largely because of the confessions and the inhibiting effect, I felt the polygraph had its usefulness, and I attempted to extend its use to civilian contractors and to certain other government personnel. For example, we were sending construction workmen to Moscow to help build a new embassy. We needed enough Americans on that job to prevent the Soviets from planting listening devices in the building.[6] I wanted all workmen who were sent to Moscow and the State Department and Marine Corps security personnel overseeing them to be polygraphed on their return home. The idea was to make certain that none had been bribed to let the Soviets install any devices. Cy Vance and Harold Brown initially acquiesced, and I got the President's approval. Later, because of the antipathy toward polygraphing, Vance and Brown were under such pressure from their bureaucracies that they persuaded the President to reverse himself.

Besides polygraphing new applicants and repolygraphing employees, the CIA uses the polygraph on foreign agents whenever feasible. In such cases it is an even more useful tool, because in the murky world of espionage the rights of the individual are not a high concern. First of all, these agents are well aware that establishing who's honest and who's not is a key element of their trade. Beyond that, they are not U.S. citizens protected by our constitutional rights. And there is little harm done if they are falsely accused by a polygraph report. Either we don't trust their reporting, and that would be our loss; or we don't employ them, both our loss and theirs, but they have no particular right to work for the CIA. Perhaps the best evidence that the polygraph does help separate true agents from false is that we know the KGB has made determined efforts to develop techniques for "beating the machine." Although there is a risk that some professionals will fool the polygraph, there is the greater one that our intelligence agencies will rely on it too heavily. If we take for granted that a person is loyal because he or she passed a polygraph test in the past, we may ignore signals that should indicate the contrary.

The most delicate part of counterintelligence is learning how to handle suspicions when they do arise. Counterintelligence experts can easily become overzealous. They can easily get carried away when they know that what they are doing is of tremendous and obvious importance to our intelligence capabilities. Beyond that, when anyone spends a long time being deliberately suspicious of

6. Some years ago another country permitted the Soviets to refurbish a building in Moscow as its embassy. Quite by accident, as the embassy staff were moving in, they discovered some unusual wiring inside the ventilation ducting. Following the wires down to the basement, they found that the wires led to an elaborately equipped listening post in an adjacent building.

those around him, it's easy for him to begin seeing clues where there aren't any. People who are intent on finding moles often see them everywhere. Grievous damage can be done when suspicion is misinterpreted as fact. There is a price to be paid when you allow counterintelligence experts to stay too long on the job; witness the fact that James Angleton was chief of CIA counterintelligence for twenty years. We've already seen one instance of Angleton's excessive zeal in his treatment of the Soviet defector Nosenko.

It is perfectly reasonable to test rigorously each new defector like Nosenko by checking and cross-checking the stories and the information he brings with him. The problem in Nosenko's case was that reasonable doubt grew into unreasonable willingness to force him to confess to being a double agent. I still feel deeply ashamed that our government treated any human being the way the CIA let Angleton treat Nosenko. It was a case of stooping to the kind of behavior we expect from the Soviets and other totalitarian societies. When I found that few people in the CIA knew about the Nosenko case and fewer wanted to be reminded of it, I insisted that reading and discussing the 1976 report on Nosenko by John Hart be made a compulsory part of every training course for senior officers in the CIA. What I intended was that they understand that counterintelligence has the potential of great abuse and that the Agency's senior people bear a responsibility not to let it get out of hand again.

Paranoia also affected the way that counterintelligence under James Angleton treated CIA officers on whom suspicion fell. With Angleton's acquiesence, members of his counterintelligence staff during much of the 1960s operated on the basis of a number of bizarre, specious theses. One was that under certain circumstances officers of the KGB would inevitably react in a certain way; that any CIA officer observing those circumstances was bound to see that reaction; if the CIA officer then failed to report such a reaction, he was holding out or covering up for the KGB person. The counterintelligence staff would then arrange to have this person treated as a suspect. Even though he was never openly or directly accused, he was barred from important or sensitive positions in the CIA. Careers were actually ruined on the assumption that failure to report something that might or might not have happened indicated guilt. The Soviets have a reputation for rigidity, but for us not to allow any deviation from a supposition was absurd and extremely unfair. When I was first told of this practice I laughed it off; it was so unreasonable, I thought, that it had to be apocryphal. After hearing it over and over again from people in the CIA whom I thoroughly trusted, I became convinced that the paranoia of the CIA's counterintelligence staff under Angleton had indeed gone that far.

Another equally bizarre thesis caused whole groups of people to be barred from sensitive positions because of reports that the Soviets had recruited a number of agents from people of their category. One report stated that certain groups of émigrés then in the CIA were spies; another asserted simply that there was a mole whose name began with a particular letter of the alphabet. Many émigrés or persons whose names began with that letter were treated as suspect and shunted into limbo by the CIA's counterintelligence staff, though no hard evidence against them ever turned up.

By 1977 some CIA retirees had come to realize that they had been wronged by the arbitrariness of counterintelligence under Angleton's management. I recall reviewing the case of an officer whose career had been brought to a dead halt by one of these specious theories. He and others were asking for compensation. I offered them as much money as I was permitted to give under existing law. Several such individuals opted instead to petition Congress for redress. In 1980, after investigating their claims, Congress passed special legislation enabling me to compensate more generously any employee who "had his career with the Agency adversely affected as a result of the allegations concerning the loyalty to the United States of such employee."[7] In short, the irrational conduct of the counterintelligence staff under Angleton was verified.

Still another area of counterintelligence that is often abused is that of dealing with Soviet "disinformation." The Soviets attempt to plant misleading information in our country through phony defectors or émigrés who give us false stories; through stories published by their Eastern European satellites that our press will pick

7. Public Law 96–450, October 14, 1980.

up; through American media people whom they supply with leaks that are sometimes genuine scoops and at other times disinformation; through attempts to recruit Americans in the media and pay them to distribute false information; and through the floating of clever forgeries. In fact, there is very little information about how much of this goes on. Most books and articles purporting to describe Soviet disinformation operations fall back on two kinds of substantiation. The first is guilt by association. That's usually association with an organization the author assumes is anti-American, though it may be just that the organization's views differ from his. Anyone who is part of such an organization or endorses its views is tagged as being an agent of Soviet disinformation. The second is a system of "proof" that can be used to support almost any thesis. If there are two or three facts that support the thesis and perhaps one to two that do not, an arbitrary judgment is made that the nonsupporting facts are Soviet disinformation intended to throw us off the track. The "fact" that the Soviets have planted them is then given as corroboration of the basic thesis!

Still, there is evidence, usually from defectors, of strenuous efforts by Soviet intelligence to shape public attitudes in our country in accordance with those favored by the Soviets, as in popular movements against nuclear weapons. There is almost no evidence of their success, other than that such movements continue to flourish, but it is seldom clear that it was Soviet support that made that possible. We, of course, make many similar efforts to plant information around the world. Sometimes it's done openly, through the U.S. Information Agency; sometimes through covert propaganda sponsored by the CIA.

The point is that we should not allow the success of Soviet disinformation efforts to make us paranoid. That is not to say that we do not face real problems. Rather, it is to warn how difficult it is to measure the amount of disinformation to which we are subjected and the damage it does, and to note that we face the same kind of risk in basing sweeping conclusions on suspicion and innuendo as we do in uncovering spies. The same kinds of defense apply to disinformation as to moles and the same kinds of cost. One added defense, though, is that any disinformation campaign must pass through our own media. Because those media are inherently probing and skeptical, and because there are so many sources of media information in our society, we have built-in defenses. There is a reasonable chance that false information will ultimately be disclosed as such by inquiring and competitive reporters.

Counterintelligence is vital if America is to be protected against those who wish to harm us by stealing our secrets or feeding us false information. Nonetheless, the potential for abuse, demonstrated in documented cases, must make us cautious. There is no area of intelligence activity more likely to abuse the rights of our citizens.

SEVEN

Covert Action:
The Dirty Tricks Department

COVERT ACTION is the term that describes our efforts to influence the course of events in a foreign country without our role being known. It is separate from intelligence — the collecting and evaluating of information about foreign countries — but it has always been assigned to the CIA to perform, by means of unattributable propaganda, sub rosa political action, or secret paramilitary support. By the mid 1970s covert action had fallen on hard times; morale had plummeted in light of recent disclosures and there was a reluctance to move boldly. It was not, however, only that the CIA was hunkering down; the country itself was confused and concerned about the role of covert action in foreign policy. And small wonder. The CIA's covert activities had so increased in the 1950s and 1960s that some of them had inevitably become public. Much of what leaked out seriously alarmed the public and the Congress, who did not condone all of the activities in which the CIA had been involved.

When the Agency was founded, in September 1947, nothing was said about covert action in the congressional debate on the CIA's charter, even though the CIA was seen, in part, as the successor to the OSS of World War II. By December of that year, the National Security Council specifically assigned responsibility for covert "psychological operations" to the CIA — and the door was opened. By 1953 major covert operations were under way to shape political and military events and to disseminate propaganda in forty-eight countries — and there were fewer than seventy countries in the United Nations at that time.[1] Just a few years later several thousand covert operations were on the books, although the majority were low-risk, low-profile actions, such as placing articles in foreign newspapers to counter stories planted by communists or paying "an agent of influence," someone to be on hand to assist us in future covert activities.

The objective of the initial covert use of propaganda and political support was to buttress democratic elements in post–World War II Europe against the aggressive pressures of communism. Anticommunist labor unions, political parties, student groups, cultural organizations, and media were funded to help them survive. They were given advice on how to help democratic candidates win elections and on how to counter such communist-inspired activities as strikes that were debilitating national economies. The impact in France and Italy was particularly favorable and extremely important for all the Western allies.

After these initial emergency efforts in Europe, programs of covert political support and propaganda increased in number and expanded to many other areas of the world. In one third world country CIA political interference became so extensive in the 1950s and 1960s that the Church Committee reported that it affected almost every level of society.[2] In another country the committee found that an aspiring politician would almost automatically go to see the CIA station chief for help in getting elected.[3]

By 1967 the cost of CIA support for useful and friendly groups overseas was more than $10 million a year. Much of this money was given to U.S. labor unions, student associations, and private foundations that, in turn, passed it to their counterparts abroad. They acted as "cutouts" or intermediaries between the CIA and the foreign organizations. This protected foreign recipients from accusations of associating with the CIA or being puppets of the

1. Final Report of the Select Committee to Study the Governmental Operations with Respect to Intelligence Activities, United States Senate, Book I, Chapter VIII, April 26, 1976.
2. Ibid.
3. Ibid.

United States. The technique also sometimes enabled the CIA to pass funds to foreign groups that needed help without those groups knowing their source was the CIA. The American organizations also arranged the U.S. side of student and labor union exchange programs. For example, the Soviet Union was particularly active in trying to organize and propagandize the world student movement. The CIA, through the National Student Association, sponsored over 250 American students who attended youth festivals in Moscow, Vienna, and Helsinki to try to counter this Soviet activity. That funding was limited to the international branch of the association, but it was so substantial that its impact was certainly felt in the organization's domestic activities, too.

Much the same was true with private foundations. Some foundations were even created as fronts for CIA funding, but bona fide foundations were also involved deeply. Excluding grants from the three largest U.S. foundations — Ford, Rockefeller, and Carnegie — nearly half of the grants made in the field of international affairs by U.S. foundations between 1963 and 1967 involved CIA money, as did one third of the grants in the physical, life, and social sciences.[4]

This kind of massive CIA involvement in domestic institutions could not be kept secret forever. The big leak came from the National Student Association in 1967. Only the key officers of the association were aware of the CIA's role in their organization, but as new ones were elected each year, more and more people came to know about the hidden connection. In 1967 one of the student leaders revealed the relationship to *Ramparts* magazine. As a consequence, President Lyndon B. Johnson appointed Under Secretary of State Nicholas de B. Katzenbach to head a small group, including DCI Richard Helms, to review the CIA's relationship with educational and voluntary organizations inside the United States. The Katzenbach Committee's report recommended against any CIA covert support to such groups, and there followed a major curtailment of CIA activities in these areas.

In addition to providing help to student, labor, and cultural organizations, the CIA used other devices to turn countries toward a Western political orientation. The most publicized was the suc-

4. Ibid.

cessful maneuver to restore the Shah of Iran to his throne in 1953. Immediately following World War II, Iran had become a testing ground in the cold war struggle between the Soviet bloc and the Western democracies. Mohammed Mossadegh's accession to the prime ministership in 1951 was viewed in Washington and London as a threat. Mossadegh was more anti-Shah than procommunist, but he became increasingly dependent on the communists. Two of the major power elements in Iran, the clergy and the merchants of the bazaar, were still supporting the Shah. This left Mossadegh dependent on the masses. Only the communists were able to rally them on his behalf. The more Mossadegh maneuvered against the Shah, the more isolated he became from the noncommunists. In May 1951 Mossadegh nationalized British oil interests in Iran. Later, when the British felt he was vulnerable, they urged the United States to join in an effort to topple him. We agreed.

The CIA swung into action by attempting to persuade the Shah to dismiss Mossadegh, which was his constitutional prerogative. But the Shah was uncertain whether he could survive the public protests that might result. It took some time and numerous emissaries to persuade him to adopt this course, but he did dismiss Mossadegh, early in August 1953. Mossadegh's supporters, largely from the left, took to the streets and demonstrated. The situation became so tense that the Shah briefly left the country. Meanwhile, the CIA encouraged the merchants and Muslim clergy to organize counterdemonstrations. Using both persuasion and bribery, the bazaar people brought onto the streets enough demonstrators to force Mossadegh's demonstrators to back down. As the tide turned, the CIA urged its contacts in the army to come down on the side of the Shah. When they did, the CIA helped bring together a more friendly government, which was waiting in the wings. The Shah appointed General Fazlollah Zahedi as Prime Minister, and Mossadegh was finished. During the entire operation the CIA employed very few people and not much money. The main point, though, is that conditions inside Iran were ripe for a change. The Mossadegh government's political base was weak and was susceptible to being toppled. The CIA simply gave it the final push.

The Agency pulled off still another successful political action the following year. A prototype of the Castro revolution of 1956–1959 was developing in Guatemala under Jacobo Arbenz. The CIA was directed to prevent Arbenz from consolidating his communist-oriented regime. It did so by convincing the Guatemalans that a "popular rebellion" was sweeping the country in support of Carlos Castillo Armas, an anticommunist army colonel then in exile. The CIA supplied Armas with enough arms for a ragtag army of fewer than two hundred men plus a few old bomber and fighter aircraft, most of them flown by mercenaries. On D-Day, June 18, 1954, a CIA radio station, masquerading as the rebels' station, broadcast word that Colonel Armas had invaded from Honduras. It continued to give reports of the movement of a supposed five-thousand-man force toward the capital. A bomber dropped a single bomb on a parade field in the capital, without loss of life. A day and a half later, as the nearly imaginary invasion force was reported by its own radio broadcasts to be nearing Guatemala City, Arbenz resigned. Armas and his few men were flown to the outskirts of the city and marched in triumphantly. Again, this favorable political outcome required only a small effort, and, again, the government that was overthrown was so weak that only a little push was needed.

The public inevitably learned that the CIA was behind these decisive political actions in Iran and Guatemala. President Dwight D. Eisenhower, in a political campaign speech in Seattle, boasted of the Iranian operation as an indication of his administration's dynamism and prowess. Such publicity began to raise concerns, especially in the Congress, about how many covert actions were being carried out and under whose control they were. And then the Congress and the public began to learn about covert efforts that were not very successful.

The most adverse exposure was a series of revelations about more than ten years of CIA interference in Chile, from 1963 to 1973. This was one of the most massive campaigns in U.S. intelligence annals. The earliest effort was an attempt to shape the outcome of the 1964 presidential election in Chile, when the CIA underwrote more than half of the expenses of the Christian Democratic Party's campaign. This support was directed at defeating the communist candidate, Salvador Allende. It was probably not known to the Christian Democratic candidate, Eduardo Frei. In addition to funding Frei, the CIA waged an extensive anticommunist propaganda campaign, using posters, the radio, films, pamphlets, and the press, to convince the Chileans that Allende and communism would bring to their country Soviet militarism and Cuban brutality. As part of this campaign, hundreds of thousands of copies of an anticommunist pastoral letter of Pope Pius XI were distributed. Frei won handily, but allegations of CIA involvement seeped out.

As a result, the CIA was reluctant to play as large a role in the next Chilean presidential election, in 1970. Not only was its role smaller; it did not support a specific candidate. The effort was directed strictly against Allende and was based primarily on propaganda, employing virtually all Chilean media and some of the international press as well. The program failed when Allende won a plurality, though not a majority, of the popular vote. Under Chilean electoral law, that threw the choice to a joint session of the legislature some seven weeks later. At the direction of the White House, the CIA moved to prevent the selection and inauguration of Allende. It attempted to induce his political opponents to manipulate the legislative election up to and including a political coup. Some 726 articles, broadcasts, editorials, and similar items were sponsored in the United States and Chile, and many briefings were given to the press. One of those, to *Time* magazine, reversed the magazine's attitude toward Allende. The overall effort failed, however, because of the unwillingness of the appropriate Chilean politicians to tamper with the constitutional process. Complementing the CIA effort, the U.S. government exerted economic pressure on Chile, again to no avail. A second approach, entirely under CIA auspices, encouraged a military coup. President Richard Nixon directed that neither the Departments of State and Defense nor the U.S. Ambassador to Chile be informed of this undertaking. During a disorganized coup attempt that took place on October 22, the Chief of Staff of the Chilean Army was murdered. The CIA had originally encouraged the group responsible, but sensing that this group was likely to get out of control, the Agency had withdrawn its support a week earlier.

Allende was installed as President on November 2. Over the next three years, until 1973, the National Security Council authorized the CIA to expend some $7 million covertly to oppose

Allende with propaganda, financial support for anti-Allende media in Chile, and funding for private organizations opposed to Allende. Other agencies of the U.S. government applied economic and political pressure. On September 11, 1973, the Chilean military staged a coup in which Allende died, reportedly by suicide. The CIA did not sponsor this coup, but how much its encouragement of the 1970 coup and its continued liaison with the Chilean military encouraged the action is honestly difficult to assess. With Allende gone, the decade-long covert action program was phased out.

More was at stake, though, than covert action in Chile. The coup-related deaths in both 1970 and 1973 and the exposure of the role of the United States in helping to topple a democratically elected government, albeit a Marxist one, brought intense scrutiny to the ethics of using covert action to change the political complexion of other countries. As a result, such covert action came to a near halt by the mid 1970s.

The use of general political propaganda also came into dispute by the 1970s. The CIA's initial propaganda efforts in Western Europe led in 1950 to the establishment of Radio Free Europe and Radio Liberty for regular, systematic broadcasting behind the Iron Curtain. If those broadcasts had been identified with the U.S. government in that cold war period, they would have lost much of their credibility in communist countries. Hence, the CIA operated the stations covertly rather than having the U.S. Information Agency do it openly. The fact that the stations were CIA operations became known in the early 1970s, and the Congress readily shifted them to the USIA. By then the broadcasts had established such credibility, compared with communist, state-controlled news organs, that their usefulness was not impaired by their open identification with the U.S. government.

Beyond these major broadcast operations, the CIA undertook hundreds of individual propaganda efforts, primarily in nations where there was no free press. It did so primarily by publishing books and placing stories in foreign media. More often than not, the information was circulated in countries where it would not otherwise have been known.

As the CIA's enthusiasm for propaganda grew, the question arose as to whether some of the material might not also get published in the United States. A news story planted in the newspaper or on a radio broadcast in another country might well be picked up by the AP or UPI and reprinted at home. Or a book subsidized by the CIA could sell in the United States as well as abroad, especially if it was in English. One of the leading CIA figures in this area in the late 1960s was the infamous E. Howard Hunt of Watergate renown.[5] Hunt testified before the Church Committee in early 1976 on the appearance in the United States of CIA propaganda originally used abroad.

> QUESTION: But with anything that was published in English, the United States citizenry would become a likely audience for publication?
> HUNT: A likely audience, definitely.
> QUESTION: Did you take some sort of steps to make sure that things that were published in English were kept out of or away from the American reading public?
> HUNT: It was impossible, because Praeger was a commercial U.S. publisher.[6] His books had to be seen, had to be reviewed, had to be bought here, had to be read ... The ultimate target was foreign, which was true, but how much of the Praeger output actually got abroad for any impact I think is highly arguable.[7]

As Congress learned more about such operations, the ones with the greatest potential for feedback into the United States were phased out.

The third technique of covert action, paramilitary operations, started with the war in Korea in 1950. Large sums of money were spent to develop guerrilla operations behind North Korean lines,

5. By one of those strange coincidences that all of us experience, I purchased a house in Washington, D.C., from Hunt in 1963, well before my time in the CIA. The real estate agent told me Mr. Hunt was an author. We noted an unusual number of unused telephone connections in the basement, and my wife repeatedly said she heard clicks and breathing on our phone and thought we were bugged. Ironically, a home I bought earlier in the Washington area was from another CIA man, Peer de Silva. More than that, at that time I found myself surrounded by CIA families. If the KGB did thorough enough research on me to uncover these facts, I'm sure they believed I was in the CIA all along and just masqueraded as a naval officer. I wasn't and I didn't.
6. Praeger was a company the CIA used to publish books in English or foreign languages for primary distribution overseas.
7. Final Report of the Select Committee to Study Governmental Operations with Respect to Intelligence Activities, U.S. Senate, Book I, Chapter X, April 26, 1976.

though little was actually accomplished. In the late 1950s, the CIA sponsored several sizable guerrilla operations against two Asian governments and provided covert military assistance to the government of a third. Then in 1961 came the well-known Bay of Pigs failure in Cuba. This paramilitary effort, conducted by Cuban exiles who had been trained and equipped by the CIA, was so large that it had to become public knowledge once the operation began. Its success depended on the assumption that many disaffected Cubans on the island would rally to the side of the invaders. They did not. Castro's military was ready and defeated the invasion force easily. It was a moment of deep embarrassment for the CIA.

Still, just after the Bay of Pigs the CIA undertook an even larger and longer paramilitary effort, providing advice, training, and equipment to Meo tribesmen in Laos, from 1962 to 1971. The Meo opposed the communist presence in their country and were willing to try to interdict the flow of arms moving from North Vietnam through their country to the Vietcong in South Vietnam. Although word of this operation leaked quite early, it never attracted much criticism. Perhaps that was because the Meo did a creditable job. As the U.S. effort in neighboring Vietnam wound down, though, there was no hope for the Meo. The U.S. withdrawal from Vietnam posed for the CIA the excruciating question of what fate the Meo would suffer at the hands of the victorious communists. Some Meo were brought to the United States, some made their way to Thailand, and others faced the music at home.

By the mid 1970s paramilitary actions had the least luster of all forms of covert action, but skepticism about any type of covert activity was part and parcel of the growing disillusionment with government that followed Vietnam and Watergate. In fact, it became so controversial that Congress could no longer treat it as lightly as when the CIA had not even been obliged to report all covert actions to it. For instance, of thirty-three covert projects the Agency undertook in Chile between 1963 and 1973 with the approval of the National Security Council, only eight were reported to Congress.[8] Then, in 1974, Senator Harold Hughes of

8. Ibid.

Iowa and Representative Leo Ryan of California set out to force the Congress to be more aware of what the United States was doing covertly. They sponsored and gained passage of an amendment to the Foreign Assistance Act of that year that required the President to approve all covert actions and report them to the appropriate committees of the Congress. The amendment was regarded by many as an overreaction, but even this tightening of controls did not satisfy Congress when the next controversial covert action was exposed.

In 1975, in the wake of Portugal's withdrawal from her former colony in Angola, three militant factions were fighting for political power. The CIA gave paramilitary support to one. The Soviet Union and Cuba supported another. By midyear the CIA's support had been increased and extended to a second faction. It was increased again in both September and November. As the congressional committees were informed under the Hughes-Ryan Amendment, Senator Dick Clark of Iowa, Chairman of the Foreign Relations Subcommittee on Africa, began objecting to any covert activities at all in Angola. By January 1976, having been unable to find a way, under Hughes-Ryan, to stop or even slow the continuing growth of the program, Clark introduced legislation flatly prohibiting any covert action at all in Angola. The Clark Amendment passed. That was the first direct congressional interference in a covert operation. The restriction enacted is still in effect. However, as we shall see later, this was not the last time congressional frustration led to action requiring the President to curtail covert activities.

The Clark Amendment was a warning against paramilitary covert action; the Howard Hunt testimony had put a damper on much of the covert propaganda effort; and the publicity about Chile had left unanswered questions about the acceptability of covert political action. The CIA, reading these signs and others, pulled back from any substantial covert activity that might lead to more controversy. When I took over in 1977 the covert action cupboard was bare and sentiment within the CIA itself was against stocking it. The majority of the espionage professionals, from what I could see, believed that covert action had brought more harm and criticism to the CIA than useful return, and that it had seriously detracted from the Agency's primary role of collecting and evaluating intelligence. There was the contrary view that a covert action network can be an aid to human intelligence collection; that is, people who do covert political work frequently end up being clandestine agents as well. How individual professionals came down on this issue often depended on when they came into the Agency and where they had served. Those who entered in the late 1940s or early fifties and were assigned to the separate covert action branch that then existed tended to remain enthusiastic. If they had served overseas right after World War II in areas like Western Europe, where covert actions had been numerous and successful, they were also supporters. If their careers had not touched such activity, they saw it as diverting time and energy from espionage. The cleavage between those holding these opposing attitudes was deep, and the advice I received about rebuilding or discarding covert capabilities differed widely.

Congress was also divided. Senator Hughes and Representative Ryan felt that no covert actions were justified in peacetime. In presenting his amendment in 1974, Hughes had stated, "According to reports in the October 2 *Washington Post* and *Philadelphia Inquirer*, these officials [Secretary of State Henry Kissinger and DCI William Colby] have said that the United States has ended covert political operations abroad, though some may be necessary in the future."[9] Hughes further commented that he viewed his amendment as only a modest first step in controlling the "cloak and dagger" intelligence operations of the U.S. government. By 1976 some of Hughes's skepticism had been picked up by the Church Committee. It stated that it had given "serious consideration to proposing a total ban on all forms of covert action."[10]

The key points behind these arguments that we should eschew covert action altogether were that covertly interfering in another country's politics undermines our own moral standards of decency, openness, and honesty; and that we have no right to impose our will on the affairs of others, because that is a totalitarian practice, not a democratic one. These seem to me to be flawed attempts to transform an idealized view of morality between indi-

9. *Congressional Record*, Volume 120, Part 25, p. 33488.
10. Final Report of the Select Committee to Study the Governmental Operations with Respect to Intelligence Activities, United States Senate, Book I, Chapter VIII, April 26, 1976.

viduals to a standard of morality between nations. We look down on a man who surreptitiously interferes with the life of his neighbor. Only if that neighbor truly endangers him — if, say, he is planning to murder him — are we likely to condone such behavior. The problem with applying this standard to the relations between nations is that nations must judge danger quite differently. The murder of an individual is a specific and decisive act, often committed with little or no warning and seldom leading to greater or more widespread acts of violence. Mortally damaging a nation, short of war, is a more gradual process. Nations believe they are justified in interfering clandestinely with opponent nations over lesser threats than would push an ethical individual to interfere with his neighbor. Sometimes nations are correct in doing this, because waiting too long might cause a detrimental trend to become irreversible or leave them at a considerable disadvantage. At other times nations simply misjudge the seriousness of the situation.

On the second point there is not, it seems to me, a moral imperative that rules out all interference in the affairs of other nations any more than there is such an imperative for individuals. We openly interfere with other nations all the time by means of USIA releases, grain embargoes, restrictions on the transfer of technology, trade barriers, threats to countries that harbor terrorists, diplomatic pressure, and so on. The political philosopher John Stuart Mill addressed this issue well in 1859, when he wrote:

> The doctrine of non-intervention, to be a legitimate principle of morality, must be accepted by all governments. The despot must consent to be bound by it as well as the free states. Unless they do, the profession comes to this miserable issue — that the wrong side may help the wrong, but the right must not help the right.[11]

The despots of today interfere in the affairs of other countries just as much as they did in Mill's day. For example, in 1977 and 1978 Cuban mercenaries in Angola stirred up tribal warfare in the copper- and cobalt-producing region of Zaire; in 1978 other Cuban mercenaries actually fought alongside the forces of the Marxist government of Ethiopia against neighboring Somalia; in 1979 Marxist South Yemen, with active Soviet backing, threatened North Yemen with both subversion and invasion; in 1979

11. *A Few Words on Non-Intervention.*

the Soviets invaded Afghanistan with eighty thousand troops; in 1979 the Ayatollah Khomeini ousted the Shah of Iran and permitted fanatical students to seize our embassy and hold hostage more than fifty of our citizens.

These were the very kinds of circumstances that have driven most recent Presidents to turn to covert action — circumstances in which resort to military force is either not warranted or feasible and in which either diplomatic or economic sanctions seem little more than a slap on the wrist. For instance, it was little consolation to the American public that we had frozen Iran's assets in this country, as we watched our diplomats being held hostage for 444 days; and we were equally frustrated at the weakness of the grain embargo as a response to the presence of Soviet troops in Afghanistan. There is an old cliché in intelligence that says the place for covert action is as an alternative between diplomacy and war. It is just such circumstances as these in which that cliché is applicable.

Thus it was that the Carter administration, despite its dedication to human rights and its considerable reservations about the morality of covert actions, turned easily and quickly to covert devices to respond to some of these despotic acts. It wasn't that there was an effort to answer each aggressive act with a covert response; rather the cumulative frustration resulting from all the acts demanded response. In fact, when choosing covert action as a response, we often find it impossible to select an action that directly replies to the aggression. We can, though, frequently tailor an apparently unrelated covert response so that the aggressor fully understands that what we are doing is in response to his aggressiveness. I believe that almost all Presidents will face similar circumstances and be impelled toward covert action.

In addition there likely will always be situations in which most U.S. citizens would applaud such covert actions as broadcasting accurate information on world affairs into countries where the people are deliberately kept uninformed by their government, infiltrating and thwarting terrorist movements and drug-trafficking operations, broadcasting and shipping antiregime materials into countries like Iran under Ayatollah Khomeini and Libya under Colonel Qaddafi, and giving financial support to democratic forces whose opposition is financed by communists.

The immediate pressures that moved the Carter administration back to specific covert actions came from different sources. Most often, when I carried back to the CIA my report on the results of a National Security Council meeting and the problems the policy-makers were facing, the CIA covert action specialists would go to work thinking up a covert approach that might help. If they came up with one and I approved, I would take the proposal back to the NSC. If it was very sensitive, I'd limit it to Zbig Brzezinski, Harold Brown, and Cy Vance to minimize the risk of leaks from a formal meeting. If they agreed, Brzezinski would take the written proposal to the President for his approval and signature. It then was returned to the CIA, and we hand-delivered it to the appropriate congressional committees.

Or Brzezinski, Brown, or Vance might originate an idea for a particular covert action and request the CIA to explore it. In fact, Cy Vance was unenthusiastic about almost all covert actions and firmly opposed to all paramilitary ones. Brzezinski was an advocate and Brown in between. The wide difference between Vance and Brzezinski reflected the philosophic gap between them. Brzezinski was much more of an activist, but when it came to intelligence operations he had far less experience than Vance, a former Deputy Secretary of Defense. Brzezinski held unrealistic expectations of what could be achieved by covert action, especially after what was by then a considerable period of inactivity. Even with agents in place, and contacts established over the years, it takes time for most covert actions to have an effect. Propaganda changes people's minds only over time; political action usually requires patient, adroit maneuvering; and paramilitary action is guerrilla warfare, a gradual wearing-down of the enemy over long periods. Even the seemingly quick, decisive, small-scale operation that restored the Shah in 1953 was but the final act of a slow process. Yet, not appreciating that, Brzezinski repeatedly called for more quick covert actions, especially during the Iranian hostage crisis.

In considering how much to turn again to covert action, the administration was buffeted between Vance's skepticism and Brzezinski's enthusiasm. In time Brzezinski prevailed, simply because there was such frustration in the White House over continuing Soviet aggressions. Well before the end of the Carter administration in early 1981, a wide variety of covert operations were in place. As I watched covert action revive this rapidly from a nadir in the mid 1970s, despite the administration's general reluctance, I concluded that it clearly was something our nation would never forsake entirely. What remains important, then, is that we define the bounds that should be placed around it, determine what should and should not be attempted, and ensure that there is careful and continual control over it.

EIGHT

The Quiet Revolution:
Machines As Spies

IN SEPTEMBER 1974, I first encountered intelligence obtained from an advanced technical system. I was then Commander of the U.S. Second Fleet, crossing the Atlantic in command of a large naval force. As our ships approached the Norwegian Sea, Atlantic Fleet headquarters in Norfolk, Virginia, warned me by message that two Soviet ships were coming out to keep an eye on what we were doing. The message predicted when they would join us and who they were. How Norfolk knew this was not revealed in the message. I assumed they were using advanced technical systems, but at that time the intelligence people would not admit to having those capabilities, even to a Fleet Commander.

Just two and a half years later, as DCI, I dealt with technical intelligence systems almost daily, deciding which should be their highest priority targets or what characteristics should be designed into a replacement system that wouldn't be deployed for four or five years. So much of our intelligence effort was becoming dependent on these systems that on October 1, 1978, President Carter decided we couldn't hide these capabilities entirely from the public, let alone from Fleet Commanders. He made the first official public statement acknowledging our use of photographic satellites. The President felt he had to acknowledge the potential of satellites in order to convince the Senate and the country at large that his nuclear arms control treaty, SALT II, was adequately verifiable. Photographs of the Soviet Union taken by satellites were essential to checking on Soviet compliance with the treaty. The public needed to know something about our satellite capabilities if they were to feel confident that we could tell whether the Soviets were abiding by the treaty. Similarly, when the Soviets shot down a Korean airliner on September 1, 1983, Secretary of State George Shultz almost immediately disclosed that we knew from electronic surveillance what the Russian pilots had been saying on their radios. This was an unprecedented disclosure of specific electronic intercept work, but only with that irrefutable evidence could he make the strong case he did against the Soviets. The short time from intense secrecy to declassification of this kind of information graphically illustrates the rapid, almost breakneck speed in the development of technological spying. Today, it all but eclipses traditional, human methods of collecting intelligence. To label it a revolution — a quiet revolution, to be sure, since many aspects of it still must remain secret — only states the obvious.

There are two technologies behind most new technical intelligence capabilities: the computer, with its vast increase in computational power, and microprocessors, which make it possible to put computers into very small packages. Computers enable us to sift, store, and manipulate the enormous quantities of data that intelligence sensors collect. Until there were high-speed, high-capacity computers, it took far too long for us to sort out much of the extremely detailed intelligence data that we were beginning to collect. Today's sensors can detect a huge variety of signals, even when they are very weak or are obscured by other signals. For example, a concealed microphone can hear a wide range of sounds, but only with the help of a computer can we separate background noises on one set of frequencies from conversations on another and thus record voices that once would have been lost in a jumble of surrounding noise. In photography we can lift from the millions of black and white dots that compose a photograph only the ones we are interested in.

The second development, microprocessing, by enabling us to put the vast computational power of computers onto microchips, allows us to reduce the size and weight of cameras and listening antennae to the point where they can be placed into a satellite or a high-flying aircraft that has limited space for payload, or to build a microphone and sorting system that is so small that it can be concealed in clothing, furniture, or other sensitive locations.

Now that we have technical systems ranging from satellites traveling in space over the entire globe, to aircraft flying in free airspace, to miniature sensors surreptitiously positioned close to difficult targets, we are approaching a time when we will be able to survey almost any point on the earth's surface with some sensor, and probably with more than one. We can take detailed photographs from very long distances, detect heat sources through infrared devices, pinpoint metal with magnetic detectors, distinguish between barely moving and stationary objects through the use of Doppler radar, use radar to detect objects that are covered or hidden by darkness, eavesdrop on all manner of signals from the human voice to electronic radio waves, detect nuclear radiation with refined Geiger counters, and sense underground explosions at long distances with seismic devices. Most of the activities we want to monitor give off several kinds of signals. Tanks in battle can be detected by the heat from their engines, the magnetism in their armor, or photographs. A nuclear weapons plant emits radiation, has a particular external physical shape, and receives certain types of supplies. One way or another, we should soon be able to keep track of most activities on the surface of the earth, day or night, good weather or bad.

Realizing that technical systems had opened vast new opportunities for us to collect information regularly with a precision that no human spy network could ever offer, I quickly became convinced that we had the capability of detecting any substantial buildup for war in any part of the world. For instance, in 1978 we were easily able to detect Cuban mercenaries massing with Ethiopian forces against Somalia in the Ogaden desert. We had forewarning when the Soviets prepared to invade Afghanistan in 1979, when the Chinese lined up against Vietnam in the same year, and when the Soviets positioned forces to intimidate Poland in 1980. If even small conflicts broke out, we could keep track of the military action. I also saw that technical systems enabled us to enter into arms control agreements that we could never have contemplated before. They gave us assurance that through regular surveillance we could check periodically to see whether the Soviets were adhering to a treaty's provisions. We build the treaties around our technical capabilities. For instance, in 1979 we were justified in accusing the Soviets of violating an arms control agreement, because our satellite photography and electronic listening devices had detected a ballistic missile test and an antiballistic missile test within a few minutes of each other.

Technical systems will in time open further opportunities. Already, for instance, an unclassified satellite named LandSat, operated by the Department of Commerce, provides valuable data for improving agriculture, forest industries, and mineral exploration. There is no reason why we cannot expand such coverage to help predict famine resulting from poor crops, provide more rapid relief after natural disasters such as floods and earthquakes, locate where prohibited crops like poppies and marijuana are being grown, and assist in road-building projects in remote areas.

As I watched us begin to exploit the new technical opportunities, I noted that the policy-makers were becoming more involved in how and when to use these systems. They became accustomed to receiving prompt and specific information from overhead photography, for instance. The results of electronic surveillance can also be made available almost anywhere in the world practically instantaneously. Occasionally the spy can be equally responsive, but the chances are that the problems of communicating with agents make quick reaction the exception rather than the rule. Technically generated intelligence, then, has become an integral part of our crisis-management system. When the State or Defense Department establishes a task force to manage a crisis, a special intelligence task force supports it. Often the policy-makers themselves will specify the technical systems they think should be employed and will wait expectantly for results. Of course, not every such request can be fulfilled. Sometimes the satellite will not be in the right location when a suspected arms control violation is taking place, or we will just not be able to get an electronic intercept antenna into position to monitor a tank battle in some remote desert. Still, the odds are high that one or another of our technical systems will be able to come through. The potential is almost unlimited.

Technically generated intelligence appeals to decision-makers not just because of timeliness but because it is highly credible. Reports from spies are subject to the strengths and weaknesses of the agent doing the reporting. Has he interpreted correctly what he saw or heard? What biases does he have? How has he shaded his conclusions about what was going on? Does he have some reason to falsify his report? A classic example is the report of the reconnaissance mission Moses sent to "spy out the land of Canaan." When it returned, Caleb reported finding a land that flowed with milk and honey and had only such occupants as the Israelites would be able to overcome. But others from the same reconnaissance party reported finding a land that "eateth up the inhabitants thereof" and that was filled with fearsome giants. Caleb and the others saw the same things, but when those facts were filtered by the perceptions of different observers, contradictory reports emerged. Technology today lets us record information and report it without passing it through a human filter.

Such reporting began about the start of World War II, when we broke the Japanese and German codes. Political leaders then received verbatim reports of private Japanese and German discussions, with only a translator standing between them and the actual data. Then, as World War II progressed, we began to use aerial photography. As contrasted with World War I, when pilots were aerial observers, the pilots' task in World War II was to bring back photos. Whether they observed the scene themselves was not important. The interpretation was done from objective photographs, not from the subjective memory.

That is not to say technology cannot be fooled. False data can be deliberately planted for us to collect. It is generally more difficult to spoof a camera or an electronic sensor than a person, but it can be done. Alexander Haig says he spoofed the Argentinians in the middle of the Falklands crisis in 1982. Of his role as a mediator, he said:

> Although the British told us nothing of their military plans, the Argentines plainly believed we knew everything the British did. Possibly this misconception could be useful. I called Bill Clark [President Ronald Reagan's National Security Adviser] at the White House on an open line, knowing that the Argentinians would monitor the call, and told him in a tone of confidentiality that British military action was imminent. The Argentines produced a new peace proposal shortly thereafter.[1]

1. *Time*, April 9, 1984, p. 61.

Another weakness is that accurately reported information can be misinterpreted. Satellite photographs usually tell very little to the untutored eye. It takes an expert photo-interpreter to tell you that a photograph of a Soviet missile silo is different from all others he has ever seen. When he extrapolates from that a prediction of a new thrust in the Soviet missile program, however, he is leading you from his field of expertise to an area where there is much room for misinterpretation. We have also found that a completely accurate copy of someone's telegram or a transcript of his telephone conversation can be accepted too readily as an indication of what he is going to do. A skilled analyst may know that the same person has sent the same kind of message or had the same conversation before, but that nothing happened as a result. Often only a person who has watched a scene over a long period of time can place an event in true perspective.

It is easy to become enamored of the quantity, timeliness, responsiveness, and accuracy of the technical collection systems. I was often accused in the press of overemphasizing technical capabilities and neglecting the value of human espionage. I did spend a good deal of my time wrestling with questions related to technical spying, and every future DCI will have to do the same. The equipment is exotic and very expensive, and the planning for new capabilities must be projected years into the future. Therefore, the choices of new technical systems are extremely difficult and receive close attention in the White House and the Congress. That involves the DCI, of course. The DCI must also be involved in managing these systems during periods of crisis, because the President and other top officials will be expecting results. These considerations unavoidably consume large amounts of the DCI's time, whereas human intelligence does not require nearly as much attention. To interpret this difference in the allocation of time as stemming from the DCI's preference is to ignore the fact that human intelligence does not need the same detailed supervision as technical. In fact, the smaller amount of supervision is a demonstration of confidence in human espionage and the way it is run.

The combination of a good human information-gathering capability and a constantly expanding technical one distinguishes American intelligence today sharply from that of all other nations. No other country except the Soviet Union has a worldwide collection capability and none but the Soviet Union yet has satellites to carry sensors aloft regularly. And, as compared with the Soviet Union, we have a substantial lead. The Soviets have made surprising progress in most military technologies, but they lag seriously in microprocessors. Even if they steal our microchips, they are inept at integrating them into working systems. We tend to overlook this problem the Soviets face, because in military hardware and space they make up for their shortcomings, usually by brute force — bigger is more powerful. That is not usually an option with small, sophisticated intelligence systems.

I came across an amusing example of this when talking with the chief of a third world intelligence service. I knew he had recently caught a Soviet spy, and I egged him into telling me how he had done it. On a summer evening in 1978, his police followed a suspected Russian spy as he drove his Volkswagen into one of the better residential neighborhoods of the country's capital. The car stopped in front of a house on a narrow street, and the Soviet opened a briefcase on the seat beside him. He was not quite finished rummaging in it when he looked up to see a police car come crashing into the front of his car as, almost simultaneously, another rammed the rear. He was hopelessly boxed in. The police found a radio transmitter-receiver and tape recorder in the briefcase. Within moments they entered the house and found a matching transmitter-receiver. The house was that of a major general in the army who was apparently committing treason by passing secret information to the Soviet spy through these radios.

Because the moment of exchanging data between a case officer and his agent is always risky, the Soviets were attempting to avoid any direct contact between the two. The plan was that the Volkswagen would stop briefly while the two radios exchanged prerecorded messages. Had the Russian not been under suspicion and the local security police so alert, it would have appeared that the car had but paused momentarily. With better technology even that would not have been necessary. Our military have "burst" transmitting capabilities in which information is compressed and large amounts can be sent in a very brief transmission. And the need for the two Soviet transmitter-receivers to be so physically close to each other showed that the Soviets lacked modern transmission techniques. The Soviets lost in this case because their technology was not up to the task.

We're ahead in technology and work hard to stay ahead. One question we must constantly solve anew is what specific capabilities to build into a new system. What may be best for detecting military movements may not be best for seeing economic developments; what may be suited for operations over land may be less than optimal over water. Bureaucratic pressures within the Intelligence Community, the White House, and the Congress make all such decisions difficult, because different people have different priorities.

Still another set of decisions concerns how much to spend in advancing our technology. The technicians are continually promising some new, tempting capability. But is it worth the cost? Again, some members of the Community are more eager than others to take advantage of specific new capabilities. Behind all innovation, however, is the need to keep advancing our technologies faster than the countermeasures that are likely to be deployed against them. We want, for instance, to have our communications devices so far advanced that the Soviets will not even suspect what we are doing, let alone trail us and pin us in a car.

Our most noteworthy successes in improving technical systems have come from a "skunk works" approach: you tell the inventors what you want and then turn them loose with relatively open funding and little outside interference. If they run into a dead end, they redirect their efforts without having to justify what they did to a whole series of committees. If they come to a critical problem for which no solution is in sight, they may undertake two or three simultaneous lines of research in the hope that one will provide a quick resolution. It costs money, but I know of no better way to encourage ingenuity, and it seems to work. The CIA used this approach with the U-2. That project started in 1954, and the aircraft was flying in 1956, a remarkably brief time for developing a new plane that could fly significantly higher than any other in the world. It was also a factor in our bringing photographic satellites into being as early as we did.

This kind of scientific freedom is hard to come by today. We tend to apply our new enthusiasm for oversight of the ethics of intelligence to micromanagement by the Congress of the development of new intelligence technologies. Ethics and technology are two quite different matters, but both the Executive Branch and the Congress tend toward microscopic review of the intelligence research budget. Once one of the congressional committees on intelligence, when authorizing a new satellite, went so far as to specify the frequency on which it was to perform certain functions. That was ridiculous and dangerous, even if it is understandable that congressional committees feel they must protect the taxpayer's money. The taxpayer would be served best if some waste and redundancy were tolerated to encourage inventiveness and to reduce the time from concept to production in this area. It might even save money by shortening the development programs.

Another false economy that congressional oversight has fostered is the frugality in stockpiling intelligence collection systems. Some systems may fail and need to be replaced quickly. Technical systems are also subject to attack, and surreptitious attacks are more likely as lasers and other advanced weapons come into use. It is not easy to persuade Congress to fund extra satellites and other systems with enormous price tags. Not doing so, however, leaves us at the risk of being without important capabilities for long periods; these systems are so complex that it takes a long time to manufacture them.

One other dangerous hindrance is that the CIA's research branch is gradually losing out to the large and clever military bureaucracy at the Pentagon. The military are eager to take over as much design work on satellites and electronic surveillance systems as possible. They believe that their inventing them will give them greater control over them when they become operational. Because the Pentagon's normal cycle of developing systems is so frightfully long, and getting longer, the more research conducted there, the less likely we are to stay ahead.

Another obstacle we face in staying ahead is the treasonous behavior of a Boyce, Lee, or Kampiles. Leaks like theirs are difficult to curtail entirely in our free society. But we must see to it that, despite all handicaps, we never allow the Soviets to counter our technical collection capabilities. We have grown utterly dependent on them, and in many applications no amount of human spying can possibly be a substitute.

NINE

Spying at Home:
The Media and Others

EN ROUTE to a conference overseas, I had dinner with the chief of a foreign intelligence service. His service is roughly the equivalent of the espionage branch of the CIA; the other elements of intelligence are scattered elsewhere in his government. As we sat by the fire after dinner in his home, I took stock of the scene. Here was a senior intelligence professional, a man probably ten years older than I, who was not far from retirement. I was a newcomer, just starting out in the profession. His intelligence service was stymied by not being able to keep pace with the technical revolution I've just described and by spiraling costs; mine was growing. I was there to learn what I could, but I wondered whether what he said would apply to the vastly different and more capable U.S. intelligence machine.

He remarked casually, "You know, of course, you want to collect all the intelligence you can on home territory." I had to confess I hadn't thought much about collecting foreign intelligence inside the United States. We talked of the risks of spying in a hostile country and of the hard truth that results are often meager because agents aren't always dependable and communicating with them is difficult. "Sometimes," he added, "the very information you ask an agent to get is available at home." What he was alluding to was that journalists, professors, and businessmen, among others, are often in contact with their counterparts in other countries. Some professors have taught foreign students who now are in important positions in their native countries. International journalists keep in touch with key thinkers and politicians in countries where they've served. Many businessmen have frequent dealings with foreign businessmen. Although contacts of these kinds aren't likely to have access to the inner secrets of the local Politburo or Cabinet, they will have an excellent feel for the state of the economy, the degree of societal unrest, or the prospects for incipient political movements. I began to ponder the advantages and disadvantages of collecting information from our own citizens, though I was amused that the old spymaster's primary lesson was not how to recruit a secret agent or to effect some other esoteric technique of espionage, but how to make use of resources openly available, at no risk to anyone.

His logic, while irrefutable, ran exactly contrary to the prevailing attitudes in the United States. Our media, for instance, had come to believe that they should have nothing to do with American intelligence. This was, however, a complete reversal from less than a decade before, when the CIA and the media cooperated closely. On foreign posts the CIA station chief and the bureau chief of a wire service or an American newspaper would usually be colleagues. The bureau chief found it useful to exchange ideas with someone who had access to different sources of information from his, and there was always the hope the station chief would let slip a good lead. The station chief often found that the newsman had a large circle of acquaintances, which the station chief hoped to tap indirectly. Since both parties were basically trying to learn as much as possible about the country where they were posted, they had much in common. Almost all the relationships between the CIA and journalists were informal. Most were no more than informed conversations on subjects of mutual interest, a comparing of notes. Some few developed to the point where the newsman agreed to seek specific information needed by the CIA. In even fewer cases the CIA paid the newsperson to work actively for it.[1]

These relationships worked well for many years; then the roof

1. Final Report of the Select Committee to Study Governmental Operations with Respect to Intelligence Activities, United States Senate, Book I, Chapter X, April 26, 1976.

fell in on both sides. The CIA found that familiarity with news-people was blowing the cover of the station chiefs. When a station chief moved from one country to another, the media grapevine would send word ahead, identifying the CIA's man. Because of this, the CIA put a stop to informal liaison on foreign posts shortly before my time. Contact was limited to briefings given at CIA Headquarters in Langley when requested by newsmen about to go overseas or simply researching a story.

The touchstone for the media's turning its back on the CIA was the Church Committee report in 1976. They were quick to note that the committee said fifty American newspersons had been on the CIA payroll and immediately began filing requests with the CIA under the Freedom of Information Act to find out which of their colleagues were involved. In response they received copies of CIA cables, which had names deleted but referred to "unwitting sources."[2] Some newsmen recognized themselves as the sources in some of these messages with the deleted names. The term "unwitting source" came as a surprise, though, and for many it struck just the wrong chord. "Unwitting" seemed to imply that they had been taken in. "Source" looked like more than a casual relationship. Clearly some excellent newspeople were distressed that their friendship with a station chief had been perceived in this light. They also worried that if it were ever disclosed that they'd been unwitting sources for the CIA, they would appear less independent than they should have been. In a word, they feared losing credibility, especially in the eyes of their colleagues.

This unfortunate jargon, combined with the general disfavor of the CIA after the Church Committee's disclosures, caused an overreaction. Most newsmen refused to share information with station chiefs or anyone else in the CIA. One day Katharine Graham, publisher of the *Washington Post*, had someone phone to see if the CIA would give her a briefing prior to a trip she was making to China. I was pleased to set up an unclassified briefing for her. When she arrived at Headquarters, I talked with her briefly in my office but did not sit through the briefing. As far as I knew, it went

2. CIA stations always identify their sources so that Headquarters can evaluate for itself the report's credibility. Code names are used to protect bona fide agents. A more casual source, like a media person or a chance encounter, would be referred to as an "unwitting source" to make it clear that the individual was not responding to direction from the Agency, and possibly wasn't even aware that he'd been in a conversation with someone from the CIA.

satisfactorily. A few months later I met her at a cocktail party. After inquiring about her trip, I asked if she would come out to Langley again and have lunch with me and the people who had briefed her. I said we would be most interested in hearing about her trip and in learning whether our briefing seemed realistic in light of what she had seen. Seldom have I witnessed such shock and bewilderment. "You know," she said, "I just couldn't do that." I couldn't help being amused and at the same time saddened by her reaction. Because some of her reporters had been tarred as unwitting sources, she was obviously setting an example of independence from the CIA. She was also reflecting the vogue that had overtaken those in the media, an exaggerated distancing from any implication of collusion with or influence by the CIA. She failed to appreciate that the public would have a difficult time interpreting one visit to the CIA as different from another.

So instead of my turning to the media for help in assessing events overseas, as my foreign spymaster friend had recommended, I found myself on the defensive. I was increasingly pressed by professional journalism societies, as well as by individuals, to prohibit the CIA from using any media person as a source. They wanted a written affirmation of an oral statement that my predecessor, George Bush, had made: "The CIA will not enter into any paid or contracted relationship with any full-time or part-time news correspondent accredited by any United States news service, newspaper, periodical, radio or television network or station."

One of the most persistent pleaders of this case was Abe Rosenthal, executive editor of the *New York Times*. Rosenthal is one of the top American journalists and one whom I thoroughly respect. Once when I was dining with him and other *Times* managers in their New York offices, he argued that the CIA should not work even with foreign journalists, let alone American. I leaned over and in a false whisper said, "Abe, I just want you to know I have the Washington representative of *Pravda* on my payroll. Is that OK?" It took him a minute to be sure I was jesting, but in that minute he recognized that it would be quite a coup for us to recruit a Russian of that stature.

An independent press is certainly essential to our democracy, but to prohibit any contact at all between it and the CIA would belie that we are both working for the good of our country and have compelling common interests. If either were to erect a complete barrier between us, each would lose an important source of information. But what seemed to me even more fundamental was that it was wrong to single out the CIA as the one influence newsmen must be protected from by regulation. Many of the sources of information newsmen depend on are promoting a particular point of view. Special favors, like tickets to plays and sporting events and rides in corporate jets, are all available and are accepted at one time or another by many journalists. None comes without some kind of price tag. Every newsperson must also decide how far he will give in to an editor's or a publisher's pressure to shift a story's emphasis, slightly or greatly, or to pull punches because of major advertising accounts or the paper's political outlook. Similarly, if a newsman talked with the CIA, he would have to decide whether that would color his reporting. If he felt, as I think most would, that he could handle whatever conflict might arise and help his country by helping the CIA, why should the CIA turn that help away? Sometimes a newsman's contacts or special access can open doors of great importance to us. What if a newsman were the person with the best access to a terrorist group holding a planeload of hostages? Should we not ask him for help?

I did write a regulation that limited the use of media people and academics to acquiring information only in exceptional circumstances.[3] There were two instances when media help was needed during my tenure and I gave my approval. Once during the hostage crisis in Iran, we found a man who had a unique access and thought he could help resolve a problem. I didn't hesitate one minute in calling on him. Circumstances overtook the situation and we did not actually use him, but we were on the verge of doing so. Interestingly, I never found a newsman who denied that it might be desirable for us to use media people in such life-and-death situations. But somehow that did not reduce the press's ardor for a regulation or law prohibiting it.

Newspeople also argued that even covert relationships would damage their professional credibility. And they were concerned

3. The regulation also pertained to the clergy, but the CIA in my experience had almost no cause to ask church figures for help.

that when they were overseas their lives would be jeopardized if anyone suspected they were working with the CIA. Those views were not persuasive to me, and frankly I couldn't believe journalists took them seriously either. Most knowledgeable foreigners, especially those in countries without a free press — and many of our allies can be counted among them — assume that the American press and the CIA work together or at least talk to each other. They know in most cases that their own media cooperate with their intelligence services. *Pravda*'s correspondents, for instance, are certainly responsive to the KGB, and many are KGB members. Even if the CIA issued a regulation prohibiting use of the media, few of our enemies or friends overseas would believe it was designed to do anything but mislead them.

Along with wanting to continue benefiting from the information and the interpretative abilities of the media, I wanted to support them better by releasing more information to them. To do this I brought a seasoned public affairs specialist, Herb Hetu, into the CIA. Herb had been a public affairs officer in the Navy and chief of public relations for the Bicentennial Commission. He set up the first Office of Public Affairs at the CIA, a single, highly visible point of contact between the CIA and those outside. To realize how radical this move was, one needs to understand the former philosophy of CIA public relations. On an overseas trip, I met a station chief who told me that his previous post had been chief of liaison with the press at Headquarters. That was a perfectly open job, one in which he acknowledged being in the CIA. Now he was back under cover again and in a position where it was important that he not be identified with the CIA. He had to be pretty low key to work openly with the media in Langley and then expect to go back under cover for his next assignment!

Herb began with a far-reaching but carefully controlled plan. He expanded the Agency's briefing program for the media, brought TV into the Headquarters for the first time with "60 Minutes" and "Good Morning America," ensured wide distribution of unclassified CIA studies to the media, arranged for groups like college alumni clubs, the Young Presidents, and the Sigma Delta Chi journalism fraternity to meet in the Bubble for briefings and question-and-answer periods, and scheduled frequent press conferences and press interviews with me. But perhaps of greatest importance, Herb answered all reasonable inquiries from the press and the public. His policy was never to limit his responses to "No comment." Questions were carefully considered. Those which could be answered, were; an explanation was given for those which could not. On the one hand I felt the CIA had to recognize that it had become a well-known part of the government and needed to correct the many erroneous or exaggerated stories that appeared in the wake of the investigations. On the other hand we attempted sincerely to provide useful services to the American media. The old practice of exchanging ideas out in the field had had its benefits, and we wanted to regain those without reaping the disadvantages of revealing our people's identity or placing the media in the position of being labeled as our sources, witting or unwitting. Expanding the exchanges in Headquarters was a way of avoiding both pitfalls.

By being more responsive within the limits of security, we developed a more stable and fruitful relationship between the CIA and the press. Unfortunately, the Reagan administration undid most of this. They started by denying almost all media requests for briefings at Langley. After a while they tempered that policy a bit, but in so doing raised the question of whether they were now seeking to manage the news. Under the Reagan policy, there are CIA briefings for the press, but usually when the administration has something to sell. Selective release of information is a powerful tool in a politician's hands. Generally it is not in the public's or the country's best interests. It is certainly something the CIA — which must remain apolitical — should avoid.

The Church Committee investigations had also damaged the longstanding relationship the CIA had with the academic community. The committee revealed that some professors had worked for the CIA without informing their universities. We received letters from university presidents who wanted to know which professors had worked or were working for the CIA. But the CIA had agreed with these professors that their relationship would be kept secret. If the professors chose to reveal their ties to the CIA, they were free to do so, but we could not and would not breach those agreements. I once had to write a letter to Amherst College, which I had attended for two years before going to the Naval Academy and toward which I felt a strong loyalty, denying that information.

Next, a number of universities began drafting their own regulations to control future faculty relationships with the CIA. On March 25, 1977, I received word that Harvard was about to issue a set of guidelines that would greatly inhibit its faculty in associating with the CIA. I had already taken a number of steps to encourage better relations with the academic community and didn't want this prestigious university to set an example that would hamper my efforts. I called the president of Harvard, Derek Bok, and told him I would like to send someone to Cambridge to discuss this new regulation and explain how it would affect us. President Bok was very cordial and accepted my offer. An hour later he phoned back; the people who were writing the Harvard regulation had told him they had already contacted the CIA and asked for the Agency's views. Much to my embarrassment, they had been told we would not comment. My enthusiasm for repairing relations with the academic world had obviously not permeated the CIA's bureaucracy. We did, however, finally have thorough discussions with Harvard. The regulation was modified, but Harvard still required its faculty to report all relationships with the CIA. Fortunately, very few other universities followed Harvard's example, and this did not become a continuing problem. Harvard also requested a complementing CIA regulation forbidding any relationships with Harvard that were not disclosed; I refused to issue such a rule.

The reason I did not comply with Harvard's request was that I felt it was not reasonable to ask an academic to disclose only his relationships with the CIA and ignore the relationships, formal and informal, he might have with corporations, foundations, or other government agencies. Any relationship can compromise a professor's objectivity and affect his teaching responsibilities, one with the CIA no more or less than one with a business that pays him as a consultant. In the business world some of those relationships involve secret, proprietary matters; some require a division of loyalty, as with screening students to recommend whom a company should hire.

I could fully understand a university's insisting that its faculty members report all external, paid relationships. After all, a university has a right to know how much time its faculty is spending on outside employment. I issued an instruction that before we engaged a professor whose university required disclosure of relationships with the CIA, we would remind him of his responsibilities to his university. If he insisted on not disclosing our relationship, that was between him and his university, not between the CIA and the university. We could not and would not be the university's policeman. However, I did require that my approval be sought before we engaged an academic who refused to act in accordance with his university's rules. It was my practice to make a distinction between universities whose regulations required their people to report all outside relations and those which required the reporting only of a CIA association. If the CIA was singled out and an academic did not want to report his relationship, I would approve it. If all relationships had to be reported, I would not.

We did find professors who were insistent that they would work with us only if they did not have to disclose that they were doing so. Sometimes this was a matter of obstinate independence; other times it was a concern over the possibility of recrimination by colleagues. A professor at Brooklyn College contacted the CIA in 1977 to ask for some unclassified information about an Iron Curtain country he was going to visit. On his return he called us again to share his thoughts. It was as simple and aboveboard as that. He had been given no assignment or remuneration by the CIA and expected none. But when word of his contact with us leaked, his colleagues almost blocked his obtaining tenure. In another case, I twice contacted a professor at an Ivy League university whom I regarded highly and asked him to accept a year's assignment in the CIA's analytic branch. My friend thought about it seriously on both occasions, but concluded that associating with the CIA could jeopardize his academic position.

What did we want these academics to do? The primary need for contact between the CIA and academia is to share ideas on all manner of world affairs, ranging from the psychology of foreign leaders to the state of world oil production to the strength of Islamic fundamentalism. The CIA, like every research and analytic institution, must be able to test its views and conclusions against the thinking of other experts. Through one-year fellowships, through committees of academics who periodically reviewed the CIA's work, and through individual consulting arrangements, we sought to tap the wisdom of academia. But the benefits did not flow in one direction. Professors who consulted with the CIA benefited from seeing how governments actually work, rather than how they theoretically work, and from gaining valuable insights into world events based on classified sources that they otherwise did not have access to. Although they could not discuss the classified data with their students when they returned to the campus, they were more richly informed and more discerning in their interpretation of security issues.

The more controversial area of contact between the CIA and the academic community concerns a much smaller group of university people, who help the CIA scout foreign students. Finding people from abroad who are favorably disposed to support American interests in their countries is a necessary part of maintaining a strong human intelligence capability. It is difficult to do this in countries with tight internal security and a disregard for human rights, which is exactly where we often most need good intelligence. It would be foolish not to attempt to identify sympathetic people when they are in our country. University personnel can sometimes help the CIA in this identification, though there clearly can be a conflict between a university official's doing that and fulfilling his responsibility to look after the student's best interests in and out of the classroom. It is largely a matter of how the situation is handled and is not different from singling out students for scholarships or jobs with business. Many of us are evaluated as having or not having the potential for all sorts of things. In the end, it is up to us, as it is with the student in this situation, to accept or reject whatever offers are made.

The argument is also raised that we are unfairly taking advantage of impressionable youngsters whom our country has a duty to protect when they are here. I respect that sense of duty, but the young, impressionable undergraduate is not usually the person the CIA seeks to win over to supporting us in his home country. He is not likely to have the maturity, the depth, or the clear career direction we are seeking. The more suitable candidates are graduate students, who are often foreign government employees studying on government grants and whose eyes are wide open.

Finally, when something of the CIA's traditional relationship with the business community was revealed by the Church Committee, it elicited the least reaction. The majority of businessmen are very pragmatic; they understand that information is needed to get along and that most relationships have benefits that go two ways. What hurt relations with them most was their concern that the CIA seemed to be unable to keep secrets. Some businessmen stopped dealing with the CIA for fear that proprietary information would be revealed or that stockholders would sue if they learned that company effort or resources had been used to assist the CIA.

The principal area of cooperation between the CIA and business is in the exchange of knowledge about what is going on overseas. Some U.S. businesses do a very good job of assessing the politics and the economics of the regions where they are operating; others are surprisingly uninformed. Overall, though, there is a good chance that we can gain valuable information merely by asking questions. The biggest problem is figuring out how best to utilize this source. The CIA has people who specialize in liaison with the business community, but their job isn't simple. Not only must they be able to ask the right questions on a broad variety of subjects, such as oil production, mining engineering, financial conditions, economic policies, and technical military developments, but they must understand the answers. It is not easy to find CIA men and women who can perform these tasks; people conversant in many disciplines are rare. For those same people to have sufficient presence and stature to meet with the top leaders of large American corporations is even more rare. Some chief executive officers are willing to cooperate with the CIA only if they do it personally to avoid any risk of the relationship getting beyond their control. I tried to locate a top-level businessman who would leave his business to head up this branch of the CIA. Interestingly, it was usually salary and prestige rather than concern about associating with the CIA that was the sticking point.

The business community has not asked for special favors, quid pro quos, regulations, or laws to govern relations with the CIA. Still, the CIA would do well to cultivate even better relations in several ways. One would be to assign more of its best people to this branch. Another would be to provide the business community with as much unclassified information and analysis as possible. For example, a study we produced on the Polish economy in

1978 turned out to have been a good guide for American banks, though unfortunately they did not follow it. Also good was one we had prepared in May 1977, on how the planned growth in the third world's capacity for producing steel was going to infringe on our overseas markets. The CIA works on many topics like these that are potentially useful to business. Volunteering to provide such work to business leaders would encourage their cooperation.

Another means would be to collect more intelligence specifically tailored to commercial interests overseas. My interest in using intelligence to further our economic interests was stimulated by a revealing conversation with one of the CIA's chiefs of station, during which he told me how one of his agents accidentally uncovered some valuable and secret business information. While probing in the economic ministry, the agent discovered the detailed bids that two European firms were making on a major procurement project in competition with an American firm. I immediately asked what he had done with this information. Nothing, he said, because there were no established procedures for handling it. Obviously we could not just rush out and give this sensitive information to the American company involved. There might have been a second American company about to enter the bidding and it could have been disadvantaged. Also, our agent's information might not have been accurate and an American company using it could have lost money. Or there might have been a risk to our source if the information was passed around outside controlled government agencies. These were real problems, but it seemed such a great opportunity to help American business that I requested the Department of Commerce to join in a study to explore what could be done in situations like this.

The result was a recommendation that we collect this kind of information if possible, that the Commerce Department be responsible for divulging it equitably, and that the CIA protect its sources by not giving any clue as to how it had obtained the information. (The recipients might be skeptical of the information the first time, but if they found that it was correct, they would be believers the second time.) I ordered that we begin collecting commercial intelligence in seven countries as a pilot project. Within a day a group of six top officials in the CIA came to my office to argue that helping business was not what the CIA had been created to do; it did not, in their view, further national security; it was not the kind of worthy cause for which they had signed up. I viewed this as a surprisingly narrow outlook on what constitutes national security, given the importance of our economic health to our position in the world. A second argument of theirs was that the CIA would be exposed to too much criticism if something went wrong. This was the old hunkering-down reflex stemming from the hearings before the Church Committee. Despite my own enthusiasm, I was stymied by institutional resistance to this kind of espionage. What I did work out with Secretary of Commerce Juanita Kreps and her successor, Philip Klutznick, was a series of briefings for U.S. business. Commerce would select a topic, such as the outlook for the electric power industry in China, and invite the appropriate businesses to send representatives to attend briefings that the CIA would prepare and deliver at the Commerce Department. Then there would be an informal interchange of ideas that was mutually beneficial. This program was only half of the loaf, but it was better than none.

Frankly, I was much less interested in stealing information about bids on specific contracts than in uncovering other nations' commercial strategies. The kind of information U.S. businesses really need is what specific market segments foreign countries are targeting for penetration and where their emphasis in research lies. Also, our government would like to know what subterfuges other countries use to cover up subsidies, tariffs, and import quotas to help their competitive position in world markets and place our exporters at a disadvantage. These matters are ideal targets for the human intelligence side of the CIA, as evidenced by the fact that we've caught the intelligence services of even some noncommunist countries doing just this sort of data-gathering in the United States. It is a sensitive and risky area, but we need not shy away from it because of that. The benefits to the country are too significant for us not to strive to surmount those risks.

My spymaster friend was certainly right in theory. There is a wealth of information no farther away than the media, academia, and commercial enterprises right at home. But in our free society any association of such institutions with secret intelligence activities may impinge on the freedoms of speech, academic inquiry, and capitalistic endeavor. The more I grappled with the question of whether associating these particular communities with intelligence was worth the risk, the more I believed that attempts to isolate them from intelligence would endanger, not protect those freedoms.

Accommodating secrecy in a democracy requires compromises with the theory of full freedom of speech, inquiry, and endeavor. The media, academia, and business need to think through the problems and participate in drawing the lines of compromise themselves, not wait to have them imposed by government, if we are to avoid tilting too far toward either secrecy or freedom.

TEN

Analysis:
What It All Means

THE ANALYTIC BRANCH of the CIA is given to tweedy, pipe-smoking intellectuals who work much as if they were doing research back in the universities whence many of them came. It probably has more Ph.D.'s than any other area of government and more than many colleges. Their expertise ranges from anthropology to zoology. Yet, for all that, they can be wrong.

On November 11, 1978, an envelope came to CIA Headquarters in Langley from the White House with instructions that it be opened by me personally. I found in it a short, handwritten note from President Carter:

> To Cy, Zbig, Stan: I am not satisfied with the quality of our political intelligence. Assess our assets and as soon as possible give me a report concerning our abilities in the most important areas of the world. Make a joint recommendation on what we should do to improve your ability to give me political information and advice. J.C.

Although this was addressed to the Secretary of State and the President's National Security Adviser, as well as myself, it was obviously an implied complaint to me about our intelligence-reporting on Iran.

The President's note was a hard blow. Just a week earlier, in a private conversation, he had told me that I was doing a fine job and that he wanted me to stay in it a long time. It was uncharacteristic of Jimmy Carter to flipflop this way. I suspected that Zbig Brzezinski was behind it. My suspicions were strengthened a few days later, when, despite the precautions taken to deliver the note privately, a story about it appeared in three newspapers simultaneously. I knew I had been set up as the scapegoat. When the Shah did fall, two months later, the easy explanation was that it was an "intelligence failure." A few years later Brzezinski confirmed my suspicion when he revealed in his book on the Carter presidency that he had "suggested" that the President write the note.[1] In fact, I had more than a suspicion at the time. Just a few weeks after the note arrived, I learned from a newsman that he was one of three journalists who had been called into the White House separately on the same day and actually shown the President's note — except that the heading had been changed to read only "To Stan."

Was there an intelligence failure over Iran that warranted Brzezinski's reaction? The answer is both yes and no. To the extent that it was yes, it was not the kind of failure Brzezinski meant. The complaint implicit in the memorandum he suggested to the President was that we had not warned that the Shah would be in as much trouble as he was by that time. Predicting revolutions, like the one against the Shah, or coups or surprise electoral reverses at the last minute will always be a chancy matter in intelligence work, as it is with the media, the business community, and scholars. Intelligence reporting on political affairs deserves to be judged on more than short-term forecasting. It is also more useful, because the policy-makers may have time to take corrective action. Still, the answer to the question of whether there was an intelligence failure in the matter of the Shah is partly yes; the CIA could have done a better job of emphasizing the deep currents that were running against him. This should have been done over the previous three or four years. Only then would there have been any real chance of our getting the Shah to change his course. Well before the President wrote his note, it was too late.

There were at least two fundamental and significant matters that we, and the Nixon and Ford administrations before us, had

1. Zbigniew Brzezinski, *Principle and Power: Memories of the National Security Adviser, 1977–1981* (New York: Farrar, Straus & Giroux, 1983), p. 367.

failed to identify and appreciate adequately. One was the extent of the dissatisfaction with the Shah and the other was the growing appeal of a renewed Islamic religious fundamentalism. We knew the Islamic mullahs resented the Shah's emphasis on secular education, his permitting activities that violated religious doctrine, such as Western-style dress and Western entertainment, and his curtailing some of the government's subsidy to the mullahs. We realized too that secular aspirants to political power resented the Shah's tight, personal control of the country's politics. And we knew that the merchant class expected a greater share in the nation's growing economic opportunities. What we didn't foresee was that all these groups would coalesce under a seventy-nine-year-old cleric then in exile in France, the Ayatollah Khomeini. Once the Shah had been deposed, the glue holding together these various factions disappeared. They began to fall apart, but the power of fundamentalism kept the revolution going. And to our surprise, the Islamic fundamentalists were strong enough to come out on top of all the dissident factions.

What compounded our failure to collect enough information about the dissidents and to appreciate the combined appeal of Islamic fundamentalism and Khomeini's personal charisma was that some of the CIA's key analysts were hung up on the durability of the Shah. The most basic reason for such a shortsighted view was that we were working from an erroneous premise. What we all saw in Iran in the autumn of 1978 was a Shah who, although beleaguered, still had control of a powerful army, police force, and secret intelligence service, the SAVAK. Our assumption was that if the dissident movements began to get out of control, the Shah would simply step in with whatever amount of force was necessary to control them. He never did that. Perhaps he was so out of touch with his own country that he did not appreciate how serious the situation was until corrective action would have caused too much bloodshed. Or perhaps he could not face difficult decisions because he knew he was dying. Whatever the explanation, our assumption that he would not hesitate to employ whatever force he needed was dead wrong. U.S. policy in that area of the world was so dependent on the Shah that it was all too easy for us to assume that he would do what was necessary to play the role we had in mind for him.

Thus, the answer to the question of an intelligence failure is also no, because it was partly a failure by the policy-makers. Intelligence had been providing some warnings. President Carter, for instance, just a year before the issuance of the memorandum, had arranged a private, one-on-one meeting with the Shah during the latter's visit to Washington. The President counseled the Shah to think carefully about liberalizing the political structure in Iran; pointing out that we saw some problems ahead. The Shah scoffed at the suggestion. In short, though we in intelligence were not sounding the alarms loudly enough, the policy-makers were not uninformed about the Shah's problems. From President Nixon on, they either did not or could not get through to the Shah.

To place in perspective the question of intelligence failure, we should note that there is little evidence that Middle East scholars and reporters were more attuned to the trends in Iran than was the CIA. The articles in academic journals and in the newspapers at the time revealed a bias like ours toward the Shah. In general, though, academics and reporters have one big advantage over CIA analysts: there is a good deal of sharing of views between them. In the CIA wide-ranging debate and exchange of ideas is not nearly so easy because of the necessary controls on the highly secret data CIA analysts use. CIA analysts are disinclined to test their theories and conclusions on people outside the Agency, who work from a less complete set of data. This problem of secrecy is genuine, but of more influence is an inherent reluctance in the CIA to go outside for second opinions. It is time-consuming to find a qualified academic willing to associate with the CIA and to make the arrangements for his security clearance. Beyond that, CIA analysts, who live day by day in a rarefied atmosphere of secret information, tend to be patronizing of outsiders, even those who are given most of the security clearances. They are not viewed as having the same depth of background as the analysts, who deal with the secret data daily.

As I watched great quantities of highly classified information cross my desk, I realized that there was excessive emphasis on the use of secret data as opposed to open information. Secret information is often highly relevant to two of the three basic categories of intelligence reports, but not nearly as much to the third — and the situation in Iran was in that category. The first category is the warning of an impending event, like the outbreak of war, a coup, or a terrorist attack. Secret photographs of military forces on the move or electronic intercepts of signals to military commanders or reports from agents who have penetrated a military headquarters are often the best or only tipoff. The second category is status reports on events in progress, like a battle, a negotiation, or an attempted revolution. In such a case, much of the relevant information is likely to be public, but it may well also take secret photos or a spy inside the negotiating team to help us keep close track of what's going on. The third category is the long-range forecasting of political, economic, and military trends. Here, so many diverse factors must be taken into account that the secret ones are relatively less important. In the case of Iran's Islamic revolution, for instance, there was relatively little secret information that was pertinent. There was no master revolutionary plan that spies could steal, no single revolutionary headquarters in which to place an agent. It was, then, a situation of a nearly spontaneous societal upheaval, and outside observers with no access to secrets could have been very useful in checking on the CIA's analysis. Most of the evidence about what was going to happen was available right on the surface. Just plain scholarly research on Iran from about 1970 onward should have forecast the problems the Shah would encounter, if not their exact timing. But secret reports, with their aura of mystery, often tend to crowd out just that kind of scholarly, unclassified work as well as respect for the scholars, businessmen, and others who do it.

If the CIA is reluctant to call for outside advice, another way to solicit it is to publish as much CIA analysis as can be declassified. It will be subjected to wide scrutiny and comment. When I first arrived at the CIA I had a strong inclination to do this for two other reasons. I felt that if the work was good, giving it to the public could only help restore confidence in the CIA. Clearly it is impossible for the CIA to attempt to raise public confidence by revealing very much about how successful our spies are. There are secrets in analytic work, too, that cannot be revealed, but they are more manageable. We can declassify a piece of analysis if we take several precautions. One is to guard against giving away some exclusive information that only we have and that gives us an

gives reasons for his
opinions

advantage over someone else — for example, what that other person's position is going to be at tomorrow's negotiation. Another is to remove any clues that point directly to the technique we used to collect it — for example, whether our agent was one of only three or four people present at a particular conversation, information that could point a finger right at him. My second reason for wanting to release more analysis was the conviction that a well-informed citizenry is the cornerstone of a democratic system. Before the Iranian crisis I encouraged more open publication, even in the face of strong resistance from many quarters in the CIA. After that crisis, my resolve to continue was much reinforced.

Actually, my initial plunge into publishing unclassified intelligence came as a result of a remark by President Carter in a television address on the world energy crisis in April of 1977. He quoted some unclassified statistics from a classified report we had sent him. The media wanted to see the full report. We went through it and found that after extracting indicators of our sources we could publish it, and we did.

The report was criticized by a number of nongovernment experts in energy matters, as I hoped it would be. I asked some of them to come to Langley to talk with us. A few of these people pointed out that we had overlooked something. Others, we could tell, were working from less reliable information than we were. All of the interchanges, though, were helpful to the analysts. They were also helpful to me in that I came away more confident of our analytic team and more understanding of where its strengths and weaknesses lay.

Another early publication I had declassified was on Soviet civil defense. I had heard so many exaggerated stories about how well the Soviets are prepared to shelter their people against nuclear attack that I considered this a useful topic to get out in the open. Study showed that only 5 to 10 percent of the Soviet urban population could be sheltered, and that percentage was declining as more people moved into cities. The plans to evacuate the other 90 to 95 percent were untested and did not acknowledge the near-impossibility of evacuating eight million people from a city like Moscow in the middle of a Russian winter. I felt the public needed to know these things to assess properly the debate that was going on.

The major hazard in publishing unclassified intelligence, and one that the CIA analysts constantly raised with me, was that it's difficult to draw the line on what should or should not be released. If information supports an administration's policy, people will suspect it has been slanted to that purpose. If it undercuts policy, the administration will not appreciate its release. Good policy should be able to withstand objective criticism, but situations do arise when the analysis that supports the current policy cannot be declassified, though the analysis that undercuts it can.

It wasn't long before I ran into flack at the White House over what we were releasing. When we issued the study of the Polish economy, alluded to earlier, it showed that the sizable funds Poland had borrowed from the West were not improving the economy's performance enough even to service the debt. Poland was a poor credit risk. At that very time, though, the White House was urging U.S. banks to lend more to Poland. Brzezinski, a Pole by birth, was livid because this report had been circulated. He argued that it was unconscionable for one element of the administration to undermine the President's policies; that by the very act of publishing unclassified reports, I was entering into the policy process; and that the DCI was not in the business of publishing unclassified, objective intelligence on his own. Brzezinski wanted to establish firm White House controls over what the CIA could release to the public. I feared that if the White House staff could stop the publication of unclassified intelligence inimical to administration policy, what next? Would they suppress information damaging to their partisan political interests? Could they tell us not to inform the Congress when intelligence was contrary to an administration policy?

Of course I could sympathize with Brzezinski's not wanting me to undercut the President's policies. I really preferred not to. It would have been easy simply to publish nothing, and that's what the professionals at the CIA wanted. Like the espionage people, the analysts were trying to avoid criticism. They were, though, subjected to more of that when we published a second study on energy, in the summer of 1977. This one concluded that oil production in the Soviet Union would start declining in the early 1980s. The outside experts who differed were eventually proved right. Production did not decline as rapidly as we had forecast.

Our report was wrong not because of faulty work, but because the Soviets changed their tactics after the report came out. They found ways to postpone the decline. But the prediction made in the report now appears to be coming true, a few years behind schedule. In any event, the report was useful in drawing attention to the serious problems that exist in Soviet oil production and that cannot be postponed indefinitely.

The differences between my view and that of the White House staff were not always a matter of my wanting to publish and their not wanting me to; there were also pressures toward publishing what would help the President. Once, I received a memo from Brzezinski requesting that I declassify an intelligence report that would provide ammunition against congressional critics of the President's Middle East policy. His memo indiscreetly requested that we declassify the report with "as few changes as possible." Since Brzezinski's memo was unclassified, I was afraid that in leaky Washington one day I would be before Congress and a congressman would attempt to discredit my testimony by producing this memo to show that I had acceded to politically motivated pressures from the White House to declassify information. I went through some bureaucratic nonsense in this instance to protect against that. I directed the CIA analytic staff in writing not to cut any corners when considering what could be declassified. When the sanitized version came back to me, I took out two more borderline items, just to ensure that we could never be accused of caving in to pressure. The White House was repeatedly insensitive, as in this case, to the importance of protecting the apolitical credibility of intelligence. And this despite the fact that Brzezinski was one of the strongest supporters of intelligence in the administration. Any number of times he came to my rescue when the NSC was about to do something that would have harmed intelligence capabilities.

Still, though I faced problems in both the White House and the CIA, I persisted in trying to open up the CIA's analytic work, because doing so clearly met a need. The Defense and State Departments publish declassified intelligence analyses regularly. Even with the best intentions, their interpretations are bound to be colored by their espousal of programs and policies. How can it be otherwise? Over and over I found myself defending the right of the CIA to publish the same kind of information when it could do so without pressures to slant the interpretation of events.

Independence of interpretation is one of the greatest advantages we have over Soviet intelligence. In a totalitarian society an analyst cannot afford to reach conclusions that would contravene the basic tenets of Marxism or Communist Party policies. We sometimes actually watched Soviet officials stationed abroad tailor their reporting to Moscow for fear of being accused of adopting noncommunist outlooks. In April 1978, the number two man in the Soviet delegation to the United Nations, Andrei Schevchenko, defected to the United States. Some months later, when I had dinner with him, he confirmed that even very senior Soviet diplomats hesitate to report frankly.

In contrast, our insistence that intelligence analysis be totally divorced from policy considerations is one of the great strengths of our system and one of our advantages over the KGB. It is, of course, a disservice to the nation if intelligence is warped to tell the policy-makers what they want to hear. Skewed intelligence-reporting can not only result in a bad decision in a particular instance, but can also erode confidence in all intelligence analysis. The Reagan administration has been plagued by inferences that analysts have been pressured improperly. In September 1982 the House Committee on Intelligence issued a report that said in part:

> Taken as a whole, intelligence on Central America is strong, and its task is both difficult and particularly important. The criticisms voiced in this report must be seen in that context. The basic concern is that tendentious rhetoric, including occasionally oversimplification and misstatement, can drive out some of the needed collection and analysis. This may occur in a context in which intelligence users demand reinforcement more than illumination, but this fact does not absolve the intelligence producer from responsibility of quality. The influence of consumer desires for "ammunition" rather than analysis can be subtle or forceful, but its effect upon the intelligence process can become costly. Therefore, it deserves the constant watchfulness of intelligence professionals.[2]

2. Intelligence Performance on Central America: Achievements and Selected Instances of Concern, Staff Report of Subcommittee on Oversight and Evaluation, House Permanent Select Committee on Intelligence, September 22, 1982.

Then in mid 1984 two senior analysts on Central America resigned from the CIA and levied allegations of political pressure on their analytic work. The fact that DCI Casey was constantly being reported in the press as a major force on this side or that of key policy issues, rather than observing the strict neutrality on policy matters that all previous DCIs observed, added to the impression of possible bias in intelligence-reporting. The greatest long-term danger that these various allegations present, whether they are justified or not, is that truly good analysts, like academics, will not remain in an organization that does not respect their freedom to report results as they see them.

Yet I can feel some sympathy for Casey in his problems with the Central American analysts who resigned. I had two cases of analysts who felt strongly about their right to stick to their guns. A few days after I became DCI, I was asked to sign an important study comparing South and North Korean military forces. Although much of it was new to me, I could tell, as a naval officer, that the presentation of naval forces was misleading. It compared numbers of units only. The North Koreans had a large number of very small ships; the South Koreans had a smaller number of much larger, more powerful ships. I marked up the draft one evening at home to show how to avoid creating an erroneous impression of South Korean naval inferiority. The next night the report came back to me again in as misleading a form as the original. The exchange went on for three days, including oral explanations by me to the analyst. It was clear that she and her supervisors felt that no one should influence the analysis, including me, even though I was to sign the report and felt as bound by the belief in independence from policy as they. I prevailed but quickly grew weary of fighting this kind of misplaced zeal for independence even in the face of error.

In the other instance an analyst, David Sullivan, became overly sensitive to efforts of his superiors to modify his conclusions. He felt that he had reached a set of conclusions of seminal importance to the country, and that his superiors were attempting to quash those views out of ideological bias. In fact, his superiors sincerely believe that he had been driven by ideological bias more than by logic. Sullivan professed later that he feared that all copies of his important work would be destroyed by those opposed to his views. He had taken a copy of his highly classified report and delivered it, by coincidence, to my former mentor, Admiral Zumwalt, who in this instance shared Sullivan's view. Zumwalt at the time was out of government. He suggested that Sullivan give the report to an aide to Senator Henry Jackson, Richard Perle. Perle presumably would at least store it in a classified safe. Fortuitously, Sullivan came up for a random polygraph test at just that time. He confessed to having given away this report. I had to fire him, and Scoop Jackson reprimanded Perle in my presence.

Preserving the right of analysts to hold differing views from those of their superiors is very important. When analysis is being done, there must be constant discussion between the analyst and his supervisors. Early drafts are usually modified some as they move up the line and are reviewed by superiors who have their own interpretations and perhaps more experience as well. Because only a single report will go to the policy-makers, there can be strong feelings about whose interpretation is most appropriate. Sometimes a persuasive or stubborn analyst will prevail in having his view be that of the report. At other times some superior, up to and including the DCI, will insist on inserting his opinion. Often there will be a compromise: the report will present one view but will include others as minority views. It is never easy, though, to decide how many minority views warrant the attention of the busy policy-makers for whom most reports are intended.

As important as it is for analysis to remain free of any influence of policy-makers, I found that the CIA's approach to the independence of analysis was frequently carried to extremes. Sometimes doing the best work possible was placed ahead of meeting deadlines. The result was analyses that were not always timely or directly relevant to the needs of policy-makers. When I once complained that a particular CIA report was late, I was told that the analysts were holding it back because they could make it a much better report if they had another week to work on it. I pointed out that, as they knew, the President would be making decisions in this area before another week went by. Doing the best possible job of research had become an end of greater importance than producing a report of timely usefulness to the policy-maker.

On another occasion, just a few months after I took office, the

President asked me for a study of the economies of the Middle East. He wanted to know specifically what the potential for economic benefit would be if Israel and the Arab world made peace and pursued a common policy of economic cooperation. Obviously the President wanted to give the countries involved some idea of what each could gain from making peace. It seemed to me an exceptional opportunity to impress the new President with the kind of work the CIA could produce. Not so. The analysts balked at researching what they considered an infeasible idea — that in the foreseeable future there could be broad economic cooperation between Israel and the Arabs. They feared that someone would distort the message and believe the CIA thought this economic forecast could be actually realized. Protecting the Agency's intellectual credibility and its freedom from being pressured into doing an analysis in which it didn't believe was more important to them than being responsive to the President. The best I could get them to produce was a vacuous, densely hedged report of little value.

The intelligence problem with Iran also pinpointed for me a couple of other difficulties. One was the inherent conservatism of a large bureaucracy. For instance, it would have been helpful to use confidence numbers to express our opinion of the probability of the Shah's survival. The analysts could have said, "Our confidence that the Shah will survive another X years is 75 percent." Instead, they preferred the categorical: "The Shah will survive another X years." This aversion to expressing results on a quantified basis had its genesis in past accusations that the Agency had "waffled" its conclusions. If a confidence level was expressed as 60/40 or 50/50, the customers would accuse the Agency of being unwilling to take a stand one way or the other. And because decision-makers would not find a 60/40 estimate weighted enough to help them select one policy over another, they could ignore the intelligence and simply follow their own predilections. Thus, the analyst felt his efforts were wasted. It need not have been that way, however. If the analysts had explained the reasons for the 60 percent probability and, again, for the 40 percent probability, the decision-maker could have applied his own judgment as to which set of reasons struck him as more cogent. But that kind of analytic work takes a lot of effort.

I also sensed that the CIA shied away from probabilities because of a lack of familiarity with handling them. In fact, probabilities are just one of a number of analytic techniques I was surprised to find that the CIA did not employ adequately. Nor was it as much in the forefront of developing new analytic methodologies as it should have been. The problem was the difficulty any large bureaucracy has in being innovative. As the analysts who should have been developing new methodologies became more senior, they were forced to be managers more and analysts less. As they fell behind in their own ability to stay abreast of new theories, they resisted letting their subordinates employ new methods they did not understand. To offset the inevitable emphasis on management as people rose in rank, we created as many positions of "senior analyst" as we could. These individuals were able to advance without assuming managerial duties. We could not afford, however, to take too many people out of the managerial stream, or the pool of potential senior managers would have been too small.

A lack of specialized analytic skills also hurt in the Iranian situation. We had an ample number of political scientists to interpret reports on what the politically informed segment of the country was saying. But the skills of sociologists and anthropologists would have been more useful in detecting the kind of societal upheaval that occurred. Such people are best equipped to analyze attitudinal undercurrents and to estimate the depth of feeling behind them. We didn't have enough of that talent. And the need for sociologists and anthropologists in the Iranian crisis is just one example. Throughout U.S. intelligence there are growing opportunities to use new analytic skills. In recent years we have been forced to expand coverage into topics not previously of great concern: the production and shipment of narcotics, international terrorism, proliferation of nuclear weapons, verification of arms agreements, trade in armaments, agricultural crop forecasting, energy sources and consumption, and arm's-length psychological assessments of foreign leaders. There is also a need for more expertise in previously neglected geographical areas. Only six times since World War II have we sent military forces into combat. They were all in previously little-known countries: Korea, the Dominican Republic, Vietnam, Cambodia, Iran, and Grenada. It takes years for an analyst to understand foreign countries like these well enough to assess societal trends that could lead to wars of the sort we've found ourselves involved in over the past forty years.

The CIA also needs to invest in developing expertise in countries that may not be of great interest to us now. We must not wait until a crisis is on us. We were caught short in the Middle East and Southeast Asia. Because we are not likely to be able to predict just where the next Iran or Vietnam will be, some analysts must study countries of relatively little interest to the United States today. The CIA's analytic branch strongly resists allocating scarce talent in this manner. The demand for more and better intelligence on whatever they've been working on for years is almost insatiable. Rearranging priorities is frightfully difficult and not without risk. The only alternative is for the analytic branch to grow continuously. It could use some growth today, but unless the branch has a better sense of priorities, growth could be infinite and undirected.

The analytic branch's biggest problem is not size, however, but prestige within the Agency. Its reputation on the outside is deservedly high. The Church Committee stated that the CIA's analytic branch "is by far the best analytic organization for the production of finished intelligence within the government."[3] Its prestige inside the Agency is clearly second to that of the espionage branch. In part, that's because only a few DCIs have given analysis more than passing attention. Most of them were either former members of the espionage branch or were captivated by it.

In part because of this, it became clear to me that the collection of intelligence, by both human and technical means, was in relatively better shape than the analysis of the information collected. Our greatest weakness was the interpretation, not the collection, of data. The more I was convinced of this, the more I emphasized my interest and participation in the analytic work. Several times a week I would call for a round table discussion with groups of ten to fifteen analysts. Sometimes the session was to prepare me for a meeting at the White House; sometimes it was to educate me on some topic on which I felt ill-informed. I always asked that junior

3. Final Report, Select Committee to Study Governmental Operations with Respect to Intelligence Activities, United States Senate, Book I, Chapter XII, April 26, 1976.

as well as senior analysts be included. I wanted to get fresh ideas and to expose the younger people to high-level discussions in the hope that they might be inspired to make their work with the Agency a career.

It will take a long time for the analytic branch to achieve the prestige of the espionage branch. It is not a question of downgrading espionage, but of recognizing that all the branches contribute to the final product. To ensure that the product is as good as it can be, each branch must play as part of a team, not independently, as is too often the case now. There is no place for elitism in such serious and important work.

ELEVEN

Marketing the Product

STAN, do you like to start work early in the morning, as I do?" the President asked as we began lunch.

Not being entirely truthful, I replied cheerily, "Yes, sir," all the while wondering how much I would like to show up at the White House at six o'clock every morning to brief him, if that was what he had in mind.

The President and I were sitting in the wingback chairs beside the fireplace in the Oval Office just a week after my first meeting with him there. We were eating from trays set on small portable tables. All I remember of the meal was that I was served one more course than the President, with no explanation. It was a bit awkward, but I wasn't very interested in eating. I had propped up on the right corner of my tray a 5-by-8-inch card on which was a list of topics I wanted to cover with him.

One item on my list was a request for a weekly twenty-minute appointment to brief him. The President pre-empted me by saying that he had in mind two or three meetings a week of thirty minutes each. After a bit of discussion, we agreed to leave the hour and day to the schedulers but would start with two meetings a week and see how they went.

Timothy Kraft, the President's appointments secretary, selected Tuesdays and Fridays at ten-thirty in the morning for the briefings. They usually took place in the Oval Office, but occasionally in good weather we moved to a table beside the swimming pool or sat in the Rose Garden or on the small terrace behind the President's personal office. The Vice President and Brzezinski usually joined us. We almost always began on time, and I learned not to run over my allotted thirty minutes, because the President kept right to his schedule.

I felt fortunate that, as a young lieutenant on my first assignment in Washington, from 1954 to 1956, I had briefed the Secretary of the Navy once a week on political developments around the world that might affect the Navy. It was a marvelous lesson in boiling down a lot of material into a few highlights, just as I had to do now. With Jimmy Carter's insistence on the efficient use of his time, I soon found that I had to be even more succinct and meaty than with the Navy Secretary. I took four thin notebooks to each briefing. In them I had a tab for each topic and usually some graphic or chart that illustrated the key points. Long before joining the CIA I had admired the graphics that are in most CIA intelligence reports, so I called heavily on the appropriate Agency people for these briefings. In my copy of each notebook I also had my talking notes.

I spent perhaps ten to twelve hours in preparing for each thirty-minute session, a heavy load, though the work helped me focus in considerable detail on the major current and long-term issues. Instead of just serving as an above-the-battle manager, I was forced to gain a solid, substantive command of the issues. It was rewarding when I felt that I had struck a responsive chord in the President, deflating when I had not. One thing that was always rewarding was that Jimmy Carter consistently listened with total concentration. Only once in four years did I feel that his mind was far off when I was talking to him. That was on February 19, 1979, shortly after a group of students in Tehran seized our embassy in what was a precursor to the hostage crisis that began with the second seizure six months later. The Khomeini government quickly threw the students out this time, but one U.S. Marine sergeant was slightly wounded and taken to a hospital. There, terrorists grabbed him and held him captive. Negotiations to free him began. The President was obviously worried and distracted. When a phone call came in, reporting that the ser-

Pocatsh

Pocatsh

Pocatsh

geant had been released, the beaming Carter immediately phoned the Marine's mother in Pennsylvania to give her the good news. I listened as his voice choked with emotion and his eyes moistened. He told us that this one incident had worried him more than anything else; he feared that the Iranians might execute the young man. Nine months later he had more than fifty American hostages in Tehran to worry about.

Another rewarding aspect of the briefings was that Jimmy Carter remembered what was said. Once, I cited a figure on the productivity of rice per hectare of land in Southeast Asia. About six weeks later I made a similar reference to India. The President instantly compared the two figures. I'd forgotten ever mentioning the one for Southeast Asia.

Initially I briefed President Carter on topics of current concern, being careful not to overlap the written briefing materials we sent to him daily. I usually selected a topic or two that were important but not quite so current. Sometimes the material was background on a current problem, like the history and status of the troublesome Israeli settlements on the West Bank of the Jordan River, or the trading patterns that tied many of the black nations of southern Africa to the Union of South Africa, despite apartheid.

On other occasions I attempted to look ahead to problems that might emerge. In 1978, for instance, I briefed him on the internal instability in El Salvador. We were not yet giving any significant attention to El Salvador, but we were to do so within the next two years. Also that year I discussed the state of the Soviet microchip industry, and that was useful a year later, when, after the Soviet invasion of Afghanistan, we considered an economic embargo on the Soviet Union. I often went a step further and included some feel for how confident we were about the information I was reporting, as well as some speculation about what might come next. I had difficulty getting CIA analysts to speculate in writing if they thought that the information might go outside the Agency. They had clearly become gun-shy from being criticized for past predictions that did not come true. I, though, could speculate orally on my own. I also used the briefings to emphasize differing points of view from ones I knew the President held. For example, our Ambassador to the United Nations, Andrew Young, was encouraging the President to support Prime Minister Michael N. Manley of

Jamaica. We had enough good information about Manley's ties to the communists to warrant my making sure that that side of the story got through, too.

In addition to presenting these substantive briefings, I described how the intelligence collection systems work. The President was new and so was I. Between us we went through a series of tutorials on satellites, electronic intercepts, espionage techniques, and the like. I would study the characteristics and capabilities of one or two means of collecting intelligence each week and then pass on what I thought would be useful to him. Because of his technical bent and his willingness to become involved in intelligence matters, he readily accepted this. The sessions were worthwhile in letting him know not only what we could do, but also what our limitations were. When SALT II became the centerpiece of his foreign policy, the President needed accurate knowledge of what our verification capabilities were; he could not negotiate without a realistic understanding of how well we could monitor Soviet compliance with the treaty.

The briefings were also my opportunity to give him a feel for how the Intelligence Community was operating and the quality of its people. I regularly brought its leaders or specialists to brief the President. I wanted him to know at first hand the kind of people who were running the intelligence organizations. It was also good for each of them to be able to tell his employees that he had met with the President and been able to describe his agency's role to him. Sometimes I brought lower-ranking officers as well. Once I was briefed by a young Army captain on a particular photographic interpretation. Both what he said and his photos were so illuminating that I told him, "I want you to be in the White House tomorrow at ten-thirty to give the same presentation to the President." At first the captain wasn't sure whether to take me seriously, but he was there the next morning and accounted well for himself.

I also tried to present some of the problems I was encountering. Sometimes these were internal problems in managing the Intelligence Community, like encouraging teamwork. Occasionally they were ticklish requests from particular senators for very sensitive information that could compromise an operation. I would tell the President how I intended to handle such issues. Sometimes he agreed and sometimes he did not. Most often on issues of secrecy he came down hard on the side of protecting secrets.

Over time the tradecraft tutorials and the long-term back-grounders had covered the most relevant material, and the briefings were then reduced to once a week; later, as the 1980 election approached, to once every other week. No other President and DCI have had this type of regular, free-ranging exchange. Is it a practice to be encouraged? From the President's point of view much depends on whether he is a person who prefers to absorb material in briefings or by reading. There are two good reasons, though, for relying on some of each.

First, in light of the technical revolution in collection, Presidents would be well advised to have a reasonable understanding of the limits and capabilities of these systems. They will call on them, hear reports based on their performance, and make decisions on large expenditures to build the next generation of such systems. They can learn what they need to about the technologies in a few special briefings, but there is an advantage in the DCI's being able to point out periodically in the course of his briefings that the information he is discussing was collected by this system or that and with what degree of success.

Second, the revolution in oversight has heightened the President's responsibilities for intelligence. Both the public and Congress expect a higher ethical performance from the Intelligence Community than heretofore. And whereas Presidents once could expect that secret misdemeanors would remain secret, that's highly unlikely in an era of congressional oversight. Presidents are much more likely than ever before to be held publicly responsible for how the intelligence organizations perform. They can attempt to forestall improper actions through various systems of controls, but one of the best checks is to have sufficient, regular dialogue with the DCI to sense the standards and attitudes he is imposing on the system. The President may see the DCI regularly in the course of various meetings on specific issues, but those will not serve this purpose as well as periodic briefing sessions, in which the President can interrogate the DCI privately, casually, and without warning.

From the DCI's point of view, personal briefings are an ideal means of marketing the Community's product to its top customer;

the President's firsthand reaction is invaluable in helping the DCI tailor future intelligence support to his needs and style. After each White House briefing, I dictated a memorandum on my reactions and conclusions in the car during the fifteen-minute drive back to Langley. In the memo I told the analysts how the President had reacted to what I had presented and instructed them on any follow-up work that was needed. The memos were greatly appreciated by the analysts, who normally get very little feedback from their customers.

Of course, all the intelligence information Presidents need cannot be marketed in just oral briefings. Every day we sent him the President's Daily Brief, or PDB. This document, of about eight double-spaced pages, was provided only to the President, the Vice President, and the Secretaries of State and Defense. By restricting the circulation to people who really needed to know what the President was being told by us, we could include highly sensitive material. President Carter received many other written reports from the CIA, the State Department, and the DIA, ranging from one-to-two-page interpretative reports on individual topics to one-hundred-to-two-hundred-page National Intelligence Estimates. (NIEs) Most of these materials passed through Brzezinski to the President. The National Security Adviser is the one person who must control the flow of reading material on national security affairs that reaches the President; otherwise he could be inundated with reading, much of it duplicatory. Only when I felt strongly that the President should see some report did I either insist that it get in to him or deliver it myself. Otherwise, we were dependent on the intelligence selling itself to the National Security Adviser and his staff so that they would send it to the President.

One other opportunity for the DCI to give advice is at meetings of the National Security Council or the NSC subcommittees that prepare for the full-scale NSC meetings with the President. On most occasions I was called on to lead off these meetings with an oral intelligence briefing. This was a substantial responsibility; I had to be fully up to date and accurate on a large number of topics. Frequently I was forced to draw the difficult line between being the President's intelligence adviser and being an adviser on policy matters. As I have noted, if intelligence is to be kept free from policy influence, the DCI should not take sides on policy issues. That was sometimes very difficult for me, having come from a career of involvement in governmental policy-making.

In June 1979 there was a debate in the National Security Council on whether to proceed with the MX intercontinental ballistic missile. Most military men held strong opinions on the MX, and I was no exception.[1] I gave the opening presentation to the NSC on the Soviet view of the MX and what the Soviets might do if we built it. I made it quite clear that they could easily counter the MX deployment that was being considered simply by fitting their existing missiles with more warheads. As the discussion went on, however, the President indicated that he had made his decision in favor of the MX. Looking around the table, he then said, "I assume from the discussion that everyone agrees." Although it wasn't my proper role to agree or to disagree on a policy matter, I could not let my silence be interpreted as agreement. I spoke up, saying that I disagreed, because the Soviets could counter the MX so easily. Under the plan the President was approving we would have built only two hundred MX missiles but rotated them surreptitiously around forty-four hundred shelters. Supposedly the Soviets would be confused as to where to shoot if they wanted to knock out the two hundred MXs by surprise. I told the President that the Soviets could increase the number of warheads on their existing large missiles by forty-four hundred and attack every shelter, not just those in which they might think there was an MX. They could do that even within the limit on warheads in the proposed SALT II treaty.

In sum, marketing intelligence to the President depends a good deal on the President's style and his confidence in his DCI. Does he prefer immediate answers to questions at a briefing, or does he prefer more studied responses to queries he pens in the margin of a written report? The system for providing intelligence has to be suited to each incumbent.

Marketing to the remainder of the Intelligence Community's customers is more complex, just because the product cannot be tailored to the needs of each and because the marketing is done by a number of separate, quite independent organizations. The CIA publishes two daily intelligence reports. The President's Daily

1. Stansfield Turner, "Why We Shouldn't Build the MX," *New York Times Magazine*, March 29, 1981.

Brief, as I have mentioned, has a very restricted number of subscribers. The National Intelligence Daily provides a similar service to several hundred readers, but because of this wider distribution does not include material as sensitive as the PDB. (We'll see later that, even so, it has been thought to be the source of serious leaks.) The State Department's Bureau of Intelligence and Research, the Defense Intelligence Agency, the four military services, and the National Security Agency all publish daily intelligence reports as well. Their readers are primarily in their own organizations, but most reports are distributed to a wider audience, including the White House.

In addition to reporting on current developments, all Intelligence Community agencies publish periodic as well as one-time reports on subjects of longer concern. They are usually in an area of special interest to that agency, but there is considerable overlap in this work. Some reports are done at the request of the analysts' superiors; some are on topics the analysts believe their superiors need to be informed about. The printing presses are constantly rolling and a prodigious amount of material is turned out. A great deal of it is read only by other intelligence analysts, but even that is useful in stimulating better analysis.

There is one publication produced by the Intelligence Community, not just by an individual agency. That is the National Intelligence Estimate, which will be discussed in detail in a later chapter. One of the perennial problems in marketing intelligence is deciding how much effort to put into long-term products, be they NIEs or individual agency efforts, as opposed to current reporting. The number of analysts who do this work is finite. Those who are working on big, long-range studies are therefore not available to interpret today's crises, and vice versa. Unfortunately most of the pressures are to work on current reporting. One reason is that busy decision-makers seldom make time to read lengthy reports on subjects they are not required to grapple with today. Another is that the wealth of data flowing in from the technical collection systems swamps analysts with requirements for current interpretation. And another is simply that interpretation of current reporting is more interesting, more exciting, and guarantees the analyst more visibility.

Every administration attempts in its own way to sort out its priorities between current and longer-range intelligence studies. In the Carter period we rejected a rather mechanistic set of over a thousand numerical priorities set up by the Ford administration. Instead, we had an annual meeting of the Cabinet-level officials involved in national security. We used that meeting to draw up a list in rough priority of twenty to thirty short- and long-term national concerns for intelligence to explore. This list guided the overall analytic effort. The results of these annual meetings were helpful, but by no means a full solution. Busy, top-level decision-makers don't have time to worry much about issues their successors may face three to ten years in the future. But only if the intelligence system looks that far ahead can it hope to detect the early-warning signs of societal upheaval, like those which led to the problems in Iran in 1978; or economic vulnerabilities, such as have been present in Brazil, Mexico, and Argentina since the early 1980s. Forecasting the potential seriousness of such problems is one of the key contributions of a good intelligence system. No single system for setting up priorities for long-range studies is likely to be adequate. Whatever else is done to help him, the DCI must set up his own internal system. Although it's no easier for him and his top people than for anyone else to shift gears into long-range thinking, unless they do it, it won't be done adequately.

A final and very important point on marketing is that vast opportunities are opening up to use new technologies in presenting the intelligence product. By using computer data processing and storage, we could have one data base for the entire Community. That would mean that differences of interpretation could be easily displayed for comparison, enhancing the understanding of why the differences exist. And through expanded use of computer terminals for consumers, marketing could be done with great speed and responsiveness. The President could just as well read his PDB on a computer terminal as in a printed booklet. It could be kept up to the minute, and if he had a question he could type it in and get a quick reply, rather than annotating a written report and waiting hours or days for the response. This technique of distribution would also help security, because there would be no paper copy that people other than the President might read or photocopy. His terminal could be tightly coded to let him have any level of sensitive information, whereas others' terminals would be set for only their level of clearance.

One reason we don't take sufficient advantage of such technologies today is that marketing is not viewed as an important element of intelligence. The excitement of intelligence is in stealing secrets others don't want you to have and in figuring out what they all mean. It's almost discovery for the sake of discovery. Finding ways to interest policy-makers in reading what is produced seems to intelligence professionals to be unworthy huckstering. Unfortunately, politicians and bureaucrats already overwhelmed by information are not out shopping for more. But, shown that the Intelligence Community can truly help them, they can be converted to relying more on the intelligence product. Is it worth the effort to find out what they need and in what form they prefer it, and then aggressively trying to interest them in the resulting product? I think the payoff — having decisions based on the best available information — makes such aggressive marketing of the intelligence product well worth the effort.

PART THREE

ADAPTING TO OVERSIGHT

TWELVE

Espionage in a Fish Bowl

PETE BROCK,[1] an espionage branch officer, had asked for thirty minutes on my schedule. He came in loaded with charts and photographs. They had to do with a sensitive operation that required my approval. We were going to surreptitiously acquire a piece of military equipment in a foreign country. There was a risk of being caught in the act; being caught would be a public embarrassment to the United States and would harm our relations with the country involved.

Pete came all the way to me to request permission because of a series of controls imposed on risky espionage operations following the Church Committee report. The CIA started this in 1976 by rewriting its own regulations to control the kinds of operations individuals could initiate on their own. When I arrived in 1977, I felt that much more was needed. The last thing I wanted was more Angletons incarcerating Nosenkos or Gottliebs administering drugs all on their own. The question, though, was which of the more sensitive operations I should personally control. Espionage operations came in such different forms, often one of a kind, that I found it almost impossible to write specific rules. I was able, however, to define certain categories of actions to be cleared with me. These included payments to agents when they exceeded cer-

1. A pseudonym.

tain dollar amounts; recruitments of foreign agents at Cabinet level or above; dispensing any lethal material, such as explosives or poison requested by an agent who might feel he would be tortured if caught; any operation where the risks were high and exposure could seriously embarrass the United States.

Pete's proposal fitted this last category. I took much more than the allotted thirty minutes to review it. I had to estimate the value of what we would learn. Would the benefits be worth the risks? In this case the answer was not clear-cut, but what was important to me was the precedent for CIA espionage. Because of the general reluctance since the early 1970s to undertake risky operations, not much like this had been attempted for some time. I was pleased that the espionage people were beginning to suggest taking risks again when the gain seemed worth it. I wanted to encourage that. If this operation succeeded, it would be easier to get White House approval when an even greater risk offered even greater gain.

So I probed the risk factor closely with Pete. How could we get the equipment without being exposed? How well had we checked the pattern activity to assess the odds that someone would detect us in the act? How could we conceal the operation while it was going on? Could we warn our people by portable radio if the operation was in danger? If the operation was discovered, could we plausibly deny involvement? Clearly I was no expert on how to do these things, but I needed to sense Pete's own confidence, understand the thoroughness of his preparations, and estimate how well he'd thought out a full range of contingencies. He'd done it well. He was a professional and was well prepared with every detail. The fact that his plan would have to stand the test of additional scrutiny at the White House had a bearing on how completely he'd prepared. He knew that if he failed to make his case persuasively with me the first time, he could always ask to try again. There might be no second chance if we were turned down at the White House. Because Pete had prepared so well, I decided to go ahead and take his plan to the White House for approval.

The Church Committee report had been explicit in blaming past Presidents for failing to exercise adequate control over intelligence activities. "Presidents have not established specific instruments of oversight to prevent abuses by the Intelligence Community. In essence, Presidents have not exercised effective oversight."[2] It was only natural, then, that President Ford saw it as wise and politically expedient to require in his Executive Order on Intelligence that the DCI obtain approval from a committee of the National Security Council for "sensitive intelligence collection operations." President Carter's subsequent order reaffirmed the requirement.[3]

Under the Carter order, it was up to me to decide which sensitive operations should be cleared with the NSC. I considered Pete's proposed operation to be within the "sensitive" category. My primary criterion was the risk of exposure, especially in situations where it would be damaging to our country's foreign relations. My next was the risk of life, either of case officers or agents. The NSC also set up a system, as indeed was appropriate, for checking on my judgment about which operations should be taken to the NSC for approval. This was an annual review of all the operations I had submitted for clearance, what they had accomplished, and where they then stood. At this review I was also required to present the ten next most sensitive operations we had conducted that in my judgment had not needed clearance from the NSC. If the NSC felt some of these ten should have been cleared, I received new guidance.

Being prepared for this annual review was one reason I had set up my own internal controls, which brought Pete's proposal to me in the first place. I did not want to find out for the first time, when preparing for the annual review, that the espionage branch had conducted operations I felt should have been cleared with the NSC. So when we prepared the list to present to the NSC of the ten next most sensitive operations, I would review twenty or more items beyond that list to see what operations the espionage branch considered below my threshold and was undertaking on its own.

My next step in preparing to present Pete's plan to the NSC committee was to review the precautions I would take to limit the number of people who saw the information about this sensitive operation during the NSC clearance process. Unfortunately, it

2. Final Report of the Select Committee to Study Governmental Operations with Respect to Intelligence Activities, United States Senate, Book I, Chapter XVIII, April 26, 1976.
3. President Reagan's order de-emphasized this requirement both by weakening it and by relegating it to a supplementary instruction.

was my experience that the most injurious leaks about intelligence came from the White House, seldom as a result of oversight briefings like this, but often from the normal flow of intelligence materials. Sometimes the President's staff was so eager to use any information that would help his political position, they "forgot" where it came from. Sometimes this was innocent; most of the time it was not. The President's people in the White House are exceedingly close to the seat of power. That can be frustrating, though, because so much of the power to execute decisions rests in departments and agencies, not in the White House itself. The White House staff, then, are tempted to leak information selectively to the press in order to pressure the departments and agencies to take actions they support or to prevent them from initiatives they don't support. President Carter, like most Presidents, found it impossible to discipline his personal staff, even when it was clear that this sort of thing was being done. In general my concern for sensitive intelligence sources led to my not discussing them in the White House in any more detail than was absolutely necessary and often only with the National Security Adviser, the Vice President, and the President.

I discussed Pete's proposal individually and privately with the members of the NSC committee, Zbig Brzezinski, Harold Brown, and Cy Vance. In this case it took some doing. Vance was naturally concerned about the diplomatic costs if the operation were detected. Brzezinski wanted all the details. I had several sessions with each, including one in which I brought Pete along so that Brzezinski could gain confidence in him, too. In due course I received the approval, and Pete went off overseas to take charge of the operation. When the actual day came, tension was high. I knew exactly what time it was to begin and end. Not many minutes after the end time we received a cryptic message: "We were not detected, but the operation was not successful." The first part was a relief; the second a great disappointment.

Pete came back and explained the problem. He developed a new scheme he believed would work if we tried again. I debated whether the fact that we were not detected on this attempt meant that we could do it again with assurance or that we'd just been lucky and the odds would be against us on a second try. I continued to have confidence in Pete and went back to Brzezinski,

Brown, and Vance for approval of a second effort. They gave it. The next attempt worked perfectly. That success has led to subsequent use of the technique to very good advantage.

The Church Committee also found that "Congress has failed to provide the necessary statutory guidelines to ensure that intelligence agencies carry out their missions in accord with constitutional process."[4] Senator Leverett Saltonstall of Massachusetts had expressed the traditional congressional attitude toward oversight of intelligence back in 1956:

> It is not a question of reluctance on the part of CIA officials to speak to us. Instead, it is a question of our reluctance, if you will, to seek information and knowledge on subjects which I personally, as a member of Congress and as a citizen, would rather not have, unless I believed it to be my responsibility to have it because it might involve the lives of American citizens.[5]

Saltonstall's concern, I suspect, was not just with secrecy, but with ethics. He knew that, though Americans might support the CIA's being deceptive or even mendacious with our enemies, they also felt strongly that the United States should live by its principles. Honesty, openness, and respect for the rights of the individual are important elements of our international reputation, and the public doesn't like to think of compromising them. Generally the public has preferred to let the CIA do what it needed to do, but only if it didn't have to know about it. Saltonstall reflected this attitude of not wanting to know the seamy necessities of surviving in a sometimes threatening and imperfect world.

The Church Committee's criticism put an end to that attitude. Senator Mathias had reminded me of this sharply during my confirmation hearings, when I had said there might be some things the committee might not want to hear about. Now, he and his committee wanted to know and expected to be kept abreast of what was going on. To reinforce this expectation, in October 1980 Congress passed an amendment to the basic charter for intelligence, the National Security Act of 1947. This required the heads

4. Final Report of the Select Committee to Study Governmental Operations with Respect to Intelligence Activities, United States Senate, Book I, Chapter XVIII, April 26, 1976.
5. Ibid., Book I, Chapter VIII, April 26, 1976.

of all intelligence agencies to keep the intelligence committees "fully and currently informed of all intelligence activities . . . including any significant anticipated intelligence activity." Informing the committees of "all intelligence activities" is, of course, impossible; there's simply too much going on at any time. Consequently, how much is reported to the Congress will always be an issue to be negotiated between each set of committees and each DCI.

When I arrived, the committees were concerned that not enough would be told to them. The espionage professionals were concerned that so much would have to be told that their operations and agents would be quickly compromised. As I saw it, the CIA professionals had to be encouraged to begin again taking worthwhile risks at the same time as they were adjusting to congressional oversight, even though they viewed the two as incompatible. Getting along with Congress turned out to be a lot easier than anyone expected, because the committees also wanted to get along with us. The residual feeling on the Hill that the Church and Pike Committees had done harm to our capabilities made the new committees eager to establish a constructive relationship with the Intelligence Community. To achieve that, Majority Leader Robert C. Byrd and Minority Leader Howard H. Baker in the Senate, and Speaker Thomas P. (Tip) O'Neill, Majority Leader James C. Wright, and Minority Leader Robert H. Michel in the House took special care in appointing the first chairmen of the committees. Senator Daniel K. Inouye, on the Senate side, had the liberal credentials necessary to assure critics that the committee would be inquiring and investigative. His war record, patriotism, and proven support for national security reassured others that the committee would be constructive. Speaker O'Neill's strong endorsement of the House committee was reflected in the appointment as chairman of his close friend and companion in the House, Edward P. Boland of Massachusetts, who was seen as an impeccably fair man. The same kind of care went into selecting the members. In addition, because these were both "select" committees, the leadership of both chambers retained the authority to appoint members without regard to seniority.

As we started to work with the committees, my first priority was to determine how much disclosure they believed they needed in order to do their job and compare that with what we thought we could tolerate as safe. We soon developed a few ground rules. The first was that the CIA need never disclose the identity of an agent. We could not let one more person than was absolutely necessary know who our agents were. Compartmentation of this information had to continue. Even I seldom asked for an agent's identity. I asked what he was like, what motivated him, how reliable he had been in carrying out instructions, and so forth. I seldom needed to know his name to assess his worth. The committees quickly saw they did not need to know names to weigh the benefits and risks of an operation. We were willing to discuss the numbers of agents of different types, such as how many people of high governmental rank were working for us, but not what countries they were in. We would reveal the types of operations they were conducting, but not the details of specific operations. We would brief the committees on the communication techniques we were employing with agents, but not which ones in which situations. We covered these topics principally in an overall briefing on the state of espionage once a year.

There were, though, operations that I felt we should inform the committees about more promptly. On one occasion I went to Chairman Inouye privately to tell him we were going to do something very risky; if it failed there would be adverse publicity and I didn't want him taken by surprise, but if it succeeded we would need more money to follow up with the next step. I pointed out that this case was unusual in that the life of one of our CIA case officers would be at stake. I could not look that officer in the eye and tell him I was going to inform two entire committees and their staffs about what he was going to do. I was, in effect, asking Dan Inouye to take it on his shoulders for his entire committee. He agreed to do that as long as we also informed the ranking minority member of the committee, Barry Goldwater. Dan Inouye was always very careful to avoid dividing the committee along partisan lines. I agreed readily, and everything went well. Two years later the Congress wrote a provision for just this kind of limited notification into an amendment to the 1947 National Security Act.

There were also times when we could say nothing at all. I once testified before one of the committees on the CIA's budget, knowing that one of the figures in the budget had been intentionally falsified. The amount of money was not for one project, which was described; it was for two projects, one not described. But I could not knowingly present something to the Congress that was deceitful, so in a secret session I told the committee about the second, hidden project. I said, however, that I could not discuss it; that the project was one of which they would be very proud; that it did not involve any degrading activities or very much money; that if one hint of its existence got out, the United States would lose a very valuable source of information; and that fewer people in the CIA knew about this program than those sitting in the committee room at that time. I further assured them that I had cleared with the President the fact that we could not in good conscience expand the number of people who knew about this program. The committee accepted that.

In the case of Pete Brock's espionage operation, I classified it as something that could wait for an annual summary briefing. Human life was not at high risk; there were no money problems involving the Congress; and if we were caught, it would be an embarrassment for us with one nation, but not a major diplomatic setback. Sometimes the committees complained that they should have been informed earlier about something like this. Sometimes we thought we were telling them too much, too soon. I do not believe, though, that there was ever a time we did not work out a way to satisfy the committees so that they had sufficient information to carry out their proper role. Yet we never jeopardized lives or critical information in explaining how we collected intelligence. Nevertheless, some fine lines had to be drawn, and tolerance, understanding, and trust were needed on both sides.

I say "tolerance" because Congress, as a coequal with the Executive Branch, would have found it difficult to accept any explicit recognition that there were areas of information the Executive could withhold from it. Finding the right balance between secrecy and disclosure to Congress will always be part of the DCI's task. For that reason it is important that an adversarial relationship not be allowed to develop between either congressional committee and the Intelligence Community. Fortunately, we never confronted that problem during my four years. There were strong differences at times, but there was always sufficient good will on both sides to carry us through. The most troublesome differences were over apparent leaks by the Congress.

When leaks do occur, it is hard to pin down their source, but there certainly are times when Congress deserves suspicion. On one occasion I testified before the House Committee on Intelligence about how we had come to a certain interpretation of events in a third world situation. The interpretation, which was controversial, had surfaced in the press. Our conclusions were based on a human source. When I was called before the committee to explain how we had arrived at our opinion, I asked for a closed hearing to protect that source. During the hearing I disclosed that our source was a human one, but I did not give enough details to identify the individual. One member of the committee took strong exception to my explanation and at the end was not convinced by my argument. That very evening the *Washington Star* carried a story saying that I had been unconvincing before the committee because I tried to lean too heavily on a single human source. Since there were no details about the source, he was not jeopardized, but I've never had any doubt about who talked to the *Star*. There was enough of this sort of thing so that at one point I asked the President to meet the four or five senior members of each committee and emphasize to them the importance of secrecy. He did, and it helped.

But the Congress is not the only part of government that needs to be reminded about security from time to time. As I've mentioned, the White House staff tends to leak when doing so may help the President politically. The Pentagon leaks, primarily to sell its programs to the Congress and the public. The State Department leaks when it is being forced into a policy move that its people dislike. The CIA leaks when some of its people want to influence policy but know that's a role they're not allowed to play openly. The Congress is most likely to leak when the issue has political ramifications domestically. In dealing with the Congress, then, we were deliberately reticent about exposing too much when there was a risk of someone making partisan political use of our information. Overall, though, I found the congressional committees on intelligence as responsible as any sector of government, especially when it came to protecting our sources.

A greater concern of mine was the passing of sensitive information to the committee staff people. Staffers come and go as other job opportunities appear. They have much less at stake than a congressman, and some may be irresponsible. One time when I arrived to testify on a rather sensitive matter in a closed hearing before the Senate Intelligence Committee, I found twenty-seven staff members present, but only five senators. I asked that the staff be pared down before I began my testimony. The chairman agreed. No matter how the committees may cooperate, though, there will be more leaks with congressional oversight than without, simply because more people know the secrets. In gauging whether congressional oversight has done more good than harm, we have to look at the benefits it affords.

Oversight was helpful in restoring the CIA's public image. If the CIA was attacked in the press, the congressional committees' standing up for us naturally carried more credibility with the public than anything we could say in our own defense. Once the committees had learned enough about intelligence to understand what we were doing and why, they were indeed willing to support us.

Congressional oversight also strengthened my hand at the CIA. If a subordinate deliberately withheld information from me, perhaps on a sensitive espionage operation, he would run the risk that a congressional committee might require him to testify on that subject under oath. He would then be in the difficult position of disclosing something to Congress that he had withheld from his director.

Most of all, the requirement to report to the Congress is valuable because it forces the DCI and his subordinates to exercise greater judiciousness in making decisions about which espionage operations are worth the risks. We have seen some of the unfortunate past excesses that can be attributed to the absence of adequate accountability. Presidents since Gerald Ford have held the espionage function more accountable through the provisions of their Executive Orders for NSC review of sensitive operations, but as valuable as that check is, it can never be a full substitute for congressional oversight. That's because there is a need for a responsible body outside the Executive Branch to make sure that the Executive is not overenthusiastic in seeking to obtain information important to the national interest. Overenthusiasm, we have seen, may lead to excesses.

Finally, contact with the congressional committees is salutary for the CIA's people because it helps them keep in touch with national views. I believe that much of the CIA's difficulty in the past was the result of its isolation from the changing attitude of the public toward what the government should and should not do. It is particularly easy to become isolated in a profession as secretive as intelligence. The need to testify frequently before the Congress helps to break that isolation.

For all these reasons, congressional oversight is a definite plus. In addition, the demand from Congress for a role in oversight reflects the altogether appropriate sense of responsibility the Congress has toward the American people, and that is not likely to disappear. It's fortunate, then, that the deep concern in the espionage branch about oversight began to lessen about 1979. The espionage people could see that the risks and disadvantages of oversight were not nearly as great as they had feared. They became reasonably comfortable in testifying before the congressional committees, and the committees, in turn, refrained from pressing too far. The espionage branch then began to propose more high-risk, high-payoff operations.

What is actually more threatening to good espionage than the possibility of leaks is the inhibiting effect on field operations of the many laws, rules, and regulations that have sprung up in conjunction with the oversight process. The case officers who direct espionage operations in the field are not, after all, usually trained in the law. One amusing example of the mix of law and spying occurred during a small war in the third world. A prime source of information for us was radio broadcasts by an American missionary who was apparently attempting to let the outside world know of the fate of foreigners in the combat area. The CIA officer in charge wondered whether listening amounted to electronic surveillance of an American. That would have required the authorization of the Attorney General. After an exchange of messages with Headquarters and discussions between Headquarters and the Attorney General's office, it was decided that as long as the missionary was using ham radio bands, we could listen without formal approval. If the missionary tried to disguise his broadcasts, thus indicating a desire for privacy, we would have to go to the Attorney General. As this instance shows, it's almost mandatory today that the Agency's lawyers be consulted before sensitive operations are undertaken and often as they progress. Lawyers have become an integral part of the operations team. There is no doubt that this can create an overly legalistic atmosphere. What can be said in mitigation is that the laws and rules apply mostly to interference with Americans and hence do not greatly affect most foreign intelligence espionage operations.

Interestingly, though, it is neither Executive Orders nor laws that have done the most to dull initiative in espionage. Tony Lapham's successor as the CIA's general counsel, Daniel B. Silver, studied the cases in which legal or presidental restrictions were alleged to have impeded important operations. He found the restrictions that impeded most were those of the CIA itself; they went farther than any requirement of law or presidential Executive Order. He concluded, "There have been very few cases (although those few were distressing) in which intelligence operations proved to be absolutely impossible from a legal point of view."[6]

What this tells us is that by the time the criticism following the Church Committee hearings had receded, the Agency had already bound itself up in self-imposed regulations. The Reagan administration came into office resolved to loosen many of the controls established by law and by the Executive Orders. They quickly learned that a general loosening of those controls was not acceptable either to the Congress or to the intelligence professionals themselves. Senator Goldwater, who has often expressed reservations about the oversight process, rejected the new administration's first draft of a presidential Executive Order as being too great a relaxation. Admiral Bobby Inman, former head of the NSA and newly appointed deputy to DCI William Casey, resigned his post after a year and a half, amid reports that he was unhappy with the slackening of controls. Where some pruning would be desirable today is in those rules prescribed by the CIA itself. I sensed that in my time but did not pursue the thorough kind of study done by Dan Silver. To loosen the regulations so

6. Daniel B. Silver, "The CIA and the Law: The Evolving Role of the CIA's General Counsel" (Langley, Va.: CIA, 1981), p. 55.

soon after they had gone into effect would have given an impression that the checks and balances of oversight were only a passing phenomenon. Now that oversight of espionage is an established practice, the CIA can afford to pare down the excessive cautions it has bound itself with. In Silver's words: "On the side of intelligence officers, I think there is a growing acceptance that a system of legal regulation can be a benefit rather than the contrary."[7] What most intelligence officers now see is that being held accountable is not necessarily detrimental and that a degree of judiciousness, encouraged by someone looking over the shoulder of intelligence, can benefit them, as well as the country.

7. Ibid., p. 56.

THIRTEEN

Catching Spies and
Meeting Russians in Tunnels

PAUL MARTIN,[1] a superior officer whom I appointed as chief of CIA counterintelligence in 1978, shortly afterward came to suspect that one of our senior officers assigned as a chief of station overseas might be a mole. I'd been through the Boyce-Lee and Kampiles cases and the damage they had caused. The prospect of a high-level turncoat was quite a different matter. A foreign source of ours claimed that a KGB officer had identified this chief of station as someone working for the Soviets. The likelihood that a KGB officer would confide such information to someone outside the KGB was extremely unlikely. Yet there were also reports that this station chief disappeared periodically for a few hours without explanation. This was unusual, and his associates were suspicious that he might be making scheduled meetings with a foreign intelligence service. Other evidence tended to corroborate that something out of the ordinary was going on. All in all, though the evidence was insufficient to convince me that I should summarily dismiss this man, as I was empowered to do by special provision of law, I felt we had to probe the case to the bottom.

I waited to see what Paul would propose, suspecting that if Angleton had been around he would have secretly blackballed the man from future assignments with access to sensitive informa-

1. A pseudonym.

ADAPTING TO OVERSIGHT / 155

tion. That would have played it safe for the country but would have ruined the man's career without his knowing why. Fortunately, Angleton's methods had died out when Bill Colby dismissed him in 1974.

Paul laid out an elaborate, detailed plan to find hard evidence if it existed. It called for deliberately giving the station chief some secret but slightly inaccurate information of a type the Soviets would very much like to have. Then he was to be placed where it would be logical and easy for him to make contact with his Soviet case officer, if there was one. We would have a failproof means of observing any contact and passage of the information.

The plan was ingenious but complex. I wanted more of an explanation than Paul could cover in a half-hour, so we met several times. I also sought advice from Dan Silver. From the legal view, there were two significant constraints on us that had not existed in Angleton's day. One was a law; the other lay in the President's Executive Order on Intelligence. They placed explicit limitations on operations like this — explicit, undoubtedly, because so many of the past abuses had been perpetrated during vaguely conceived counterintelligence activities.

The law, the Foreign Intelligence Surveillance Act, was passed in October 1978. It controls wiretaps and other forms of electronic surveillance inside the United States. To the extent that Paul's plan involved such surveillance, the law stipulated that we had to use the least intrusive technique that would do the job; that we had to seek only genuine intelligence or counterintelligence, not private information; that the needed information could not reasonably be obtained by normal investigative techniques; and, most important of all, that there had to be cause to believe that the United States person being placed under surveillance was an agent of a foreign power.[2] I immediately began agonizing over

2. A "United States person" means not only an American citizen but a foreigner living in the United States. The precise definition, from the Foreign Intelligence Surveillance Act of 1978, Public Law 95-511, October 25, 1978, 92 State 1783, Section 101(i), is: " 'United States person' means a citizen of the United States, an alien lawfully admitted for permanent residence (as defined in section 101(a) (20) of the Immigration and Nationality Act), an unincorporated association a substantial number of members of which are citizens of the United States or aliens legally admitted for permanent residence or a corporation which is incorporated in the United States, but does not include a corporation or an association which is a foreign power, as defined in subsection(a) (1), (2), or (3)."

that last requirement. How positive did I have to be that the station chief was an agent of a foreign power in order to comply with the law? It was a bit like insisting on having proof of a crime before investigating it. I wrestled with my conscience as to whether this man's behavior was sufficient justification for what amounted to entrapment. I decided that there was enough evidence to proceed under the law and so certified to the Attorney General.

An alternative would have been to confront the man and hope he would confess. That was unlikely if he was a true double agent. Moreover, if he fled the country, he could do us more damage and we would have little chance of finding out what he had passed to the Soviets. We needed to build a legal case, arrest him, and hope to get a confession in the course of prosecuting him — all if he was a double agent.

So we proceeded down the legal route. The next step under the FISA was for Griffin Bell to certify as I had done and send his certification to a special court, one that is unique in American jurisprudence. Manned by federal judges hand-picked by the Chief Justice of the Supreme Court, it meets in a special, secret room in the Justice Department whenever it is needed. One judge is on call twenty-four hours a day for emergencies. The court's function is to check that no one tries to cut corners on the FISA. It does that by reviewing the certifications furnished by the Attorney General to ensure that all of the provisions of the law have been followed. The court, incidentally, has never yet found a request to be deficient. What the FISA did in this instance was force me to think deeply about the importance to the country of acting on our suspicions and subsequently invading the man's privacy. Then I had to convince the Attorney General. This process was intended to protect the suspect, but it also protected us in the Intelligence Community from being carried away by either an excess of zeal or bad judgment.

Sometimes, however, the very people who supported the FISA rules when they were drafted champed under their restraints later on. A foreign visitor to the United States once had some information on which an important presidential decision depended. I was instructed to get that information promptly. We knew that the visitor was talking to quite a few people and were confident that in a reasonable time we could learn from one of them what the information was. Since the FISA required use of the least intrusive means, that seemed the proper way to achieve our end, rather than spying on the visitor directly. I proceeded but was immediately put under pressure by the White House staff to place a tap on the visitor's telephone in the hope of getting more immediate results. For almost a week I was accused of being a "petty bureaucrat" for not using the more intrusive telephone tap. Finally, I received written instructions that redefined the needed information. I was told to learn what the visitor himself was saying about this situation. Only direct intrusion into his privacy could satisfy that requirement. Now, it was technically legal for me to use the more intrusive method. To me this seemed a deliberate flouting of the spirit of the law while conforming to its letter. I could have resigned in protest, but that would have been extreme. I could have appealed to the President, but he was under tremendous pressures at the time. I chose to comply and inform the President when matters quieted down that, in my opinion, we all had egg on our faces.

The President's Executive Order imposed additional restrictions on what we could do in checking on this chief of station. Fundamentally it divides counterintelligence responsibilities between the FBI and the CIA. In most democracies there is a healthy reluctance to entrust one agency or individual with both domestic and foreign spying; the potential for abuse is just too great. Our European cousins usually divide these functions between two separate organizations, one for counterintelligence and one for foreign intelligence, each doing its work wherever necessary, at home or abroad. We, in contrast, make a geographical separation. The FBI does counterintelligence and most foreign intelligence inside the United States; the CIA does both outside the country. If either must operate in the other's territory, it must have the approval of the other. This system takes advantage of the CIA's network of intelligence agents abroad, but it keeps the CIA out of domestic activities. It requires good teamwork between the two agencies, something that has not always existed. From a nadir in the later days of J. Edgar Hoover, who for a time forbade virtually any communication with the CIA, the relationship has improved steadily.

In early 1978 President Carter appointed William H. Webster as

Director of the FBI. There was more to be gained in the counterintelligence field by this appointment than met the eye. Bill Webster and I had been classmates and good friends at Amherst College from 1941 to 1942, before World War II interrupted our education. More than that, we had kept in touch through the intervening years. Building on that friendship, we determined to improve relations between our agencies even more. About once every eight weeks we had lunch with a small number of people from both staffs to demonstrate our personal commitment to harmonious relations. We were careful to assign people to the job of liaison with the other agency who would promote teamwork. Bill Webster is a man of such high character and exceptional ability to get people to work together smoothly that it all came easily. Perhaps what was most important was that our staffs realized that neither of us was going to permit any infighting. As one of Bill's assistants said to me once, "Admiral, when both staffs found out that you and Director Webster often played tennis with each other before coming to work, we knew we'd better not let any trouble develop between the two organizations."

Besides dividing counterintelligence between the CIA and FBI, the President's Executive Order, following suggestions from the Church, Pike, and Rockefeller investigations, also limited what we could do to check on a suspect. The CIA could not conduct any electronic surveillance inside the United States; it could only initiate requests under the FISA and then turn to the FBI to carry them out if the FISA court approved. No intelligence agency could conduct TV surveillance, physical searches, or mail surveillance in the United States without permission of the Attorney General for the specific operation and prior approval by the Attorney General of the agency's internal rules for conducting such operations. All agencies were under explicit rules concerning the collection and storage of information about "United States persons." There were restrictions on examining tax returns, on experimenting on human subjects, and on contracting with private companies or institutions without disclosing the intelligence connection.

Dan Silver in time agreed that Paul Martin's plan conformed to all of these limitations. We went ahead. I asked to be kept posted at each stage. As I waited, I wasn't sure which result I was hoping for. If we found the station chief a traitor, I'd be relieved because we'd be stopping the presumed loss of secrets. If no evidence developed, I'd be relieved because we did not have a mole after all and the man could be exonerated. The trap was set. The chief of station responded step by step, just as we'd planned, up to the last step. There was no evidence that he contacted the foreign power. Now, could I be confident that we'd been wrong in our suspicions? Or had he outwitted us? Had our procedure for observing a transfer of information really been failproof? The stakes were high in terms of the damage he could do. How certain did I have to be in order to protect national interests? Should we attempt another trap? Could I get the Attorney General to go along with a second certification that we still had cause to believe this man was an agent of a foreign power?

A halfway measure would have been neither exonerating him nor starting another operation, but keeping him away from sensitive information. That, though, could have ruined his career unjustly. At last I decided that our entrapment effort had been sufficiently well executed for me to rest my suspicions. I then ordered that no record of our suspicions and the ensuing investigation be put in the man's personnel record. Thus, his seniors would not be prejudiced when they decided where he would be assigned next and whether he would be promoted. A record of the investigation was to be kept, but it would be isolated from his personnel file and from people involved in his career. If new suspicions arose, the old file would be reactivated.

This was a typical counterintelligence case, where the rights of the individual had to be carefully balanced against the interests of the state. The KGB would have had no scruples about how they investigated an individual like this — no presidential Executive Order, FISA, or Attorney General approval. Nor would they have hesitated to blackball such a person if there had been a shred of doubt. But the KGB's advantage in counterintelligence has its downside. Soviet disregard of the individual is one cause of dissatisfaction with the Soviet system, and that dissatisfaction helps us recruit Soviet citizens as agents and convinces knowledgeable Soviets to defect. Both are of great help to our counterintelligence efforts.

There are, however, critics who believe the balance has tipped too far toward protecting the individual. Hank Knoche said in 1978, in reference to Colby's firing of Angleton, "There is no counterintelligence anymore."[3] Senator Sam Nunn of Georgia, whose views I respect highly, said to me in 1979, "You know we really have no counterintelligence."[4]

These views, coming from sensible men, reflect in part a reaction to the dissolution of Angleton's strong, centralized counterintelligence operation. Colby split up the responsibilities of the counterintelligence staff because it had reached into so many areas that virtually no espionage operation could proceed without its approval. This had alienated most of the officers in the espionage branch. The result was that they disdained counterintelligence so much that the practices of good counterintelligence had fallen into disuse. Colby retained a central counterintelligence staff to handle defectors like Nosenko and to search for moles among Americans throughout our government, but he delegated primary responsibility for checking on the validity of foreign agents to the sections of the espionage branch that recruited them. The central counterintelligence staff did retain the right to review each case and voice its opinion. Although there is a disadvantage in having people judge their own work, the branch people are the ones who are most intimately familiar with the individual agents and hence have the best information for judging them.

Colby also selected George Kalaris, a highly respected professional officer, to revamp the central counterintelligence staff. Kalaris introduced a methodical and organized approach and placed CIA counterintelligence on a more productive, balanced footing. It was during Kalaris' time that a series of major counterintelligence studies, like the John Hart survey of the Nosenko case, were made. They were used as the basis for the reorganization. I chose to keep Colby's mix of centralized and decentralized counterintelligence, because it was more effective than the previous system and because I wanted very much to avoid any risk of being unfair to our employees. When Kalaris left counterintelli-

3. Thomas Powers, *The Man Who Kept the Secrets: Richard Helms and the CIA* (New York: Alfred A. Knopf, 1979), p. 374.
4. Personal conversation.

gence, it was running well, but I made sure that his successors were people who would not allow a revival of the Angleton period.

The myth that counterintelligence had suffered a grievous blow with the departure of Angleton lived into the beginning of the Reagan administration. The Reagan transition team that descended on the CIA in late 1980 was as unbalanced and uninformed a group on this subject as I can imagine. They badly wanted to "unleash" the CIA. Their original leader, Lawrence Silberman, a former Ambassador to Yugoslavia, told me that I certainly would not be reappointed DCI, because I had supported passage of the FISA. His deputy, Lieutenant General Edward Rowny, U.S. Army (Retired), told me the new administration intended to submit a bill on Inauguration Day to repeal the FISA. What they objected to was the special court that has to approve each wiretap. In fact, I had objected to the court as a possible source of leaks when it was first proposed within the Carter administration. I was overruled by the President. Today I do not believe anyone can point a finger at the court as having been the source of even one leak. In addition, the FISA has been essential to continuation of any wiretap operations. In the wake of the Watergate investigations, we found that the FBI agent who did the wiretaps and the commercial companies who let the FBI have access to their facilities had become reluctant to cooperate, for fear of being taken to court for committing a crime. Passage of the FISA provided a legal foundation for wiretaps and solved that problem. I explained to Rowny that no matter how much the new administration disliked the idea of a court, they had better learn to live with it. Not only had it not caused us any problem; it had reopened the wiretap business. Before the passage of the law we often would settle on a wiretap we needed only to find that we could not get it installed without the cooperation of a telephone company. After the establishment of the court, our requests for help in installing wiretaps were honored because the companies were clearly backed by the law. The new administration dropped the idea of tampering with that law once it understood that the FISA had actually improved our counterintelligence capabilities.

What's more, the new administration's original desire to repeal the FISA was founded on the fallacious belief that counterintelligence needed new emphasis. We should never be complacent about the possibility of having moles in our midst, but our record since World War II is exceptionally good. I never saw any indication that British and West German counterintelligence was any better than ours, even when Angleton had our counterintelligence going on frequent wild goose chases. Since Angleton's departure, we have uncovered Boyce and Lee, Kampiles, Truong, and Barnett rather quickly after they became traitors, and that is a reasonable indication that our counterintelligence is working well. Again, that does not mean we can let down our guard. Important secrets have indeed been lost through foreign espionage, and efforts to steal our secrets will not cease. I am convinced, however, that the counterintelligence staff under Kalaris and his successors reached a very high level of performance. Because a new emphasis on counterintelligence operations against human penetrations was not warranted, by 1978 I shifted my concern to an area of counterintelligence that was not getting the attention it deserved. That was the stealing of our secrets by technical means.

We had not yet adjusted our counterintelligence efforts adequately to the technical revolution. I started a change by initiating a review of the security of our embassy in Moscow. After all, Nosenko had led us to uncover fifty-two Soviet microphones there in the mid 1960s. It was also well known that the Russians had been bombarding our Moscow embassy with electronic emissions off and on for over thirty years. This interest in Moscow led in May 1978 to a confrontation with the Soviets in a tunnel under our embassy.

During a special check of the embassy building, after a fire destroyed part of it in 1978, an alert member of the embassy security team noted that a chimney on an adjacent building backed up to one side of our building. On a hunch, he poked a hole in the chimney from our side. Inside, he found an antenna mounted in a pulley with cables to raise and lower it. Apparently the Soviets were using the antenna to send signals into the embassy or to listen. In either case, they were eavesdropping. Our man decided to climb into the chimney and lower himself to the bottom on a rope to see what was going on before the Soviets knew we had found them out. At the bottom he found himself in a small room with a large amount of monitoring equipment. There was also a tunnel leading into the adjacent building. With a flashlight in his hand, he began crawling through the tunnel. Midway he encountered a Russian with a flashlight coming toward him! Both men immediately turned and scurried back, and there was no incident. This event was such a graphic example of the levels to which the Soviets will stoop that we considered publicizing it. The State Department was concerned about possible countercharges, since we had on occasion been caught in embarrassing circumstances. Also, State was worried about the possible impact on the SALT II negotiations. The department did issue a terse press release recounting the facts. Surprisingly, it received very little play in the media. Within two days of the incident the Soviets actually had the effrontery to send us a note of protest. They claimed we had violated the lease on our embassy building by breaking into the chimney! [7]

We know the Soviets also collect information inside the United States by extensive use of technical systems. There are, for example, arrays of antennae on their embassy in Washington and consulates in New York, San Francisco, and Chicago to intercept domestic telephone calls transmitted by microwave. They have placed a huge antenna in northwest Cuba to intercept telephone calls relayed by satellite across the United States. Unfortunately, one of our greatest counterintelligence vulnerabilities is our misuse of the open telephone to discuss classified information.

Far too much classified information is "double-talked" on open telephones. Our government has too few "secure" telephones with scrambler systems, and people are loath to accept the modest inconvenience of using a scrambler when it is available. We need to buy many more scrambler telephones and to put up with the minor inconvenience of using them. Ironically, we have been willing to let counterintelligence against human spies violate the basic rights of our citizens, but we have not been nearly willing enough to accept a minor inconvenience like this to thwart technical spying.

Another practice that makes us vulnerable is our heavy reliance on local employees in our embassies and other facilities overseas. We probably would not find it easy or inexpensive to get Americans to go to Moscow, or to places like central Africa, to do the menial chores of housekeeping in an embassy, but we should make the attempt. As it is, we hire some seventeen thousand foreign nationals in our embassies around the world to do these jobs and even to fill clerical and lower management positions. In the Soviet Union we employ over two hundred locals. We can't even select the employees we want, but have to take those whom the Soviet government assigns to us, undoubtedly after training by the KGB. We give such employees the opportunity to report what they see and hear and to plant sophisticated technical devices in our midst. In contrast, the Soviets have no Americans in their installations in our country.

There are many other relatively minor inconveniences that would deny the Soviets and others the opportunity to employ technical intelligence devices against us. We need to be sure that sensitive military operations, like the opening of the doors on an ICBM silo, are not performed when Soviet photographic satellites are overhead. We should use only American labor to construct our embassies overseas. We should ship all sensitive equipment overseas in diplomatic pouches, which cannot be opened. For instance, as part of the review of the embassy in Moscow, we found that the State Department had shipped in a new typewriter for the ambassador's secretary, using normal customs procedures. The machine sat in a Soviet warehouse for three days awaiting clearance. When we learned that, we immediately shipped it home in a diplomatic pouch and gave it a thorough inspection. Fortunately, there were no bugs or transmitters in it. The Soviets had missed the opportunity, but we could not count on their doing so in the future. We began shipping sensitive equipment into the Soviet Union in diplomatic pouches, just as the Soviets do to the United States.

One problem in tightening standards for defense against technical spying is that the responsibility for doing that is diffused throughout our government. Many different departments, agencies, and contractors have to understand and follow whatever standards are set, and they must be supervised to ensure compliance. It is also difficult to impress on our own people how important it is not to be casual about following security procedures designed to prevent leaks. Sometimes it is hard to impress them, because we cannot tell them all we know about the enemy's techniques and how successful they can be. Doing so might reveal our counterintelligence techniques.

At the same time we run a risk of being overzealous in coping with technical counterintelligence, as we once were with human counterintelligence. The experts tend to see a bug under every table. Given their way, they would prescribe defensive measures that would make it almost impossible to carry on the business of government. Still, we are so lax today that we can afford to take many more precautions than we do now. The threat is real, and it grows as Soviet technological ingenuity improves. What is especially worrisome to me is that the Soviets may be using techniques that we are unaware of. We believe we are ahead of them in technology, but we would be foolishly complacent if we acted on the belief that their dedication to this kind of spying may not have led them to inventions in areas we have not explored.

FOURTEEN

Covert Action: How Hot?

ON DECEMBER 21, 1982, Congress, in frustration over its inability to influence the course of covert action, passed the Boland Amendment:

> None of the funds provided in this Act may be used by the Central Intelligence Agency or the Department of Defense to furnish military equipments, military training or advice, or other support for military activities, to any group or individual . . . for the purpose of overthrowing the Government of Nicaragua.

A year earlier the CIA had briefed Representative Boland's committee about a new covert paramilitary action to provide support for a five-hundred-man guerrilla force to operate against the government of Nicaragua. After the briefing, Chairman Boland, without dissent from his committee, wrote a letter to DCI Casey, criticizing the covert action. Although we do not know how Casey responded to Boland, he did not change the program. Rather, he increased the size of the group twentyfold, to something like ten thousand guerrillas. What originally was described to Boland as a small "strike team" turned into a major military force. Ed Boland's hesitancy at the smaller operation turned to anger at this marked change in its character. What can the chairman of an intelligence committee do when he is flouted like this? He can attempt to get the Congress to enact legislation curtailing the President. Boland did.

The Boland Amendment, like the Clark Amendment before it, was something no DCI would want. Both amendments confirmed to the world that the United States was undertaking a covert activity. In both cases Congress could have enacted secret legislation, but that's not an easy process. Disclosing the Angola operation didn't make much difference, since Congress terminated the covert action anyway. With Nicaragua, the legislation only curtailed the covert action. Because the operation had grown so large so quickly, it had already been widely reported in the press, but the Boland Amendment officially confirmed that the press reports were true. The CIA was left with no plausible way of denying its involvement.

Nonetheless, the operation continued to expand, from ten thousand men to fifteen thousand. The only perceptible change the amendment brought about was in the rhetoric justifying the covert action. The administration first stated that it was not trying to overthrow the government after all, just preventing it from supplying arms to the guerrillas fighting against the government of nearby El Salvador. When evidence of arms shipments to El Salvador grew slim, Secretary of State Shultz said the new purpose was to stop the Nicaraguans from exporting revolution in the region. Much of the Congress remained anxious about where this was leading us. The House, under Boland's prodding, voted several times to discontinue any funding for the guerrillas, called "contras." There were repeated battles over what, if any, support the Congress would approve for them.

For two and a half years the administration eventually got most of what it requested, but it did so at the expense of growing suspicion and mistrust in the Congress. For instance, when the Congress passed the fiscal year 1984 appropriations bill for the CIA, it was so worried that the CIA might find ways around the congressional funding limits that it enacted legislation prohibiting the CIA from soliciting funds for the contras from private donors or from the intelligence services of other, sympathetic countries. Despite this, it was reported that the CIA had encouraged Saudi Arabia and Israel to provide funds, obtained equipment from the Pentagon in lieu of purchasing it, urged U.S. civilians to contribute to the contras, and overspent its congressional funding limits. In mid 1983, Chairman Boland said the CIA was "almost like a rogue elephant, doing what it wanted to."[1] The similarity between that remark and some comments made during the Church Committee investigations just seven years earlier was inescapable and a sign of a distressing deterioration in the Executive-Legislative relationship on intelligence.

A crisis in the deterioration came on April 9, 1984, when Chairman Barry Goldwater of the Senate Intelligence Committee lashed out in a letter to DCI Casey, "It gets down to one, little, simple phrase: I am pissed off!" What infuriated Goldwater was that he was not aware of the CIA's extension of its covert action to include the mining of Nicaragua's harbors. His letter went on:

> I understand that you had briefed the House on this matter. I've heard that. Now, during the important debate we had last week and the week before, on whether we would increase funds for the Nicaragua program, we were doing all right until a member of the committee charged that the President had approved the mining. I strongly denied that because I had never heard of it. I found out the next day that the CIA had, with the written approval of the President, engaged in such mining and the approval came in February!

Whether the administration was remiss or Goldwater not alert in this situation can be argued; the bottom line is that the administration's inept handling of Congress had alienated one of its strongest supporters. Why? Because the administration had fulfilled the letter, but hardly the intent, of the procedures for notifying Congress of covert operations. Those procedures are based partly on law, partly on practice. The law, the Hughes-Ryan Amendment, requires that the Congress be notified "in a timely manner" of any new covert action and that the President "find" that the action is "important to the national security of the United States." Hence, the term "finding" is used to designate the formal presidential approval of a covert action. When the CIA prepares a finding for the National Security Council to approve and the President to sign, it must choose between a very broad and a very specific wording. In this case, the finding could have been as broad as "Conduct covert paramilitary operations to dis-

1. Don Oberdorfer, *Washington Post*, August 6, 1983, p. A13.

courage the government of Nicaragua from interfering in the affairs of its neighbors." Or it could have been as specific as "Assist anti-Sandinista forces in mining the harbors of Nicaragua."

Under a broad finding, an operation can be expanded considerably; with a narrow one, the CIA has to go back to the President to obtain a revised finding if there is any change of scope. The Congress is wary of broad findings; they can easily be abused. The CIA is afraid of narrow findings; they can be a nuisance. What has evolved is a working understanding that whenever the activity being carried out under a finding is widened past the original description to the Congress, the CIA will advise the committees. In this case the mining was just such an expansion, and Congress was right in expecting to be informed. The CIA did go through the motions of informing, but it wasn't speaking very loudly. According to Senator Daniel Patrick Moynihan, ranking minority member of the committee, there was only one sentence on mining in an eighty-four-page transcript of the briefing.

This error brought to the surface a feeling in Congress, latent for a while, that it should be notified in advance of any covert action, not just "in a timely fashion." Some congressmen even wanted to require the President to obtain the approval of Congress before proceeding with a covert action. These issues had been raised with me back at my confirmation hearings. The committees were still worried that they would end up being held responsible but would not know about an action in time to stop it.

In my confirmation hearings I had declined to agree to advance notification. Three years later I was glad I had. The CIA was called on to provide covert support for an operation by another branch of the government. Secrecy was vital to the entire mission. Because the CIA's support was technically a covert action, not intelligence collection, we were required to report it to the Congress. Had we done so before the operation, it would have been the only way the Congress found out that the operation was being planned. It probably could not have been kept secret. (The argument can be made that the Congress should be informed of any operations undertaken by the Executive Branch. In fact, the Congress has attempted to ensure through the War Powers Act of 1973 that it is informed of military operations, but inadvertent informing of Congress through reporting on covert actions is not the way to accomplish such a purpose.) Accordingly, I strongly opposed a move by the Senate Committee on Intelligence to insert into the Intelligence Oversight Act of 1980 a requirement for "prior" notification of all covert actions. Another reason I opposed prior notification was that I felt it unreasonable to ask a person to risk his life and then tell him I was going to notify some thirty congressmen and their staffs about what he was going to do. In the end, the Congress tightened the wording on notification but did not require prior notice. They did stipulate that whenever the President declines to notify Congress in advance, he must submit a separate statement explaining why he considered the delay essential to national security.

When the Nicaraguan mining case came to light, the Congress had reason to claim that the intent of the 1980 law had been slighted. It used that to its advantage in extracting concessions from DCI Casey. First, he was forced to apologize formally to Goldwater's committee for the way the notification had been given. Then he had to agree to new rules for informing that committee. One member, Senator Walter D. Huddleston, said, "We had 'prior' notice to begin with. Now we've extended that, tightened up what might have been loopholes." Huddleston was, of course, purposely exaggerating about prior notification. The loophole we insisted on in 1980, that the President can delay notification if he subsequently provides an explanation, is still there. But the Congress had edged a bit closer to prior notification, though the Boland Committee wasn't satisfied even with that. It announced plans for drafting legislation to require prior notification. If, because of the mistrust resulting from a situation like this, the Congress someday does legislate prior notification, the CIA may cease some useful covert activities for fear of premature disclosures, or it may just back away from risky covert actions altogether to avoid the danger of arousing the Congress again. In either case, the country loses.

Why, though, did the mining run into such opposition? After all, the contras had been conducting other military actions against Nicaragua for some time. The Senate, dominated by the President's own party, voted 84 to 12 to call for its cessation. This reflected a sense of embarrassment felt by much of the American public. Our ethical standards in dealing with our Central American neighbors were revealed as not being what we would like them to be. The world saw that we had endangered the lives and property of countries that were not involved in or concerned with the dispute between us and Nicaragua, and that we were deliberately interfering in the internal affairs of Nicaragua to the point of undeclared war to enforce our will in that region. The Soviets, of course, have done this kind of thing routinely, especially in Eastern Europe. What embarrassed Americans was that we had stooped to the Soviets' style. The fact was that seven months earlier we had condemned the same kind of action when 241 U.S. Marines and other military personnel were killed in Beirut by a truck bomb driven into their barracks. We told the world that was "state-supported terrorism" and pointed the finger at Syria and Iran. Surely theirs was a more heinous act, but not different in kind from our supporting the people who planted the mines in Nicaraguan harbors. To those ships' crews whose lives were endangered in those harbors, the contras we were supporting looked every bit like state-supported terrorists.

The mining issue receded, only to be succeeded six months later by a dispute over a manual for guerrillas that the CIA had distributed to the contras. Some of the instructions on how to conduct guerrilla warfare were offensive to many Americans. One section advocated "neutralization" of Nicaraguan civil officials, like judges and police. Unhappily, in the American vernacular "neutralization" is understood to mean "assassination." Even to imply that assassination is an acceptable practice violated a standard of morality for covert action. Starting with President Ford, three Presidents have in their Executive Orders on Intelligence specifically prohibited the CIA's carrying out assassination either directly or indirectly. Here, then, the CIA had overstepped the bounds. It was rightly accused of being out of control. Casey again found it necessary to apologize, and he admitted "negligence" in supervising the contra program. He said he would institute new controls, and he reprimanded or suspended five lower-level CIA persons.

Several factors were responsible for this covert action's getting out of control. The contras had their own objectives and style, and our control over people like this is limited. Also, Nicaragua from 1981 to 1984 was not an Iran of 1953 or a Guatemala of

1954, where the political situation was crying out for change. Many Nicaraguans were becoming dissatisfied with the Sandinista government, but the euphoria of the revolution of 1979 had far from worn off. Thus, the CIA's operatives were undertaking a mission that was close to impossible, and in their effort to succeed they stretched to find additional ways to employ the contras. That they came up with some unacceptable ones, like mining and assassination, was a result of the Agency's having recalled a number of old covert action warriors from the retired ranks of the CIA and the military for this task. These people were accustomed to conducting covert actions that were kept covert; they were not used to being held accountable, as they must be when covert action is conducted under oversight. Witness the fact that they ignored a specific presidential directive against even encouraging others to commit assassination.

The continuing contretemps over the contras was unfortunate in two respects. First, it severely aggravated an already deteriorating relationship between the Intelligence Community and the Congress. In the long run, Congress has the power to work its will in ways that can unduly restrict intelligence operations. Second, the specter of a CIA out of control was raised before the American public only a few years after we had worked so diligently to regain the confidence lost through the earlier excesses. The public's confidence in its intelligence organizations is absolutely essential to their success. How could the Reagan administration turn this all around so quickly?

The administration's willingness repeatedly to flout the Congress reflected a view that oversight was an impediment rather than a necessity for good intelligence in a society like ours. This new proof of the importance of oversight was that the first thirty years of American centralized intelligence without oversight had ended in a halt to most human intelligence activities. Why had the halt been called? Because wrongs had been committed and, as is almost inevitable in our open society, disclosed. The disclosures brought such opprobrium that either the Congress or the White House ordered the halt, or the intelligence professionals did so on their own for fear of further condemnation. This generalization applies equally to covert action, to counterintelligence, and to espionage. In thirty years we had shown that the secrecy of intelligence presents temptations and that oversight is needed to keep people from overstepping the bounds tacitly stipulated by the public.

That the Reagan administration did not understand this was evidenced in a speech Casey gave to the Association of Former Intelligence Officers in October 1984. He said: "With few exceptions, the highly publicized charges made against the CIA during the mid seventies turned out to be false. The charges were on the front pages and their refutation buried away so that few people noted them."[2] That statement may have pleased his audience of old intelligence hands, but it was both inaccurate and dangerous. There was, of course, much exaggeration in the media about the errors of the past. I railed against it regularly myself. But the record of errors is fact. Even if there are arguments over how many mistakes were made, one need only visit the building that contains Nosenko's cell to understand that whatever the number, they cannot be taken lightly. Treating them as imaginary implicitly says that oversight is not needed. It was that attitude which led the Reagan team into public controversy, with considerable risks for the future of our intelligence.

Very likely, the Reagan model of intelligence was the OSS of World War II. The OSS, though, operated when our national objective was unconditional surrender. Almost any covert action to help win the war was considered acceptable, and the more the better. Translating that attitude to the peacetime conditions of the 1980s was a serious mistake. The Church Committee had learned a lesson about the limits of usefulness of peacetime covert actions when it said in its report: "The Committee has found that when covert operations have been consistent with, and in tactical support of, policies which have emerged from a national debate and the established processes of government, these operations have tended to be a success."[3] What's been missing in the Reagan-Casey approach is attention to the provision in the Hughes-Ryan Amendment that covert actions must be "important to the national security."

2. *Periscope, Journal of the Association of Former Intelligence Officers,* Volume IX, Number 4, Fall 1984.
3. Final Report of the Select Committee to Study Governmental Operations with Respect to Intelligence Activities, United States Senate, Book I, Chapter VIII, April 26, 1976.

It was not unreasonable for President Reagan to state that it was important to our security to change the situation in Nicaragua as it then existed, even though there were good arguments on the other side. There was, though, good evidence that he treated the criterion of "important to the national security" pretty cavalierly in at least two other instances. In 1977, the White House, for some reason, commented publicly on a covert action concerning Mauritius. Later, a press story concerned a proposed covert action to unseat the government of Suriname. Covert actions in such insignificant situations as Mauritius and Suriname can hardly be described as "important to national security."

A key reason for that provision of the law is that we should not bypass the normal processes of government for less than important benefit. Compared with the way the rest of foreign policy is controlled by public opinion and by congressional scrutiny, there are relatively few checks on covert actions. We don't want Presidents to be tempted to use covert action as a way of doing things that would not stand up to congressional or public review.

Another problem of resorting to covert action is that there is a fundamental conflict between any covert action and the accepted practice that intelligence must stay clear of policy and its execution. The CIA is responsible for developing a covert action plan, for supplying the intelligence about whether it will work, and, later, for carrying out the covert action and for reporting on whether it was successful. That there can be conflict was clear from the Bay of Pigs. There the Agency's reporting was far too optimistic about the likelihood of dissident Cubans rallying to the cause of the invasion. Their not doing so was one cause of the failure.

The DCI himself must decide how much emphasis to place on his roles as chief intelligence officer and chief of covert operations. He can put primary emphasis on providing good, unbiased intelligence while also informing policy-makers about the possibilities of covert action. Or he can be out in front, advocating the use of covert action while at the same time doing his best to keep the intelligence reporting unbiased. Casey, with his OSS background, opted for the latter. With a background in systems analysis for the Navy, I chose the former path. The most compelling argument for the DCI's favoring the production of intelligence over covert action is that he is the only one of the President's advisers who has even a chance of presenting unbiased intelligence to him. All the other advisers are direct participants in the policy-making process who are bound to favor intelligence that supports their policies. For that reason alone the President should keep his DCI from advocating one policy or another, as is bound to happen if he becomes deeply enmeshed in covert action.

Some people contend that this dilemma could be avoided by removing responsibility for covert action from the CIA and placing it in an entirely separate agency. That might help solve some problems, but it would create others. The CIA's intelligence agents overseas are often the same people needed for covert action. It would be confusing, and at times dangerous, to have two agencies giving them orders and managing their activities. And if one agency did only covert action, what would it do during periods of slack demand? Might it not act like most bureaucracies and fill the time by making work, by encouraging more use of covert operations? Rather, the answer is to accept the idea that covert action not only can operate under congressional oversight, but is the better for such oversight.

If Presidents define "important" more carefully, they will not be passing up many worthwhile covert projects, because the environment for covert action has grown less favorable anyway. For example, because of the worldwide revolution in communications, it is not nearly so easy to use political action as it was when we restored the Shah to power in 1953. Even in developing countries the public knows much more about internal affairs and world events than heretofore. Politicians are more reluctant to accept covert funding from the CIA because the risks of being found out are higher than in the past, and few politicians can afford to be accused of being puppets of the CIA. Covert propaganda is also not as effective as when there was much less information available. And even relatively small paramilitary operations can't be kept secret very long in an era of investigative reporting and dense press coverage. So covert activities of all three sorts are more risky, more likely to become known, and less likely to succeed. At the same time, doing things openly is more feasible and sometimes just as effective. The transfer of Radio Free Europe and Radio Liberty to the U.S. Information Agency has not diminished their impact.

I conclude that in this changed environment we can expect two things from covert action in the future: first, a continuing, very limited contribution to our foreign policy from the lower spectrum, such as propaganda, antiterrorist actions, and modest funding of democratic causes; second, an occasional very important contribution at the more controversial end of the spectrum, that is, political or paramilitary interference in other countries. The introduction of oversight and the increased national awareness of the ethical issues involved in covert interference has restricted these latter opportunities, but we would be foolish to forsake them entirely. When conditions are ripe, the reward can be significant.

I saw a number of examples. We created a radio station to broadcast into a country that was virulently anti-American. The Voice of America reached that country also, but it lacked credibility because of the volume of anti-American propaganda in the local press. In addition, the CIA's broadcasts were specifically directed at refuting the local media's false stories about the United States, whereas the Voice of America prided itself on presenting all the news objectively.

In another case we attempted to influence the direction of a third world country that was teetering between its limited form of democracy and something quite authoritarian. There was a struggle going on in the country's capital: Should the government turn to the Soviet Union for military assistance for the first time or continue to rely on Western sources? We knew that one of the country's representatives at an international meeting was a strong supporter of continued reliance on the West. We hoped that he would be in the capital when the issue came to a head, but it appeared that that was not going to be the case. We therefore made certain that he received a message indicating that the Soviets might demand his removal from his post if they took over the provision of military assistance. The man immediately took the next plane back to his country and joined the fray on our side. Unfortunately, he lost, but we had made an effort with little risk or expense.

And when the U.S. Navy provided the helicopters for the Iranian hostage rescue mission in April 1980, they did not have a suitable overland navigation system for the helicopters. The CIA's paramilitary branch did, and installed them in the Navy aircraft, thus making the mission feasible.[4]

These, and other even more rewarding operations, convinced me that the talent necessary for covert action is available in the CIA and must be preserved. I was convinced, though, that squandering that talent on insignificant projects would only jeopardize it. We must be willing to hold it in readiness until the right conditions exist. Such conditions are not likely to coincide more than once or twice during an administration. Presidents and their advisers will be tempted by covert action more often, but a major benefit of congressional oversight should be the tempering of such enthusiasm.

There is one overriding issue in all three forms of human intelligence activity: espionage, counterintelligence, and covert action. That is, to what levels of ethical behavior will we stoop? The only specific guidance the Intelligence Community has on this question is the prohibition on assassination contained in three successive presidential Executive Orders. The remaining specific limitations in those orders all concern whether and how much the Intelligence Community will intrude into the lives of Americans. That is more a matter of how much personal sacrifice our citizens are willing to make than one of ethical standards. The only other guidance on ethics is that received in specific situations from the committees of Congress.

The absence of more specific instruction in law or presidential Executive Orders to guide those who oversee human intelligence results in part from the difficulty in setting absolute standards of ethics in intelligence. In some circumstances, such as during

4. There was an amusing incident involving the installation of these navigational systems. A CIA expert, accompanied by a naval commander, was sent out to the aircraft carrier in the Indian Ocean to check out the equipment. The two men had to stage through the island of Diego Garcia. While awaiting an aircraft that would take them from there to the carrier, the commander met a Navy enlisted man he knew. The enlisted man told the commander in a whisper that he had deduced from the number of people and the equipment passing through Diego Garcia to the carrier that there was going to be a hostage rescue attempt. The commander told him that he was correct — and then took him along to the carrier so that he couldn't tell anyone else, who might let the cat out of the bag.

World War II, we have condoned the plotting of assassinations. Yet in other circumstances, such as the CIA's plotting against the lives of several international figures in the 1960s, we have not. There are, then, two schools of thought on the acceptability of certain kinds of intelligence activity.

One contends that those who oversee intelligence should be free to decide ethical issues purely on the basis of what is necessary to combat the enemy. They believe that those who are well informed about the threats posed to our country should make ethical decisions on behalf of the citizenry, not merely reflect the opinion of less informed citizens. James Jesus Angleton epitomized the extreme of this school of thought in 1975, when testifying before the Church Committee. The question under discussion was toxic poisons. President Nixon had ordered the CIA to destroy all stocks of such poison. It was later learned that some toxins were not destroyed. Angleton in testifying to Congress on this had said, "It is inconceivable that a secret intelligence arm of the government has to comply with all the overt orders of the government."[5] Angleton admitted in subsequent testimony that this was a statement he should not have made, that it was "rather imprudent," and that he wanted to withdraw it. He refused, however, to say that he had not meant it when he said it. This view — that defense of the country is so vital that the CIA can use the President's public words as a means of deceiving others — is at the heart of this school's reasoning.

The other school, to which I subscribe, says that there is one overall test of the ethics of human intelligence activities. That is whether those approving them feel they could defend their decisions before the public if the actions became public. This guideline does not say that the overseers should approve actions only if the public would approve them if they knew of them. Rather, it says that the overseers should be so convinced of the importance of the actions that they would accept any criticism that might develop if the covert actions did become public, and could construct a convincing defense of their decisions.

We are a democracy, one with high ethical ideals. We should

5. Hearing before the Select Committee to Study Governmental Operations with Respect to Intelligence Activities of the United States Senate, Volume 2, p. 72, September 23, 24, and 25, 1975.

never turn over custody of those ideals to any group of individuals who divorce themselves from concern for the public attitude. The crimes against mankind perpetrated by zealots who did not need to answer to the citizens are too many. Even American intelligence, operating in the past in the confidence that it would not be held accountable, committed errors that disgraced our nation and, in the longer run, imperiled our very intelligence capabilities.

The importance of oversight over intelligence activities in democracies has been accentuated by the number of our allies who have followed our lead in some measure. West Germany, France, Italy, Australia, and Canada have all within the past eight years taken steps to bring their intelligence organizations under closer control of their political authorities. And in early 1985 Great Britain was rocked by accusations against her counterintelligence organization, MI-5, for improper tapping of telephones, maintaining files on citizens suspected of radical leanings, illegal break-ins of private premises, and infiltrating domestic political groups. It seems certain that British intelligence will be forced out from under its traditional blanket of near-total secrecy. Again, in Britain as in the United States, without accountability the temptations of acting in secret were too great.

PART FOUR

MANAGING THE COLOSSUS

FIFTEEN

Three CIAs, Not One

EARLY IN MY TENURE as head of the CIA, I realized that managing the agency was unlike any management experience I had ever had, or any I had studied at the Harvard Business School. Here are some matters that brought me to that conclusion.

Hank Knoche had not informed me of the bombshell of Lowell, Hilliard, and Edmund P. Wilson that was sitting on the shelf when I arrived. Although Wilson was not the focus of public attention in 1977 that he came to be, Knoche must have known we were dealing with a person of questionable background. Wilson had quit the Agency under a cloud in 1971 and then was fired by naval intelligence, where he went next, in 1976. Knoche and the branch chiefs thought these three cases were internal affairs for the branches to handle, even though there were questions of whether laws had been broken and murder abetted, and even though the CIA was bound to be subjected to more adverse publicity.

Almost the entire personnel system was also considered to be out of the director's purview. Major appointments, such as chiefs of station, were being made without my approval. Once, when I requested the heads of the three operating branches to submit to me a list of their most promising, versatile people in the top pay grades, I had a near-rebellion on my hands. I wanted to consider these people for special assignments outside their branches to broaden and develop their potential for top Agencywide leadership positions. The branches were indignant that I considered interfering with "their" people's careers.

The Presidential Daily Brief was one of the most important reports. What we told the President had to be correct. I was the one the President, Vance, Brown, or Brzezinski would call if an item in the PDB was unclear or if it sounded like an argument against a policy one of them favored. Yet there was no provision for clearing what went into the PDB with me each day. Since I certainly had to read what we sent to the President anyway, it seemed preferable for me to do so before the fact rather than after.

When John Blake, the head of the support branch, one of the six top positions in the Agency, told me he was going to retire, he also told me who he thought his replacement should be. His advice was welcome, but I soon found that he had arranged it so that only the man of his choice had been given the requisite experience to qualify for the job. When I called in Jack's nominee and told him I was interviewing others as well as him, he said that if I didn't select him within one week he would retire also. (I let him do just that and found a highly experienced outsider to bring in instead.)

When the first annual budget came to me for approval, everything had been decided. The three branches expected me to rubber-stamp what they wanted. What's more, the comptroller was not in a strong enough position to question the submissions of the branches, even though there was widespread evidence of excesses. For example, a senior espionage branch officer took his secretary with him literally halfway around the world to write up his notes at a supersecret conference, because he did not want to trust a secretary from the local station. For another, there was so much travel money that the head of the European section of the espionage branch was able to leave Headquarters and spend several weeks traveling in Europe to talk with his station chiefs every three months.

From what I could discern, these were all practices of long standing. As I began to express concern that I was not consulted on decisions in these areas and others, many became defensive and cautious about volunteering information to me. After all, there was a ready image of military men liking to be thoroughly in charge. My apprehension at the DCI's lack of involvement was shared by my new deputy, Ambassador Frank Carlucci. I had asked Frank to leave his post as Ambassador to Portugal and come help me. He replaced Hank Knoche, who had left six months earlier. Unfortunately, Hank had not worked out. Our differences had become irreconcilable before I had been on the job four months. One of the major differences between us was just this matter of how involved the DCI should be in the management of the CIA. Hank could not understand my insistence on making such decisions as what to do with people who were moonlighting for Edmund Wilson. Moreover, rather than changing the system in the way I felt necessary, Hank assumed that in time I would come round to doing things the way they had always been done.

It wasn't long after Frank Carlucci arrived that he came to share my concerns. He told me he had come to perceive that running the CIA from the director's office was like operating a power plant from a control room with a wall containing many impressive levers that, on the other side of the wall, had been disconnected. We decided that we were not really in charge of a single CIA, but of three separate organizations operating almost with autonomy. Neither of us had ever seen anything like it — and Frank had served in a variety of government posts.

The three independent organizations were the three operating branches: espionage, technical development and operation, and analysis.[1] The autonomy of the three operating branches from the DCI and their separateness from each other derived first of all from the different times each was formed and the distinct evolution of each; second, from compartmentation, which had kept much of what each did secret from the others; and third, from the different and often conflicting requirements of each to accomplish its assigned tasks.

For instance, the espionage branch must operate in maximum

---

1. There is actually a fourth branch, which provides administrative support — communications, supplies, and personnel accounting — to the other three. Although it is essential to the Agency's success, I will concentrate on the three other branches, which are especially vital to the CIA.

secrecy to protect its agents. Yet this is the area of the Agency's activities where abuse has most often occurred in the past. Naturally, it is here that oversight has concentrated. Oversight, though, reduces secrecy, so this branch is in a constant struggle between adequate oversight and adequate secrecy. Most of this branch's activities take place overseas, and it thinks and plans in terms of personnel living and working in foreign countries.

In contrast, the analytic branch has few overseas assignments and little need for oversight. And, though it has a need for secrecy, the need is not as crucial as with espionage, where lives are at risk. As I've noted earlier, it is desirable to have outsiders check on the quality of analysis and interact with the analysts, even at some risk to security.

The technical branch fits somewhere in between. It shares with espionage a concern that oversight will compromise its secret work. It shares with analysis a desire to be open enough to tap the resources of American industry and its technology. It operates mainly in the United States, but has just enough people overseas to share some of the pertinent concerns of the espionage branch.

These differing outlooks give rise to a lot of pushing and pulling on what position the Agency as a whole should take on specific questions. In any other organization such disputes would be brought to the person at the top, who would have to adjudicate them. Not so in the CIA. There, the branch heads go a very long way to compromise with each other rather than let an issue reach the DCI for resolution. The last thing these three want is for the DCI to become a strong central authority. In adjudicating between them he might favor one or the other, and the others would lose some of their traditional freedom. Most particularly what two of them feared was that the DCI would favor the espionage branch and that it would become even more dominant than it already was. From the evidence I could gather, this concern had shaped views for a long time, perhaps especially during the tenure of DCIs Allen Dulles, Richard Helms, and William Colby. They came from the espionage branch and could have been suspected of harboring a natural partiality.

The espionage branch had been dominant so long, the others felt they must stand well clear of it or risk being absorbed. People differ in their views on just how powerful and separate that branch has been, but when I arrived there was no question that the analytic and technical branches were decidedly inferior in prestige and influence. The espionage branch, for instance, would never acknowledge that its role was to collect information for the analytic branch to analyze, which it was.

In most large organizations an elite evolves over time. In the Navy it has long been naval aviators. In the CIA, it has been espionage operators, as borne out by the rise of Dulles, Helms, and Colby from their positions in the espionage branch to that of DCI. In the Navy, technology has brought nuclear submarine officers to the point of challenging the aviators for premier status. In the CIA, both the analysts and the technical people have grounds for challenging the espionage people, but are still far from doing so. In part that's because the technical revolution has not yet been fully appreciated, and in part because DCIs have tended to rely on the espionage branch for analysis as well as espionage. After all, the espionage people in the field do get a very good feel for the countries they serve in. In short, because past DCIs could and did rely primarily on the espionage branch, it remained far more prestigious than the others.

If the branch chiefs feared having a DCI who would settle differences between them, what did they want their directors to be? What they had in mind was someone who would fight the political battles for them with the White House, with Congress, and with the public, but would leave to them the management of the Agency and its operations. Only when I came to understand this did I comprehend why there were so few of the normal management mechanisms available to the DCI; why so few of those levers were connected.

There were many reasons why I could not accept this system. I felt it my responsibility to assure the American public that I knew what the CIA was doing and how it performed. Most important, I felt personally responsible for preventing any repetition of the kind of error the old system had failed to prevent. I owed the President the assurance that the old practices would not be revived. He had never specifically stressed "cleaning up" the CIA to me, but it was clear that he expected high ethical standards from all of us who worked for him. And I owed it to the CIA to keep it out of trouble, for I believed in the CIA's importance and wanted to maintain its usefulness.

It was also not practical to condone so much autonomy within the CIA. The revolution in technical collection demanded a higher level of teamwork between the technical and human collection efforts than was possible with three largely autonomous entities. And the espionage branch could no longer do adequate analysis because so much of the information it needed quite properly went directly from the technical collectors to the analysts, leaving the espionage people without a complete picture. The oversight revolution also made it important that the Agency avoid new errors that would bring more debilitating criticism. That meant my exercising positive control.

Until I thought of each man individually, I had difficulty understanding why previous DCIs had tolerated the independence of the branches. Allen Dulles, the giant who held the office for eight and a half years during the formative period of the Agency, was a man keenly interested in spying and covert action and quite uninterested in management. Helms and Colby, between them, managed the Agency for another eight and a half years, but, being intelligence professionals, they had lived with the system of independent branches and knew the pain they would have caused had they tried to upset it. Just bringing Angleton's power under control had been a major undertaking for Colby. John McCone, the other DCI who had a reasonably long tenure, concentrated on getting the technical branch established, rather than on managing the whole. These four presided over for two thirds of the CIA's thirty-year life. A number of others served for such short terms that they had little opportunity to influence management style.

I wondered whether there was something in the nature of the profession, instead of in the personal disposition of these men, that made tight central control undesirable to them. The best reason I could find was that central control might make the organization too bureaucratic to be innovative and daring. It was not unreasonable to argue that too many checks, controls, and procedures might induce caution. That argument did not hold up, however, when I saw how bureaucratic the CIA had become as a consequence of the very independence of the branches. To prevent one branch from intruding into another's territory, they had established as complex a maze of bureaucratic procedures as I have witnessed anywhere in government. For instance, the espionage branch wouldn't abide by the overall CIA regulations. Instead, it reissued as its own directives whatever Agencywide regulations applied to it. Unless I could rely on someone to check, I could not be sure that my directions were being transmitted faithfully to the espionage branch.

I also never saw evidence that the wildest and most daring schemes of the past, hatched under inadequate supervision, had actually produced useful intelligence or covert action. What I did find was that the secrecy which surrounds spying engendered a mystique, one that misled people into believing that you could spy well only if you were totally unsupervised. That simply was not so.

The only valid reason I could find for the degree of decentralization that Frank Carlucci and I encountered was that the Agency had grown haphazardly, without strong direction. From the moment of its inception it was overcommitted, with pressing requirements for intelligence, counterintelligence, and covert action. Its people were highly dedicated, and they concentrated on getting the job done, not on building a management system for the long run. Besides, many were fresh from OSS experience and were inclined to be operators, not managers. Because they were also highly capable, the machine ran in spite of the poor management. Now the first generation was leaving. The CIA had grown in size, the nature of intelligence had grown in complexity, and as the older professionals retired, the younger replacements found themselves adrift in an unstructured system.

As the Agency continues to grow, it will become unmanageable unless it acquires a more solid foundation. The possibility is very real, since few CIA personnel are natural managers or get much experience in management. Spies tend to make good decisions on immediate operational issues involving only a few people. When they must deal with broader, long-range issues, they are apt to depend on what they know, crisis management, rather than on advance planning. In addition, CIA stations are relatively small and afford espionage people very little experience in managing. Scientists want to get their dollars and go off and invent without having to worry about managing anything. Analysts are like academics and have little interest in or skill at managing. What each group needs is common standards and procedures, set by central management, to which each manager would have to subscribe.

And there must be enough central direction to bring them together as a single team.

The CIA was a long way from that ideal when I joined it. That was where Frank Carlucci came in. I was extremely fortunate in being able to persuade Frank to take the job and to talk the President into relieving him of his ambassadorial post. I had met him only briefly, but from my time in Naples I knew of his reputation in Europe as one of our toughest and most competent ambassadors. He seemed to me right for this job because of his service in other high-level positions of the government. He had a good deal of experience in administering large organizations, as well as a professional foreign service officer's savvy about world affairs. He lived up to every expectation.

Frank spearheaded a major effort to establish a sound, central management system in the CIA, and did so with great tact. But because we were infringing on the autonomy of the three branches, he encountered resistance at every stage. There was nothing malicious about that resistance: it was a natural reaction to change. And these Agency professionals were facing not just the internal changes that Frank and I were pushing on them, but the entire gamut of change that came with oversight and controls. It was not easy for them to see so much of their traditional self-rule slipping away.

We began with an effort to build a more corporate form of decision-making, especially for deciding what direction the Agency should take in the future. Heretofore what little planning there was had been done exclusively in the three branches. The resistance to Agencywide strategic planning was great. The best we could do in our three years together was set up procedures to review and coordinate the plans of the three branches, not to start from the top with an Agency plan from which the branch plans would derive, as would have been logical. We began in such areas as Agencywide personnel policies, priorities for research on new intelligence collection techniques, and means for maintaining cover as enemy counterintelligence techniques improved. We also made a major effort to reshape the four personnel systems into one.

Beyond these changes in management procedures, I tried to get better control of the Agency by bringing in a number of key persons in whom I had confidence, of whom Frank Carlucci was one.

Next, the area of the CIA I thought needed the most attention was analysis. In large part this was simply because espionage had commanded so much attention that the analysis branch had been neglected. I wanted a chief analyst with a very broad-ranging, inquiring mind who would set high intellectual standards. Robert R. Bowie, a senior Harvard academic who had spent considerable time in the government, combined common sense with deep intellect. His writings were extremely thoughtful, and whenever I had been with him at conferences, I found that he was the one who asked the most trenchant questions. I knew he was on the verge of retiring from Harvard and felt fortunate in being able to persuade him to come back to Washington and to the CIA as head of analysis. His outsider's viewpoint and perceptive mind did much to broaden the horizons in that branch.

I also brought with me from Naples two of the three Navy commanders whom I had called on for advice in that brief period between the phone call telling me to come to Washington and my departure for the airport. George Thibault stayed in the CIA the full four years I was there. In addition to preparing speeches and doing research projects directly for me, he played a major role in helping to infuse into the personnel training system some of the intellectual rigor that he had helped me with at the Naval War College. Bernie McMahon ran my outer office for a year, until he had to go back to the Navy. These two men and Rusty Williams, the civilian I brought in as a special assistant, were very helpful to me in making the transition from the Navy to the CIA. They knew intimately my style of managing. They could interpret my orders, needs, and frustrations to the people at the CIA, and they could listen and learn from the CIA professionals, helping me to more quickly understand the Agency.

I also shifted some of the CIA professionals around so that key spots were filled by people with whom I had rapport. When I had to replace the chief of the espionage branch after nine months, I brought in a CIA professional from outside the branch itself, John McMahon. John had spent a brief period in espionage, but had moved on to a career that had taken him to all the branches of the Agency. I wanted someone in charge of risk-taking who had that kind of broad outlook, and the espionage branch had not permitted many of its people to gain such experience.

Finally, I found it necessary to establish a means of communicating directly with the people of the CIA. The three branches had such exclusive control over the information that went out to the employees that I was soon frustrated by my inability to let people know what we were doing and why. Whenever I changed some policy or procedure, the reason for my doing so was not transmitted down the line if the branch heads did not agree with it. They simply carried out their orders, making no effort to hide their negative feelings. That, of course, undercut what I was trying to do, and the mixed signals confused subordinates. I finally decided to bypass them by instituting informational notices to go on the bulletin boards. These Director's Notes discussed the reasons behind any changes being made, informed employees of what the facts were when the Agency was falsely accused in the press, quelled the bad rumors that often cropped up, brought new opportunities to the attention of employees, and generally attempted to keep people informed about how things were going. They became so popular that we had to print enough for each employee in Headquarters as well as for our people overseas.

I also wanted some means of getting feedback from the employees, of sampling attitudes. This seemed especially necessary, because if the managers were not sending my signals down the line, they certainly weren't letting come back up any signals they did not like. Yet I knew that there was confusion in many employees' minds as to where the Agency was going in the wake of the investigations of 1975–1976. One device I used for learning how they felt was to establish a rule that any employee could communicate with me directly by writing a note and delivering it in a sealed envelope to my office. I assured them I would open such communications personally and handle them discreetly, but that they were only for my information. I would not try to resolve personal problems by this route. Naturally this procedure worried the intermediate managers, who were bypassed, although this channel was used sparingly, and never to criticize individuals. When I received a suggestion that merited consideration, I sent it down the chain of command for review, making sure that the person who had written to me remained anonymous.

Another way I got feedback was by developing an interchange with the chiefs of our overseas stations, very important people to the success of the Agency. I asked each to write me a letter of not more than two pages, once every six months, describing what was going on in his area of the world and at his station. From these letters I could deduce who were the good thinkers and who were the ones willing to call the shots as they saw them. Although I made it clear that the letters were not to include any requests for action on my part, the espionage branch deeply resented my talking directly with "their" people.

I got an even more direct feel for employee attitudes from a series of discussions with various groups of middle-management people, like espionage officers at midcareer, secretaries, analysts at the desk level, minorities, and the handicapped. I appreciated well that the captain of a ship doesn't know what the attitudes and morale are on his ship if he talks only to the executive officer and the department heads. Since morale in the CIA was supposedly low, I felt it was important for me to learn as early as possible just what that meant. I wanted to know what the CIA's equivalent of the Navy's junior officers and chief petty officers were thinking. George Thibault, whom I asked to set up these discussions, decided which cross-sections might provide different insights, met with the participants to help them organize their sentiments and encourage them to be hard-hitting and candid, and then scheduled their meetings with me. Then he and I would meet with them, without anyone else present.

All in all, then, Frank and I initiated three standard managerial techniques to bring the three-headed colossus of the CIA under centralized control: revamping the organizational mechanisms to gain control of people, budgets, and future plans; placing our people in key spots; and opening up communications from top to bottom. Unfortunately, we couldn't put these significant changes fully into place before we both left, in 1981. Bureaucracies have many ways of resisting change, and as the 1980 presidential election approached, those who resisted us simply dragged their feet until they found out whether we would be around after the election.

In this case resistance was more than the standard bureaucratic impulse in favor of the status quo. It was in part a factor of the uncertainty wrought by the two revolutions in oversight and technical collection. It also was a consequence of a sociological change that had been taking place for some years. The CIA was shifting from an elite, establishment institution, almost a club, to a normal professional organization where people were admitted and accepted on the basis of their credentials and abilities, not their associations. It had grown to a size where many relationships had to be relatively impersonal. Little wonder that an organization in this kind of transition resisted further, deliberate change. Yet it was not all an uphill battle.

Three months before I left the CIA I engaged a management consultant firm to survey the organizational arrangements and management procedures as they then existed. After extensive interviews with all the top people, the consultants concluded that the need for the changes we had made was widely accepted, that the changes which had been achieved exceeded by far what could have been accomplished in most private sector corporations in a comparable period, but that there was a very strong desire for a period of stability.

Whenever I describe these management adjustments, the question I am most frequently asked is "Did you reach the point where you felt confident that you knew everything that was going on, that they weren't doing things without telling you?" My answer is that I believe we moved far enough toward central management of the three branches that, except for very small projects (little money or few people), there was simply no way for anyone to hide ill-conceived activities. And, because I moved people like John McMahon into top leadership positions and brought in new, younger people in whom I had personal confidence as chiefs of station, I had no fear that the organization was operating behind my back or hiding things from me.

But being confident that the organization was not *out* of control was not the same as feeling that it was adequately *under* control.

SIXTEEN

The Halloween Massacre

THE DISCUSSION MEETINGS George Thibault organized with mid-to-upper-level CIA employees were modeled on Admiral Zumwalt's skull sessions with junior naval officers and chief petty officers. Many of the issues raised were problems endemic to most bureaucracies: how to get good ideas forward, whether grievances were being fairly considered, and whether the information employees wanted to have was being disseminated properly. I would take up problems like these later with the right people in the chain of command. Two other themes that ran through almost every meeting were very unusual and attracted my close personal attention. One was a complaint about overstaffing in the espionage branch. The other was a deep cynicism about the entire personnel system.

Realizing that tampering with an organization's personnel system might set off an explosion, I girded myself for the worst as I dug into these two problem areas — and got it. There was so much evidence of overstaffing that I decided to go after it first.

Almost from my first day at the Agency, I could just feel that there were too many people. When I sent out a written question, a huge volume of replies would come back almost instantly, indicating that there were plenty of people who could drop everything; and every internal memorandum was letter-perfect, suggesting an excess of secretarial help. What the younger people were complaining about, though, was a stifling amount of supervision of their work and a disheartening lack of prospect for promotion. Too many old-timers were hanging on. Hank Knoche confirmed that we were top-heavy when he came to me with the delicate problem of demotions for some senior people. For instance, Cord Meyer, an old CIA hand with a distinguished record, had risen to the top civil service grade, but there were no jobs left for him that called for that grade. He was acting as a special assistant to Knoche, which was far below his abilities. We had to drop him a grade so that we could promote someone else who was serving in a job that deserved the grade. Several more people had been sent abroad as station chiefs because there was no other place to put them. They had to be demoted, too. And I remembered Jim Schlesinger's telling me that the Agency was still overstaffed. That was surprising, since Schlesinger had slashed the Agency by more than 630 people during his five-month tenure. I had been impressed by the emphasis he had used when mentioning the problem to me.

It was at this point that I learned about a study the espionage branch itself had done on its personnel situation in mid 1976, while George Bush was DCI. It called for a reduction in the size of the branch by 1350 positions over a five-year period. No action had been taken. Bush had not rejected it, but neither had he faced up to it. I asked William Wells, who had become chief of espionage just after the study was completed, what he thought should be done. He had little enthusiasm for grappling with the problem but did not argue against the recommended reduction. I then conferred with a large number of top CIA people. Again, I found neither enthusiasm nor opposition to carrying out the study's recommendation.

I finally turned to James Taylor, the comptroller. Taylor had come to the CIA with Schlesinger and was enough of an outsider to look at the subject objectively. He cautioned me not to go ahead with the entire cut of 1350, but proposed instead that I reduce staff positions by only 820. He pointed out that in the time it would take to effect that reduction, we could determine whether we wanted to go further. I decided to do as he recommended but to accomplish the reduction over two years instead of the five suggested in the original plan. I didn't want the organization beset for five years with uncertainty about who might have to leave. I also wanted to restore incentive to those bright, impressive younger people who now had too many supervisors. The future of the CIA depended on them.

Accomplishing the reduction in two years rather than five made one big difference. The reduction was to be 820 *positions* (not people), most of which would be vacated as people left through normal retirement, resignation, or death. The estimate was that 820 posts would be vacated by this kind of attrition if we took five years to accomplish the reduction. But there would not be enough attrition in merely two years to eliminate 820 positions, so we would have to push some people into early retirement or out of a job. The press has repeatedly reported that anywhere from 820 to 2000 *people* were summarily fired as a result of the decision. The actual number of people fired was 17. An additional 147 were forced to retire early (and most were actually better off financially for doing so, owing to anomalies in the government's retirement system). The remaining positions were vacated by normal attrition or by the transfer of people to other branches in the Agency. In short, the espionage branch's authorized number of people shrank by 820: all of the reduction except the 147 forced into early retirement and the 17 dismissed was effected by attrition.

On August 7, 1977, I gathered the top people in the CIA in the Bubble to announce my decision on the reduction. Fortunately, I had some good news, too. In April I had asked Special Assistant Rusty Williams to do a thorough review of how the espionage branch was operating. In view of all the public discussion of past mistakes, I felt I owed it to the President and myself to check carefully to see whether there were any questionable practices still in use. I gave Williams carte blanche to inquire wherever necessary and to take however long he needed. Just a few days before the meeting in the Bubble, he and I met with the President and were able to report that the espionage branch was being run ethically and soundly. I passed this report on to these top people and then explained my reasoning for the elimination of 820 positions in the espionage branch.

This reduction comes from a conviction of the DDO [acronym for the espionage branch] management that since the major cutback

in Southeast Asia, the Headquarters element has not reduced pro-
portionately. Since I have been here, I have listened to and talked
with groups and individuals and find there is a great deal of opinion that the DDO is overmanned and has a lot of people who are
underemployed. If there is one thing I would like to be sure of, it is
that every employee in this Agency feels a full sense of challenge, a
full sense of contribution. Let me emphasize that this reduction of
820 positions is an effort to be leaner and more effective. It will be
carried out in as considerate a way as we possibly can. For instance, we will take as much by attrition as we possibly can. Beyond that we will try to take from early retirement. And beyond
that we will reach down to those people who have been consistently graded in the bottom of their category — those ranked
within the bottom 5 or 10 percent. There will be a higher proportion of cuts in the more senior grades than the junior ones, because
there is a tendency when you cut large organizations to end up
being top-heavy. This is a virile, young organization and our future depends on attracting and retaining the same type of high-
quality people that we have today.

I repeated the entire session the next day in order to reach as
many people in Headquarters as possible, and I also sent a message, summarizing the meetings, to all the field stations.

Bill Wells and I had agreed that he would take until November 1 to work out the details of how the two-year plan would operate, but I wanted everyone who would be affected during the next
two years to know it right away.

During the three-month interval between August and November not one CIA official counseled me against proceeding with
this plan. Interestingly, I announced the planned reduction to a
group of fifteen press people at a breakfast interview on August 9.
None considered it newsworthy and none of them wrote it up. But
as soon as the names of those affected were announced on November 1, all hell broke loose within the Agency and in the press.

The first problem was that, although I had directed that the
notices not be sent out on October 31, they were. The affair became known as the Halloween Massacre. On top of that, the way
the individuals were notified was unconscionable. Because
the Agency had gone through a large reduction under Schlesinger, I had assumed, incorrectly, that procedures for dismissing
people as humanely as possible were well organized. In fact, it was

quite the reverse. The note was an abrupt two-paragraph bureau-cratic letter that said, in effect, "It has been decided that your services are no longer needed." It was not the kind of sympathetic, regretful letter that these people deserved, especially those who had served for many years. On learning of this, I wrote out by hand a two-page letter to go out over my signature; I explained the need for the reduction, offered thanks for the individual's past service, and expressed my genuine regret that this step was neces-sary. Unfortunately, just as I was leaving for the airport on a trip, I was talked out of sending it by Bill Wells and Jack Blake. They were concerned about the legal implications of my saying more than was in the form letter. I regret to this day not having seen to it that these letters were written and delivered properly. The way the notification was handled only confirmed the complaints about the impersonal nature of the personnel management sys-tem.

The first hue and cry in the press was that this reduction emas-culated the country's espionage capabilities. There were charges that some of the CIA's most talented espionage people and much of the Agency's corporate memory had been eliminated. I cannot reveal the number of people who were in the espionage branch, but it was large enough that a reduction of this size couldn't pos-sibly have been cataclysmic. And individuals who were rated by their supervisors as being in the bottom 5 to 10 percent could hardly have been as valuable as the media said they were. One of those transferred to another branch of the Agency, for instance, proved to be an alcoholic who was in the habit of working only half a day. The espionage branch had been willing to carry him and could afford to do so. Of course he was an exception. And it would be unfair not to acknowledge that some of the people asked to leave because they ranked at the bottom were quite capable, steady employees who did a competent job, even though they had little prospect of moving to higher positions. In any event, com-plaints about the loss of the 147 by forced retirement were beside the point. Almost all of them would have retired within a year or two anyway.

A more sophisticated argument against dismissing intelligence officials is that in their anger they may turn against the Agency and sell the secrets they know to the highest bidder. A senior British official actually politely reprimanded me for having fired them. He said that his organization always eased out an individual gracefully, usually with financial inducements. The CIA is strongly influenced by British practices, and some of the opposition to the reduction undoubtedly sprang from this. Hanging on to poor performers and people who weren't required, or even easing them out with bonuses, made no sense to me. If you keep such people, you run the risk that the organization will assume that such low standards of behavior are acceptable or that overstaffing is the norm. If you pay them off, they know very well that you're easing them out, and if they really are prone to retaliate, they may do so anyway to make more money. But the most compelling argument against those tactics was that they had not worked well for the British.

Britain, which has had far more than its share of damaging, high-level spies, is understandably self-conscious about the matter. At a social event former Prime Minister James Callaghan asked me whether we still had any concerns about British security. What he was hoping to hear, I'm sure, was that we felt all that was behind them. I was noncommittal, although what I would have liked to say was that the British were still vulnerable because of their unwillingness to clean house now and then. Since they see that nothing is done about it, British intelligence professionals are less likely to report abnormal behavior. It wasn't long afterward — in 1982 — that the British record turned even blacker with the uncovering of Geoffrey Prime. He had been a Soviet agent inside their highly secret communications intelligence organizaton for years. His unusual behavior, like unexplained trips to Vienna, should have alerted his colleagues, but no one reported it. Britain paid dearly for being unwilling to let go poor performers, malcontents, or those exhibiting aberrant behavior. I rejected the British policy as naïve, unworkable, and dangerous.

Another protest made by the press, despite the espionage branch's own study to the contrary, is that the 820 positions were desperately needed. Almost all intelligence "failures" since the reduction have been blamed on a shortage of experienced people in espionage. The argument is doubly strange. First, no outsider can estimate what contributions better human intelligence might have made in those instances that reporters called failures because of lack of emphasis on human intelligence. Because a spy may theoretically overhear just the right conversation does not mean that he is likely to do so. In my experience, human intelligence occasionally got a superbly useful piece of information. More often it provided helpful background information about a country and its politics, but nothing to aid with an immediate decision. Second, no positions overseas were eliminated. Besides, no outsider, be he a reporter or a student of national security, has an accurate idea of how many people the secret CIA needs. Because of compartmentation, few even inside the CIA, except those at the very top, can make a sound estimate. The press simply was parroting the views it received at second hand from people who purported to know.

What was really behind the outcries from such people inside the CIA and from outside it — from the CIA retirement community — was outrage at my challenging the traditional independence of the espionage branch. If I could summarily reduce the size of the espionage branch, I might next begin to supervise what it did. The cry was over power and turf, not over the number of people required, nor was it sincere sympathy with individuals, each of whom had been selected by the branch itself for dismissal.

This is not to say there were not some genuine concerns in and out of the CIA over the reduction. The most valid was that I was closing off the possibility of a massive increase in covert actions. Here it was largely the old hands, in retirement, who protested, and they were indeed right. I did not foresee that as being something the country would need or want. The media, however, went along with them, even though it is doubtful that they, let alone the public, wanted more covert activities. Although I explained the rationale and the numbers to scores of reporters from the nation's major newspapers and television networks in personal interviews, not one ever reported the facts correctly for almost seven years.

The most serious effect on the CIA was that morale dipped even farther as the press and others circulated unfounded rumors of more cuts ahead. It took some time to quiet the apprehensions, because some of the old die-hards in covert action continually fed the rumor mill. Their empire, which was surrounded by a moat of secrecy, had been invaded by an outsider who they believed would never understand or appreciate it and therefore could not properly change its ways. The retired people convinced themselves that it was of overriding importance for them to save the CIA from any change, so they put to work their training in manipulating people. The press was malleable, and the fantasy endures.

In fact, the reductions improved our espionage capabilities. Since the cutbacks were exclusively in Headquarters' overhead, the case officers in the field were freed from some of the unnecessary supervision directed at them from Langley. For instance, when the chief of the section for Europe traveled to Europe every three months to see his people, he was giving more personal direction to his subordinates than sound management called for. Moreover, when managers like him became so absorbed in the details of current actions, they did not have time to concern themselves with the broader issues, such as the value of what they were doing or its ethics. In my experience a bigger staff does not help such a person step back to look at the big picture; instead, it gives him time to become mired in the details of directing his subordinates. What is needed is a better management technique. A manager can develop it with a smaller staff, because he will have to learn, under pressure of an increased work load, to delegate details.

There were, of course, some real shortages of people, but these were problems of distribution. Africa, Southeast Asia, and the Middle East, which had grown recently in importance, were understaffed, but Europe and Northern Asia, which had deserved great attention after World War II, were now overstaffed. Personnel had not been shifted as needs changed, because the subsidiary divisions of the espionage branch had kept about as much autonomy and independence from the chief of espionage as he had from the DCI. Everyone's fiefdom was nicely intact.

Next, I turned to the more systemic problem of the CIA's personnel system. In fact, the crux of the problem was the existence of four personnel systems rather than one; that is, one for each of the three operating branches and the support branch. Between them these four systems did not meet the needs of the Agency or of the individual employees. There was no plan to ensure that we would have the people we'd need in the future. In 1977, 30 percent of all espionage officers were over fifty years old. Since the average retirement age was 53.5, a lot of trained people were going to leave within a short period. If a business corporation loses many of its top people in a short time, it pirates replacements from rival corporations in the same field. Not so in espionage! It is very much like the military: one cannot go to IBM to recruit a general to lead troops into battle; one has to develop that talent inside the organization. It is the same in espionage. The only people experienced in espionage outside the CIA work for the KGB, British intelligence, or the intelligence organizations of other foreign countries. The espionage branch was unwilling to face the problem caused by its lack of a steady, planned flow of personnel. It was obvious that as 30 percent of the old-timers left, we would have to take in a lot of recruits at the bottom. I immediately ordered a sixfold increase in the number of recruits each year to get ready for the big exodus at the top.

The autonomy of the four personnel systems also caused problems in recruiting. The central recruiting office's function was only to locate candidates. The branch personnel offices decided which candidates to accept. As a result, it took an extraordinary amount of time for most candidates to be interviewed. If they were not accepted by the first branch office the recruiting office sent them to, they were sent to another. On average, it took nine months for an applicant to be rejected or accepted. The son of one of my closest friends applied in early 1977. I privately monitored, but did not intercede in, the process of his application. After putting up with ten months of indecision by the Agency, the young man simply gave up and went into the business world.

I found from simple observation that the personnel system had many other problems. I was curious, for instance, when I heard the term "walking the corridors" dropped in conversation. I was aghast when I discovered what it meant: individuals returning from an assignment overseas often spent weeks or months walking from office to office, looking for one where they were needed. With no central planning system, valuable talent went unused. When there was a shortage of skills in one branch but extra people in another, there was no system for arriving at a solution beneficial to both. When secretaries and communications clerks felt they were stagnating in their grade, no effort was made to retrain these people for jobs that held better opportunity for advancement. The central personnel office didn't have the authority to solve such problems within the branches.

What was needed was one personnel system that could look after the needs of people as well as of the organization and handle staff in an equitable manner. Frank Carlucci and I set out to make the necessary changes, with primary emphasis on improving the way we treated people. We instituted such procedures as compiling lists of candidates who could move up into key jobs when they were vacated and then developing training programs so that those candidates would be properly qualified; making instruction in leadership part of all training courses to encourage staff to pay attention to the needs of people; mandating the rotation of personnel around branches to develop leaders who understood the whole Agency, not just one branch; arranging for better career-counseling to help employees chart their own careers in an informed way; and making the entire system sufficiently clear that people knew when they were likely to come up for promotion or reassignment, what prospects they had, and so on.

What we really wanted was one set of standards and procedures for the entire Agency and a central personnel office with the authority to enforce them. Only such a system could negate both the fact and the perception that cronyism influenced the decisions about who got ahead and who did not. For instance, promotion supposedly was based on annual written evaluations of each employee. But whenever I studied an individual's evaluation file, I realized the format was designed to reveal as little as possible about his capabilities. All it told was where he had served. What really counted when the promotion panel met was the oral and informal evaluation by his superiors. Consequently, the superiors could make or break their subordinates. Because of this, they could and did command them; they did not have to lead them, because the employees knew that pleasing their boss was ultimately more important than producing results.

Carlucci and I installed a new evaluation report form, set certain standards for the entire Agency, established accounting systems for determining what numbers and kinds of people would be needed over the next decade, and strengthened the central personnel office. The resistance from the bureaucrats was immense.

Power over people is something all bureaucrats seek, and the branch chiefs would not easily give up what they had. It was all part of one struggle: whether the CIA was going to be one Agency under the control of an active DCI and his deputy or three agencies under the control of the three branch chiefs. We did not get as far as we would have liked, but we made the Agency more sensitive to its people and to the ways in which it treated them.

The CIA needs people not only with skills, but with high moral standards, with the confidence to be independent, and with the desire to be innovative. Attracting and keeping such people is not as simple today as in the past. The Agency is still coasting on the very high quality of the people who joined it after World War II and during the cold war. Today's youth are inclined to question rather than to follow blindly, and that is good. But as a result they require clearer explanations to motivate them than many of us did in the past. I saw a good example of this at an unusual luncheon I had with five young officers who were still in the Agency's initial training program. One of them had phoned my office and asked if the five could meet with the director. The trainee said they did not want to register any complaints; they wanted to see what the Agency's top management was like. I arranged a luncheon for just the six of us. I asked each one why he or she had joined the Agency. The responses reflected such patriotism and so strong a wish to serve the United States, to contribute to their country, that I was very moved.

People who probe deeply into an organization they join will stay with it only if it offers them a clear understanding of their career path and a well-defined sense of where they, as individuals, fit into its mission. The CIA has some of our finest young people coming into its ranks, but unless it moves smartly to modernize its personnel procedures, it will not keep them.

SEVENTEEN

Men versus Machines

THE CONVULSIVE REACTION to the elimination of 820 positions in the espionage branch reflected the broader concern that human intelligence was being downgraded or pushed aside. In fact, no significant resource or operational authorization that the espionage branch requested was refused. I did, though, give more of my time to the technical systems. Technical systems cost infinitely more money than human ones, and once the Congress appropriates the money for something like a new satellite, the commitment is set; you cannot modify a satellite once it is launched, and it may be up there for years. And there are plenty of "experts" around the government who are ready to modify the plans for satellites set by the DCI and his staff. All this inevitably involves the DCI intimately in decisions on future technical systems. Beyond that, the DCI is called on almost daily to make decisions concerning technical collection, because it has become such an integral part of crisis management.

Seeing the DCI's attention diverted elsewhere for the first time in its history, the espionage branch came to feel neglected. And, while busy feeling neglected, it failed to define where human espionage fits into a new era of intelligence collection dominated by technical systems.

The espionage branch is still a bit stunned by the new reliance on technical systems that can collect data without exposing the life of an agent and that can respond very quickly. What espionage people have not accepted is that human espionage has become a complement to technical systems. Espionage either reaches out into voids where technical systems cannot probe or double-checks the results of technical collection. In short, human intelligence today is employed to do what technical systems cannot do.

Advocates of human intelligence commonly say that what technical systems cannot do, but human espionage can, is to discern other people's plans or intentions. Uncovering intentions is the strong point of human espionage, but it is an exaggeration to say that only espionage can do that. Reading another country's messages through electronic intercepts or listening to its leaders talk to each other through a concealed microphone can reveal intentions, often with greater accuracy than an agent's reporting.

Human spying has the advantage, though, of allowing us to go right to the horse's mouth; we can recruit an agent who has access to the people making decisions. In some cases the agent will be able to talk directly with someone in the know; in others he'll establish contact with someone who is present when decisions are made; in still others he'll find someone who will give him access to written reports of what's intended. As I noted earlier, there are two limitations that are frequently overlooked. One is the difficulty of placing an agent in just the right place at just the right time. The other is the question of whether there are any reliable sources who can divulge a country's intentions.

On the first point, those issuing some of the strongest complaints about "intelligence failures" don't consider that it can be immensely difficult to recruit someone who has access to exactly what we want to know. For instance, in late 1983 the Long Commission, investigating the terrorist attack on the Marine barracks in Beirut, complained of the failure of human intelligence to provide warning. That was an uninformed slap at the Reagan administration's use of human agents. It was unreasonable to expect the CIA to have anticipated this particular threat far enough in advance to have placed an agent in every terrorist organization. Spies cannot be recruited overnight. A suitable candidate must be identified, his friendship and trust nurtured over weeks and months until he is willing to work for us, an opportunity found to insert him in the organization we want to learn about, and enough time allowed him to gain the trust of that organization. In Lebanon the CIA would have had to elevate terrorism to a very high priority perhaps a year or more before the actual attack. There were many terrorist groups to infiltrate, and the one that carried out the attack may well have come into Lebanon from Iran only a few months before the attack. And terrorist groups are usually composed of fanatics who are not easily fooled by imposters. All this is not to say that the CIA should not have been trying to place agents in Lebanon or that it could not have done better. It is to say that even had it had the prescience to make an all-out effort, its chances of success were low.

The problems of placing agents are particularly severe when we consider that our prime intelligence target, the Soviet Union, is able, in its authoritarian society, to exercise tight control over the contact its people have with foreigners. That, as well as the severe penalties levied on Soviet citizens for spying, makes our recruitment of Soviets a challenge, especially if we hope to get one inside a particular office, missile design bureau, or whatever. Against tough counterintelligence you usually settle for recruiting anyone you can, whether or not he has access to specific information you would like. Still, though such efforts are difficult, they can be worthwhile. When you hit it just right, the payoff, as with successful prospecting for gold, can be immense. But the public complaints about a lack of human intelligence in specific incidents, like the fall of the Shah or the terrorist attack in Beirut, are unfair. The public expects something more than human collection is likely to produce, except in the most fortunate of circumstances.

The second limitation on using human agents to ascertain intentions is that there may be no one who knows just what will happen. There was, for instance, no master plan for unseating the Shah; it was simply a protest that gained momentum. In late 1980, when the Soviets moved military forces to their border with Poland, there was probably no Soviet leader who could say with assurance whether they would invade or not; it was likely a day-by-day decision. We tend to look on authoritarian countries like the Soviet Union as making unequivocal decisions. Many decisions, in fact, result from the push and pull of pressure groups.

Those are not electoral pressures, which can be reasonably measured, as in the United States. They are pressures of the military, business, the government bureaucracy, or special interests. Thus, it is not easy for us to know who speaks authoritatively on foreign policy in a country like the Soviet Union.

If we have a feel, though, for the various pressures, we may be able to forecast trends. Even in the Soviet Union, opinion can be sampled by foreigners who travel, read provincial as well as national newspapers, and by those who take advantage of opportunities for contacts with Soviet citizens. We can exploit cultural and scientific exchange programs, tourism and merchant ship visits, just as the Soviets do in the United States. Admittedly, such contacts do not represent highly influential views in the government; they will not produce any "hot tips" on specific near-term developments. What would be valuable, though, is a sampling, made over a period of years, of the views of a cross-section of Soviets. Marked changes in attitudes could well signify trends that might influence government actions, even in that society.

After leaving the CIA, I talked with an academic friend who visits the Soviet Union periodically. Over about fifteen years he noticed a pronounced deterioration in the quality of Soviet society — lack of respect for authority, drunkenness, and black-marketeering. Although observations of such trends are valuable, they can be missed by case officers and agents who are looking for discreet pieces of information. The espionage branch is the ideal instrument, though, for uncovering such trends, even if doing so is almost an overt activity.

There is a need for sampling opinion and detecting trends in far more places than just the Soviet Union. Today we don't have an adequate understanding of the prospects for political stability in the Philippines, Saudi Arabia, Khomeini's Iran, and Argentina's new democracy, to name a few. Problems of internal dissatisfaction leading to political change in such countries are going to be with us for a long time. If we are to protect our interests, we must somehow anticipate such developments and understand them. Traditional espionage is not usually the best way to get a feel for undercurrents of change in a society. Rather, in many countries public opinion can be sampled openly.

In authoritarian nations, of course, there are limits on the kind of opinion-sampling a U.S. government official can carry out. The Shah, for instance, would never have tolerated a political officer from the U.S. embassy going into the mosques or bazaars to talk to the followers of the Ayatollah Khomeini, the man intent on overthrowing him. But such sampling could have been done by CIA case officers not known to be affiliated with the United States or by agents recruited by the CIA for just that purpose. Using either undercover case officers or agents, the espionage branch could assess public and governmental trends in almost any country. Case officers who "work the street," recruiting agents and picking up useful intelligence, develop a keen knowledge of the culture, attitudes, and language of their country of assignment. I found them very knowledgeable about the inner workings of other countries. Whenever I held a meeting with analysts to discuss a country or region, I always insisted that someone from the espionage branch familiar with that part of the world be there also. I knew he could make a useful contribution. It's that kind of broad knowledge of what's going on in a country that we need in order to forecast the probability of upheaval well enough in advance to do something about it. You don't get that only by attempting to recruit agents who are so well placed as to give us a blueprint of another country's future.

This is not to suggest that sampling opinion and detecting trends be done in lieu of conducting espionage, but that it proceed side by side with it. The espionage branch, however, strongly resisted my efforts to employ it to take the pulse of foreign countries. First, because semicovert collection was not in its tradition; that activity was not considered espionage by the professionals. Second, because the CIA had become too accustomed to living and working in comfortable cities abroad; not enough of its people were out in the remote areas.

To anticipate societal change, the espionage branch must place case officers throughout a foreign country so as to get a feel for all shades of opinion. It also must equip them with the polling skills of George Gallup as well as the seductive ones of Mata Hari. Unless it makes these kinds of adjustments, espionage will continue to have a hard time finding its niche alongside technical collection systems.

In addition to concentrating on ascertaining intentions, the espionage branch should work on complementing technical systems in four other ways. First, it should focus on those areas where technical systems raise questions they cannot answer. For instance, if overhead photography uncovers a new factory that looks as though it could produce nuclear materials, we can use electronic intercepts to confirm that the factory communicates regularly with the Ministry of Nuclear Affairs. When we have that much information, we can send a spy inside the ministry to determine if the factory is talking to the nuclear power division or the nuclear weapons division. That sort of activity enhances the power of espionage by concentrating its efforts on limited, specific information that cannot be had by technical means.

Next, it should back up technical systems that fail, either because of a flaw or because of enemy interference. The human intelligence people can carefully analyze which are our most vital technical systems and which are more likely to be compromised, and then prepare to substitute for them.

Third, it should verify what is collected by technical means. Both electronic surveillance and photos can be deceived. As noted previously, Secretary Haig attempted to mislead the Argentinians with false messages. It is always reassuring to have a human source confirm that intercepts are valid. The espionage branch needs to study where deception is most likely and attempt to recruit agents who can provide confirmation in those areas.

Finally, it should devote more effort to implanting technical devices, for audio pickup, electronic intercept, infrared sensing, or other. When such devices must be placed in proximity to the target, often only a case officer or his agent can do the surreptitious positioning. As technology continues to improve the devices, they will become increasingly important. The teamwork between the CIA's technical and espionage branches will be vital. The technical people need to talk more with espionage experts so that they understand the purpose of the implanting.

The espionage branch has so far resisted moving in any of these directions purely and simply out of pride. Having been the center of the CIA's collection (and analysis), it resents any other intelligence effort being elevated to its level. When it finally faces up to being a member of a team, it will have to change profoundly the way it recruits and trains its people. A redirected espionage branch will need to make a greater effort to recruit agents with specialized knowledge and specific access. For instance, the agent needed to penetrate the hypothetical Ministry of Nuclear Affairs would have to know something about nuclear physics and have access to that ministry. A study of which niches are best filled by human espionage would probably disclose that we should be recruiting more scientists, economists, sociologists, and labor leaders, rather than foreign policy experts. Similarly, people newly recruited to become CIA case officers should have those skills.

Traditionally the CIA's espionage branch has staffed itself with case officers who are liberal arts graduates. In large part this is a policy of recruiting one's replacement in one's own image. It is an article of faith that people educated in the liberal arts are better at dealing with people and hence can do a better job of recruiting agents than can scientists or engineers or economists. Skill in recruiting is not like skill in surgery, possessed by only a few. Recruiting is salesmanship, and lots of people can be good salesmen. A good case officer needs sound ethical principles, initiative, an ability to communicate, and a quickness of mind that will enable him to react well under pressure. People with all sorts of academic backgrounds possess those traits. The CIA should look for case officers who have such qualities and who also have academic training in the disciplines most appropriate to human intelligence collection. This is where sociologists and anthropologists would be ideal, for sampling public attitudes. Economists, computer engineers, and others with technical skills are likely to be in high demand also. Many such people, incidentally, are already employed in the analysis branch and could be lent to the espionage branch for a few years now and then.

The new role for espionage is no less important than the old, but it is never easy to redirect the thrust of an established, proud, and successful organization. The technical revolution will in time force the espionage branch to become a team player. The longer it takes, the more often espionage will be sidestepped, worked around, and ignored. The potential contributions of espionage are too important for the country and for the Agency to let this happen. The practitioners of espionage need to be reminded that they are neglecting their future because of their fixation on their past.

EIGHTEEN

Why the CIA Is Unique

IN WRITING THE STORY of almost any organization, one must explore some of the failures, problems, and mistakes in the organization's history. Those are often what led to shaping it into what it is. That's especially the case with an organization whose history is as controversial as that of the CIA. In telling the story of most organizations, though, one can usually balance past problems with accounts of successes. That's not so with the CIA. It is all too likely that the greatest accomplishments will be the greatest secrets.

While I was DCI I came to expect exceptional performance from each of the branches because of the high quality of the people. My yardstick for measuring this quality was the many military and civil service people I had been associated with before joining the Agency. In terms of dedication, competence, self-sacrifice, and readiness to take risks involving themselves, the CIA's people were, I found, a match for any other group.

Frank Carlucci, who had served in a greater variety of government posts than I, also rated the Agency's people very highly. During the first year that he and I worked together, he repeatedly commented on the dedication and responsiveness of the staff, and he stressed how well and rapidly they reacted to orders. Each time Frank spoke of this to me, I agreed, though I did not consider it a big thing. Finally, I realized that Frank was seeing something that I was missing. He had been with the State Department, the Department of Health, Education, and Welfare, the Office of Management and Budget, and the Office of Economic Opportunity in the White House. I had served exclusively in the Department of Defense. In Defense there is a tradition of responsiveness that derives from the operational environment, where action often cannot be postponed. I recognized that Frank was not accustomed, from his work in civilian agencies, to the kind of superb responsiveness he was seeing in the CIA, but that I accepted it as normal.

I expressed my view of the quality of the Agency's people frequently in public when the question of morale at the CIA arose. There was much talk about bad morale in the 1970s, and morale was bound to sag when there was so much public criticism. What I said, over and over, was "If I ever have to run another organization with bad morale, I hope that it will be just like the CIA. I've never noticed any letdown in performance, no matter what the state of morale." Whenever I thought of morale, I thought not only of the impact of public criticism, but of the special sacrifices the CIA demands of its people in the name of secrecy. There are secrets in the military, but most are technical details one does not need or want to share with friends or family. In the CIA, the secrets touch what many people do and preclude the kind of reward that feeds morale.

In early 1979 I pinned a medal on a CIA career officer. The ceremony was in my office, not in the larger conference room, where we usually gave out awards. And there were only four people present to hear me tell Dick that I considered him a real hero. Dick was a middle-grade officer who, along with a small group of CIA people, had been in a foreign country on a secret assignment when public order broke down. Anti-Americans came into control of the remote area where he and his group were. We feared for their lives. Dick, with a display of astuteness and bravado, stood up to the leader of the insurgents and demanded transportation and safe passage to the capital. His composure and presence carried the day, and everyone got home safely. I was commending his calmness and resourcefulness under pressure. It was because of the secrecy of what he had been doing that only four of his coworkers on the project were there for the presentation. He was getting credit for his performance, but it was a very quiet pat on the back. He could not even take the medal home, because it would disclose that he worked at the CIA. He could tell his wife he had received it, but not why. Dick had to be satisfied with knowing that the good job he'd done had been recognized privately.

This case was not unique. In the entrance lobby of CIA Headquarters one of the marble walls is inscribed with forty-seven gold stars. Underneath them is a small glass case with a book that contains the names of CIA men and women who have died in the line of duty; in some instances there is just a blank space for someone whose role in the CIA can never safely be told.

The sacrifices of CIA professionals and their families go far deeper than not getting much public recognition. Sometimes people like Dick have to bear the cross of appearing to their friends and families as less than successful in their work. Working undercover, a case officer ostensibly is employed by some organization other than the CIA, but he never appears to achieve much status in that organization. He's never the top man, the president, the manager. It looks as though his career is stagnating. Before children can be told of their father's true occupation, they may think him something of a failure. Matters can become even worse when the children finally know. One officer described to me the trauma his family underwent when he first told his teen-age son that he worked in the CIA. The son was at an Ivy League college and had become swept up by the antimilitary, anti-CIA vogue that prevailed on many college campuses in the early 1970s. Suddenly this heavily committed young man learned that his father was part of all that he opposed. It took time and patience for the father to bring the son around to accepting his role. Not many families can manage that kind of stress.

I had noted other types of family stress back in the 1950s, when I happened to live across the street from a man who acknowledged to us that he was a CIA case officer. He was on home assignment after he and his family had spent most of his career overseas. My wife and I often remarked that we could almost see Tom thinking twice before he answered the most simple question. That kind of stress affects wives, too. In this case it was a standing joke with my wife and me that we could anticipate Tom's wife phoning our house if her daughter had been over to play with our children for more than an hour or so. Occasionally we even answered the phone, "Yes, Betty, Mary is here and just fine!" When Betty lived overseas, she had worried that someone might find out what her husband did and harm her children. Betty had also faced times when she worried that Tom might not come back from a risky espionage operation. As I've noted, most of the risks to life and limb are taken by agents, not CIA case officers. The CIA's espionage professionals occasionally face physical risk, but more often another kind of risk.

That is the risk of giving in to the temptation to cut corners. Some cut corners in an earnest effort to get their job done better, some for personal gain, and some for personal pleasure. It is almost impossible to keep tight rein on an espionage officer in the field, because so much of his work is done without supervision. If he is given a large amount of money in cash to pay an agent, we cannot expect him to return a signed receipt, showing that it all went to the agent. It isn't possible to have a foolproof accounting system under such circumstances. And sometimes the officer works with people who offer him various bribes or deals. The Edmund P. Wilsons, Lowells, and Hilliards succumb to such temptations; most do not.

One instance of a case officer who gave in to temptation for personal pleasure came to my attention early in my tenure. An officer on an overseas assignment had developed an amorous relationship with a woman agent, whom he had earlier recruited to help us. His becoming involved with her was, of course, unprofessional conduct. Mixing business with this kind of pleasure in the profession of espionage leaves a case officer open to blackmail or may expose his identity. It is, we know, an old trick of the trade to entrap a rival intelligence officer by revealing him in a compromising situation with a woman. The Soviet KGB would have no hesitation in doing that whenever it could. Also, one of the most difficult aspects of espionage is knowing whether your agent is a bona fide agent, a double agent, or an opportunist who is putting you on for money. Clearly a case officer who has an amorous relationship with an agent cannot report objectively about him or her.

I fired this officer, in part because of his unprofessional conduct, but more because, in attempting to extricate himself, he lied to his superiors when they confronted him. As I saw it, if this man could lie to his superiors and get away with it, his superiors might conclude that they could lie to their superiors, and so on up the line to me. What was at stake was control of the Agency.

Conscientious case officers who are above giving in to the temptations of personal gain or pleasure still face difficult ethical decisions, because they often cannot refer back to Headquarters for guidance. Very early in their careers they may have to decide for themselves whether to refuse to participate in an activity like the inhumane treatment of Nosenko. Sometimes they make an honest but unwise judgment call on such an ethical issue; sometimes they make just the right call at the time, only to find that it is subsequently criticized. For instance, the Agency opened lots of U.S. mail back in the 1950s. At that time, I suspect, the American public would have accepted that as a price of the cold war. But when it was disclosed in 1975, it was soundly condemned by the public, because the norms of that era were different.

Hiding your accomplishments, leading a double life, regularly facing difficult moral issues, and being subjected to criticism for doing what was acceptable at the time one did it can all take their toll. In many ways, a clandestine career can be said to deform the person involved. The unusual pressures and temptations of espionage can produce some deviations in performance. Look at the bribery and unethical performances uncovered in U.S. business operations overseas in recent years. The demands and temptations of espionage are even more unusual; espionage is an unusual profession. If we expect to recruit and retain a sufficient number of highly ethical, dedicated, and competent individuals over a long period of time, we must treat it as an unusual career.

The place to start is with the length of a career. We should limit the number of years that case officers are subjected to the strains and pressures they will inevitably face. Something between a twenty- and twenty-five-year career would be a good compromise between exposing the individual too much and not taking full advantage of his expertise. That means that case officers would join the CIA at about twenty-two to twenty-five and retire at forty-two to fifty. The Congress has already recognized this need for shorter careers by establishing a special retirement program for case officers. Those who have served overseas for five years, have a total of twenty-five years in the CIA, and are fifty years of age or older can retire. That's quite a bit before the normal civil service retirement age. This has been helpful, but there is no provision for forcing people to leave once they've crossed those thresholds.

What is needed is the establishment of a norm of twenty to twenty-five years for a career in espionage, with the employer, the DCI, having the discretion to keep enough people to provide the needed top management of espionage. The DCI and his deputy, though, could ensure that the few who did stay past twenty or twenty-five years were those who would set the right tone of responsibility and ethics. Siphoning off this much talent and expertise may seem wasteful, and to some extent it is. But there are limits to how useful a senior case officer can be. After twenty years or so, it is very difficult for a senior case officer to maintain a reasonable cover. Surely by then the KGB and most other unfriendly intelligence services have deduced who the CIA people are. Thus, though the senior people may have many contacts, built up over the years, the risks of dealing with them may be too high. In addition, doing undercover espionage work at all hours of the day and night and in all manner of unusual circumstances is a young man's game. Finally, shorter careers in the espionage branch would also help prevent the kind of stagnation that resulted in 30 percent of that branch being close to retirement age in 1977.

Under this plan it would be necessary to raise both the current pay and the retirement annuity for espionage branch personnel above normal civil service standards. Starting a second career after a first one in espionage is never easy. Often a man cannot disclose much, if anything, about his past work, and his experience can rarely be translated readily into legitimate business skills. The high probability that a man entering the CIA's espionage branch under this plan would have to start over again in such circumstances at about age forty-five should be taken into account and compensation adjusted appropriately. Besides, I believe that we would be well advised to consider higher pay for those in espionage. It is not easy today to attract the right kind and number of people into this profession.

It's a rigorous life lived largely overseas, where opportunities for spouses' careers are slim. And the national attitude toward our doing espionage has become much more ambivalent than it was even twenty years ago. The last thing we want is to find that only the likes of Edmund P. Wilson are willing to join the espionage service, as a preparatory school for smuggling and other illegal activities. The country would be far better off paying whatever is needed to attract the relatively few individuals of high capability and high ethical standards that the espionage branch needs.

The CIA has tried for years to find ways to pay its people more because of the special challenges they face. The usual recourse has been to obtain a higher grade or rank for CIA people than is held by those in other agencies. This, however, is a poor way to achieve the objective of paying this particular profession more than others in government. It leads to inequities within the CIA, since there is no clearly established procedure for allocating pay, and it leads to resentments and jealousies among other government employees.

The espionage people also deserve better protection from the Congress and the White House. That could start with an up-to-date charter for the CIA that establishes the country's endorsement of the conduct of espionage, counterintelligence, and covert action, and that sets forth the basic rules for those activities, rules that are not as likely to shift with administrations as are Executive Orders. Next, it is to the advantage of the professionals to have vigorous oversight. To the extent that they are sometimes held retroactively responsible or are unjustly accused in the press, the fact that two congressional committees and the National Security Council are responsible for knowing what is going on helps cushion the impact of public reaction. In addition, oversight, especially by Congress, can give helpful guidance to the CIA as to what is and what is not acceptable conduct in the pursuit of secrets.

Most important, the CIA professionals deserve our understanding of the special quality of the responsibilities we place on them. They are asked to take actions that the public often does not want to acknowledge its country does. In the course of such activities they may have to make very difficult decisions about how far to pursue the information they are seeking. Many of them individually are confronted with a variety of temptations. And the veil of secrecy that shrouds what they are doing may make such temptations even more tempting. Highly capable and dedicated men and women may make errors under these circumstances. When there are errors, we, the public, must accept some of the responsibility for having given these people the assignments they had to undertake. And we should not forget that we owe the professionals of the CIA a debt of gratitude for having accomplished all that they have done in the relatively few years since the inception of the Agency, in 1947.

At the same time, we also owe it to them to watch what they are doing today with as close attention and as healthy a skepticism as we can, and to insist that our surrogates in the two intelligence committees of the Congress do so also, to a degree that the public cannot. The CIA professionals need and deserve such scrutiny, not because we mistrust either them or the organization, but because what we ask them to do carries the burden of possible errors in judgment or falling prey to temptation.

PART FIVE

MANAGING THE OCTOPUS

NINETEEN

The Spy Plane in a Yam Patch

STAN, you have all those exotic technical systems. I would like to see some photographs of what is going on in that war," said the President. This ordinary request was the beginning of a fiasco. The war the President referred to was a small conflict that had recently begun between two third world nations. Since the fighting was not of major concern to the United States, I suspected that it wasn't so much interest in the war that stirred the President as it was his wish to see how well the intelligence wizardry at his disposal could perform and whether I could make it work. We were both new, and it was a good time to experiment; not much was at stake.

As soon as I returned to my office I called in Hank Knoche and told him the President had just asked for some photos of the war. "Call the right people and get some overhead reconnaissance on it." I didn't stress urgency, because it seemed redundant when the President had personally made the request. How wrong I was. Hank assured me this was a piece of cake; we would have the photos quickly. My next scheduled briefing for the President was in three days. I expected to go to it armed with a sheaf of photos.

The day before that briefing I asked Hank where the photos were.

"The overhead systems just aren't finding anything, Stan. This is a pretty small war in a remote area. We don't have a good fix on where the fighting is taking place."

I gave my apologies to the President the next day and assured him I would have results for him at the next briefing, in four days.

I wondered a bit whether Hank appreciated sufficiently that we were being tested. I decided to emphasize the urgency of obtaining photos by raising the matter at the daily staff meeting of top CIA management. It included Hank, the operating branch heads, the support branch head, the general counsel, the public affairs officer, the legislative liaison officer, and one or two others. In addition, John McMahon, who had temporarily replaced Admiral Dan Murphy as the deputy for the Intelligence Community, attended as the representative of the Community. I kept asking when we were going to get some results from the overhead reconnaissance. The answer kept coming in: "Not yet." No one seemed to know why not yet. After another briefing with the President, at which I was again embarrassed by not having photos to produce, I displayed increasing exasperation at the staff meetings. That didn't seem to goad the photo people into much action, but it did stir up the chief of the CIA's espionage branch, Bill Wells. He suggested that his people could get us the photographs we needed. I asked him how.

The plan was to lease an aircraft, hire a pilot in one of the warring countries, give him a camera and some training with it, and have him fly out over the battle area to take pictures. Wells contended that this would be even better than overhead reconnaissance, since the small aircraft could fly under most cloud cover that might block high-altitude systems. It seemed like a Rube Goldberg way to do things when we were spending fortunes on sophisticated gadgetry, but I was getting desperate. When I asked what the risks were, I was assured that there would be no evidence of any U.S. connection to this aircraft. The plane would not have U.S. markings or documents, and the camera would not be traceable. The chance that the United States would appear to be meddling in the war if something went wrong was slim. I was a bit startled when Bill told me we would have to assume full liability for the aircraft — $2 million. Nonetheless, I gave my approval.

I anxiously awaited the takeoff of this Red Baron. The clandestine people proved their ability to move quickly, and within a few days, while the overhead systems were still producing nothing, the plane was in the air. Our first report was simply that it had taken off. Hours later the next report came in: it was overdue in returning to base. The next day we received the unhappy news that the plane had crashed in a yam patch, not as a result of antiaircraft fire over the battlefield, but because of poor flying by the pilot, who had survived. Since he had flown over the battle area before crashing, there was hope that we still might get our photos. In a few days the film was developed; it showed only forests and roads, no troops or weapons or battles. With the overhead reconnaissance people still not producing photos, my embarrassment was now acute. And when the $2 million bill came in, I wondered if it really had been an accident or whether we had been taken for a ride to finance a new plane for someone.

To make matters worse, it turned out that there were other Red Barons in the area. At about the same time our plane was over the battlefield, the local U.S. military attaché, a colonel, decided to get some photos on his own. He didn't know about the CIA's effort and didn't ask anyone's permission or even tell his superiors what he was doing. The colonel flew the aircraft assigned to him, resplendent with U.S. identification, right over the battlefield and took lots of good photographs. At least he knew how to point the camera. The colonel was unaware that it was the President who was asking for the photos; he was just demonstrating his initiative and hoping to earn himself some credit. With the photos in hand, however, he had second thoughts. Not having asked permission to fly this mission, he suggested to his superiors in the Defense Intelligence Agency that discretion was the better part of valor. They quietly filed the pictures away. I didn't know until months later that while I was frantically looking for photos, the DIA had them right in Washington.

As the weeks rolled by, I took a merciless beating, half-jocular, half-serious, from the President and the Vice President at every one of my twice-weekly briefings for them. Not only did I feel silly and frustrated, but we certainly weren't building confidence that we were even halfway competent. Impatient with shallow excuses at one point, I called a team of photographic experts into my office to explain what was wrong.

The explanation was simple. The overhead reconnaissance

people weren't even looking at the battlefield! It was a small war. In its early days, when their systems looked at the expected battlefield and found nothing, they hypothesized that the war consisted so far only of small-scale skirmishing hidden from overhead cameras by the forests. They felt they could prove their worth by giving warning of the arrival of tanks, personnel carriers, and other military equipment that might tip the outcome of the conflict. Thus, they turned the photo systems away from the battlefield and toward the approaches. This decision was made by a committee on photoreconnaissance that worked under John McMahon on the Intelligence Community staff. Perhaps the President's request had not penetrated down that far or, more likely, the committee in its own wisdom had decided that it knew better what would best serve the President. Their approach was not entirely illogical, but it did not give the President what he wanted. Once I issued instructions on precisely where to search, we had photographs almost immediately. It was more than a month after the President had asked for them. The photos didn't reveal much, because there wasn't much combat going on, but establishing even that was something. The whole experience humbled me. It also left me wondering what kind of a team I was leading. Here I was, the head of the whole Intelligence Community of the United States, and I couldn't produce a few pictures of a Mickey Mouse war.

There were three different organizations for photography involved in this disaster: the overhead reconnaissance systems managed from the Pentagon, the military attaché's aircraft managed by him in the country, and the CIA's civilian aircraft run by the CIA station chief. Not one performed well. The overhead reconnaissance committee responsible for coordinating the efforts wasn't responsive. Although the attaché and the CIA team operated from the same airfield, neither knew what the other was doing. The CIA took special precautions to avoid identification with the United States; the attaché flaunted his American identity. The three organizations lived in separate worlds.

At the same time I was having similar experiences with the organizations that operate the technical systems for electronic surveillance. Another way to follow the course of a battle is to listen for signals from military radars and communications systems.

Just knowing where the signals originate can often tell you where the lines of battles are drawn. Identifying the radars can tell you what kind of equipment is being employed. Listening to unclassified communications can sometimes tell you what the commanders are doing and planning.

Fortunately, the National Security Agency, which does most of our electronic surveillance work, had a listening post within reach of the battlefield. The war had hardly begun, however, before I was asked at the morning conference to approve the assembly and dispatch of an eavesdropping team. The idea was to move it even closer to the battle area than NSA's team in the hope of intercepting short-range signals. It seemed to me to be a long way to go at great expense for a small increment of intelligence, but I was new, so I agreed.

In a few weeks, as the war began to wind down, I became increasingly skeptical as to whether we should continue both the CIA team and the NSA operation. I had difficulty getting an evaluation of what the two were achieving. Electronic surveillance people are always entranced by their ability to intercept signals and want to do more, regardless of whether it is useful. And the analysts who use intercepts almost always tell you that the intercepts they've been given are valuable, because analysts have an infinite appetite for information. At one of the morning conferences I asked, "How much overlap is there between what NSA is doing and what we're doing? Is there really something important that the CIA team can do and NSA cannot?" The questions met with blank looks and stammers. There was no NSA representative present to speak for that agency, but it was clear that the CIA didn't know what the NSA was doing or how much duplication there was. I had spent enough time with intercept work in the Navy to be confident that we were not gaining much by this double effort, so I brought the CIA team home. I had learned that these two agencies could work on the same problem only a few hundred miles apart and not talk to each other. Why?

Because, just as with the photos, there was intense competition and little cooperation. Both the NSA and the CIA have been in electronic surveillance for a long time. The NSA generally deals with powerful, long-range signals. The antennae to intercept such signals can be placed at some distance from the origin of the signals. In placing its antennae, the NSA works with the military services, which also intercept tactical military signals in and around battlefields. Often, though, the signals we want to intercept are weak and an antenna must be placed quite close to them. We may need to use a CIA case officer or one of his agents to put it in place. Thus, both agencies are important to our intercept work, but there is a lot of overlap. The NSA is many times bigger than the CIA's electronic intercept component. Despite the very good justification behind the CIA's role in this work, the CIA was paranoid about being dominated, if not absorbed, by the NSA.

This small battlefield operation served as my introduction to the rivalries, overlapping jurisdictions, and lack of cooperation between the agencies responsible for technical collection. I simply didn't have the levers to pull to ensure a team effort. Whenever I tried to deal directly with the person who had the information I needed, it always seemed necessary to call for one more person. Often there wasn't time to do that. I was astounded, for instance, that I was expected to make decisions about renting Red Baron aircraft or dispatching a CIA intercept team at a morning conference when most of the people present were not qualified to compare the relative capabilities of overhead reconnaissance and civilian aircraft on hire. I constantly found myself confronted with advocates for one system, but never anyone who had analyzed the advantages and disadvantages of the alternatives. In my previous experience as a Fleet Commander, my operational staff weighed for me the relative merits of doing a particular task with submarines, surface ships, aircraft, or other means. They listened to the advocates of each, and then laid out the pros and cons. I tested their reasoning against mine and made the decision, comfortable that all reasonable alternatives had been examined and that my decision was being made as much as possible on fact, not emotion or partisan interests. In contrast, at the CIA, when deciding between technical intelligence systems, I personally was expected to think up the arguments against what every advocate presented; that is, to weigh on my own all possible alternatives. I certainly knew I could not translate military procedures, lock, stock, and barrel, into the world of intelligence collection. Yet I came away from this experience convinced that better teamwork was mandatory.

TWENTY

Intelligence Reporting Run Amuck

TECHNOLOGY HAS SO INCREASED the amount of information we can acquire that a whole new set of problems has resulted. On the one hand, analysts are inundated with data and must find ways to filter, store, and retrieve what is significant. On the other hand, analysts must be concerned with whether they are receiving everything that is collected in their area of interest; with whether the members of the Community — the CIA's espionage branch, the NSA, the Defense organizations responsible for overhead reconnaissance, the CIA's electronic surveillance component, the State Department's diplomatic-reporting system, the FBI's foreign intelligence branch, the Defense Intelligence Agency's attachés, the intelligence organizations of the military services, and the intelligence offices of the Departments of Treasury and Energy and the Drug Enforcement Agency — all share what they collect. An unfortunate example of information not being shared adequately came in the summer of 1979. It led to the most serious intelligence failure of my tenure. The failure to forecast the fall of the Shah earlier that year was of far less significance than our mishandling of the report that a "combat brigade" of Soviet troops was in Cuba. Had we predicted the Shah's fall from power even six or seven months ahead of time, there was little the United States could have done to prevent it. The reporting on the combat brigade, however, did play a direct part in scuttling the SALT II arms control treaty with the Soviet Union.

In June 1979 President Carter had met with President Brezhnev and signed the SALT II treaty. The Senate was preparing to hold its initial hearings on ratification when, on July 18, the *Washington Star* reported, "Sen. Richard Stone, D-Fla., yesterday said Soviet combat troops may be in Cuba in violation of the agreement that ended the Cuban missile crisis in 1962." The obvious implication was that if the Soviets could not be trusted to abide by an old agreement, the Senate should not ratify a new one with them. While SALT II was stalled over this issue, the Soviets invaded Afghanistan, in December 1979, and the treaty was scuttled. If the leak had been the truth, its effect on the treaty might have been justifiable. But it was not. The chain of events it triggered was unfortunate.

That chain actually began in the spring of 1979, when Brzezinski directed a review of all intelligence on Soviet military activities in Cuba. He was concerned about increasing Soviet and Cuban activities in Central America. In response, I told the Intelligence Community to review files for information that may have been overlooked. In early July the NSA came up with something old but new. What was old was a conclusion buried in its files that the Soviets in Cuba had a unit designated a "brigade." What was new was that this conclusion had never been shared with the rest of the Intelligence Community. Some of the clues the NSA used to reach this conclusion came from its own signals intelligence, some from photo and espionage information given it by other agencies.

The United States was well aware that the Soviets had a sizable training mission assisting the Cuban military. What the new White House–directed search did was remind the NSA that one unit in that training mission was referred to by the Soviets as a brigade. On the grounds that the term "brigade" is normally associated with combat units, rather than with training, the NSA jumped to the conclusion that the unit had a combat function. That was a big inference from a sparse fact or two. To emphasize its conclusion, it coined the term "combat brigade" to identify the unit as what it thought it was.

Next, the NSA published the conclusion as part of its daily distribution of new, raw intelligence data. When readers saw the designation "combat," they imagined a unit preparing to move out of Cuba and go to war in Central America. We were already worried about Nicaragua, whose government was on the verge of collapse. Because intelligence had never before reported a Soviet combat unit in Cuba, people assumed that the brigade had just arrived. It looked like a threatening move made by the Soviets just after they had signed a treaty with us.

The NSA report was hardly out before it found its way to Senator Stone. This was a deliberate leak by someone in the Executive Branch; the report had not been distributed to the Congress. Stone, with a large constituency of anti-Castro Cuban refugees, had reason to stay alert to developments in Cuba. He also had a constituency of conservative Floridians who disliked his having voted for the Panama Canal Treaty in 1978. To placate both constituencies as he faced an uphill battle for re-election in 1980 (a battle that he lost), he needed an opportunity to demonstrate that he could be tough on the Soviets and the Cubans.

On the morning of July 17, at a public hearing of the Senate Foreign Relations Committee, Stone alluded to the fact that he had intelligence on a previously undisclosed Soviet military presence in Cuba. Later that day in a secret hearing he pressed Harold Brown, myself, and several others for more details. Brown stated that "there is no evidence of any increase in the size of the Soviet military presence in Cuba over the past several years." I agreed with that. Brown went on, though, to assert that "intelligence does not warrant the conclusion that there are any other significant Soviet military forces in Cuba" besides a training group. This went a good bit further than I thought warranted, in view of the NSA's categoric assertion that there were Soviet combat forces in Cuba. The rest of the Intelligence Community, though, had just begun to check on the NSA's opinion.

In the meantime, the quotation appeared in the *Washington Star,* clearly leaked from the secret hearing. ABC's Ted Koppel covered the story a day later; John Scali on the same network discussed it a few days after that. Fortunately, it was not picked up anywhere else and faded from public attention. That gave us in the Intelligence Community some breathing space. We were glad to have that, because we were not only reviewing files, but had new intelligence that the brigade was going to participate in a special field exercise in early August, just a few weeks away. If we could watch that exercise, we might learn something new and more conclusive. We, of course, did just that. What we learned was that this unit was doing field training on its own, not simply training Cubans. That was a possible indication that it was preparing for combat. If this kind of training had taken place before, we had not detected it.

Our surveillance of the Soviet brigade's exercise was a satisfying contrast to the yam patch incident of two and a half years earlier. This time the teamwork was superb. One technical sensor gave the initial clue, a second was keyed to that, and so on, until we had a very good picture of what was taking place. The Intelligence Community could be justifiably proud of its performance. That pride strengthened the conviction that the NSA was correct in saying that this unit was different from anything we'd seen before. A few days after the exercise, the CIA published an independent evaluation saying that the unit was indeed a combat brigade.

The CIA's confirmation threw the administration into as much panic as can be generated in Washington in mid August, when most officials are away on vacation. Cyrus Vance, still on holiday, immediately recognized that when the word got out, the SALT treaty would be in trouble. He was right. The CIA's report was published in the widely distributed National Intelligence Daily. Because the subject was sensitive, the CIA took the unusual step of checking with the staff of the National Security Council before publishing. Approval was given. On August 29, less than a week after the item appeared in the NID, Clarence Robinson, a writer for *Aviation Week* magazine, phoned Richard Baker, on the staff of David D. Newsom, the Under Secretary of State, for confirmation of a story he had heard about a new Soviet military unit in Cuba. It was clear that he had a copy of the item from the NID. Baker told Robinson that the State Department had no comment.

Newsom immediately contacted Vance for permission to notify key members of Congress that the story was bound to come out soon. Congress was in recess, and the lawmakers, some of them overseas, had to be reached by phone. Newsom urged each one not to let the story get blown out of proportion. All of them took the news as a matter of course except Senator Frank Church of

Idaho (who had been chairman of the Senate committee that investigated allegations of intelligence abuses). Church was rather more liberal than his Idaho constituents. Like Stone, he was facing a tough battle for re-election in 1980 (which he also lost). He too was looking for ways to show that he could be more firm with the Soviets than most of the people of Idaho thought he was. He immediately saw that going public with the information Newsom had given him was a good means for doing that. He asked Newsom if he could. Vance, who was resigned to the item's imminent release and knew that he needed the support of Church, as Chairman of the Senate Committee on Foreign Relations, to get the SALT II treaty approved, acquiesced. Church called a press conference. *Aviation Week* had gone to press before Church's press release but, ironically, did not run the story. The editors apparently did not feel they had sufficient confirmation to print it. Thus, the administration had more time to deal with the problem than it realized. Vance could have restrained Church for a little while anyway.

Instead, Church at once took the position that the Senate should postpone debate on SALT II until the Soviets withdrew the brigade. More than a month was consumed in the attempt to work out some arrangement with the Soviets that would satisfy the Senate. The Soviets were not flexible. On October 2, unmoved by a major presidential speech on the subject the night before, the Senate voted to postpone consideration of SALT II until the President assured them that Soviet troops in Cuba were not engaged in a combat role. On December 25 the Soviet Union invaded Afghanistan, and all consideration of ratifying SALT II ceased. Whether the Senate would have ratified it if there had not been the delay over the combat brigade, we can only speculate.

The unnecessary panic in the White House and State Department about notifying Congress and mollifying Senator Church was harmful. The issue became hot before they were ready to handle it. It turned out that in 1963 the Kennedy administration had agreed to a Soviet brigade's remaining in the location where we identified the combat brigade in 1979. The White House and State Department had lost track of that. With some research into this history, State should have been able to present the intelligence to the Congress and the public in a less alarming light. The CIA and the NSA had in their files reports going back to the late

1960s that used the term "brigade" in connection with Soviet activities in Cuba. These too had been forgotten. As a piece or two of this old information emerged at the NSA, it was not illogical to conclude that the brigade had a combat function, especially after it was seen doing independent, combat-type training. That, however, was not the only possible conclusion that could have been drawn. It could have been a unit that provided an opportunity for the several thousand Soviet soldiers in Cuba to get occasional refresher courses in basic soldiering skills, such as driving tanks or firing artillery. Or the brigade could have been preparing to put on a demonstration for the Cubans. Our playing up this combat training exercise as something new was misleading. It was new to us, but such exercises might have been going on unnoticed. After all, we detected the one in August only because we had begun paying special attention to the brigade and because the Intelligence Community's collection effort had been particularly well coordinated in predicting and tracking the exercise.

The NSA bears most of the blame in the case of the Soviet brigade, but the rest of the Intelligence Community did not respond well once the NSA's report was out. Professional jealousy was at work. The NSA had got a scoop. The CIA and the others feigned a lack of interest in the report until it became obvious that it was too significant to ignore. That, I believe, is the only explanation for the CIA's dragging its feet in searching its files and discovering that it too knew there had been a brigade in Cuba for a long time. Most of all, though, everyone became defensive.

In part this was because analysts dug in their heels at what they perceived as pressure from policy-makers to play down the significance of the brigade. In part it was reluctance to admit error and weaken the Community's credibility in outsiders' eyes. The *Washington Post* in a retrospective on this crisis summed it up well: "Intelligence officials later explained that the 'Soviet combat brigade' was so described to distinguish it from a training outfit. Once the words had been repeated in internal documents with wide circulation and even public statements, 'we can't back off' an inquiring official was told."[1]

Why did the Intelligence Community present an incomplete

1. Don Oberdorfer, "Cuban Crisis Mishandled," *Washington Post,* October 16, 1979, p. 14.

picture on the brigade? The fundamental mistake was in the NSA's doing its own analysis. The next was in publishing it. The NSA is mandated to collect intelligence, not to analyze it. It must do enough analysis about what it has collected to decide what it should collect next. In intelligence jargon this level of analysis is termed "processing." Processing is regularly stretched by the NSA into full-scale analysis. In this instance, the abuse of processing was flagrant. The NSA's first report on the brigade was based on old information that had previously been processed. Having rediscovered it, the NSA had the responsibility to turn it over to the analysts at the CIA, the DIA, and State for evaluation. This is not purely a matter of bureaucratic turf. Although the NSA has excellent analysts to do its processing, it does not have the range of analytic talent needed for responsible analysis, nor all of the relevant data from the other collecting agencies needed for a comprehensive job. The NSA's analysis is bound to be biased in the direction of what signals intercepts tell, and is less likely to take account of photographic or human intelligence. The NSA and other collecting agencies also do not have the consistent contact with policy-makers that the analytic agencies do. In this case, it meant that the NSA was not sensitive to how the policy-makers would interpret the term "combat."

A dangerous side effect of the NSA's regular transgression from processing into analysis is that it leads to deliberate withholding of raw information from the true analytic agencies. The NSA wants to get credit for the scoop. Even when the NSA does release information promptly, it is frequently so digested that other analysts can't use it. The NSA excuses these practices by saying that it must protect its methods of collecting data. It is true that the NSA's collection techniques must be carefully protected and therefore that the information it gathers must be handled very carefully. If, for instance, a report of a particular telephone conversation ever got back to the two people who had it, they might conclude that their phones were tapped or that one of them was a traitor. On the other hand, if the NSA's report of that conversation was too sterile, analysts would not give it much credence. There is a fine line to be drawn here, but there is no question in my mind that the NSA regularly and deliberately draws that line to make itself look good rather than to protect secrets. Somehow the point does not get through at the NSA, any more than it does at the CIA's espionage branch, that it hurts the overall intelligence effort if a collecting agency does not properly share its information. And when it delays sharing until it can give the information directly to the decision-makers, we run into the very kind of problem we've seen with the Soviet brigade.

The NSA, with its military orientation, also collaborates with the military services to keep the CIA out of the analysis of major military issues. For instance, on joining the CIA I quickly recognized that the Agency was not up to date on the latest developments about some very secret aspects of the Soviet Navy. I went to the Secretary of the Navy, Graham Claytor, and explained the benefit to the Navy of having a second opinion on what was happening with the Soviet Navy. Graham immediately agreed to try to get the Navy to release more data to the CIA. Over a period of years, the two of us were able to open the door only a small crack. Many of the needed data were collected by Navy ships and aircraft, not by intelligence elements under the tasking control of the DCI. The material collected was therefore technically outside the DCI's jurisdiction. Some of it, though, was electronic intercept material processed by the NSA for the Navy. I directed Vice Admiral Bobby Inman, Director of the NSA, to share that information with the CIA. He said he could not, because the Navy contended that it was tactical, not national intelligence. The Navy had placed it in a special code word compartment to which the CIA did not have access. This, of course, was a bureaucratic ruse, and the loser was the United States. Not only is it highly desirable to have two views on any subject, but the Navy has vested interests that may well bias its interpretation. For example, if the performance of Soviet ships and submarines is seen as being poor, the Congress may feel that we don't need a big Navy after all; if the Soviet Navy is seen as being highly capable, the Congress may also not want a large Navy because it would be too vulnerable.

TWENTY-ONE

Unbalanced Competition in Analysis

NEXT THURSDAY we're going to have a meeting of the Special Coordinating Committee to review your proposed testimony to the Senate on the verifiability of SALT II, Stan," David Aaron announced to me in late August 1979. David, a young, bright Mondale protégé, was assistant to Zbig Brzezinski. He consistently used his agile mind to develop logical reasons for doing things the way the administration wanted them done. That was his job, and he was good at it. In this case he was worried that I would be too independent and say things in my testimony that would hurt the chances for ratification of SALT II. Brzezinski, Hamilton Jordan, and Lloyd Cutler (a prominent Washington attorney who had been brought into the White House especially to shepherd SALT II through the Senate) were also worried about me. They may have suspected that I shared the reservations of many military men that another arms control agreement with the Soviets would weaken resolve in the United States to maintain an adequate nuclear deterrent of our own. If so, they were wrong.

They were particularly concerned about what I would say, because my testimony was going to be important. As much as anything else, the fate of the SALT II treaty hinged on whether the Senate believed we could verify Soviet compliance. As Director of Central Intelligence, my testimony was bound to carry a great deal of weight, since it is through our intelligence apparatus that most checks are made. The treaty itself stipulated that neither side would interfere with the other's "technical means of verification," by which it meant primarily photographic satellites. Those satellites are the most important part of our system for keeping track of the Soviet's nuclear arsenal. Satellites tell us how many large intercontinental ballistic missiles (ICBMs), submarines, and bombers the Soviets have and a good deal about their size. We also use electronic intercepts, especially of telemetry. Telemetry is the means by which performance data generated inside a test missile are signaled back to its launch pad so that the engineers can monitor the missile's performance in flight. Because the data sent by telemetry can tell us a great deal about the missile's inner workings, they help us verify specifications covered in a treaty, like a missile's total carrying capacity, or "throw weight." Almost all other collection techniques are used as well, including human espionage. What is required for verification as much as anything, though, is great analytic skill in piecing together many small fragments of information. I was repeatedly impressed by the ability of CIA analysts to do this with enormous skill. My testimony would center on how effectively the Intelligence Community, using all these resources, could detect and deduce what the Soviets were doing.

Specifically, that meant testifying about our ability to check on a whole series of individual treaty provisions. For instance, there is very little doubt in our minds about how many large, 200,000-pound ICBMs the Soviets have; they are hard to hide from satellite photography. But it is more difficult to determine whether each of those ICBMs has one, ten, or thirty warheads hidden inside. We cannot x-ray the missile's nose cone from a satellite. We can watch it being tested and we can deduce from other indicators, like its estimated throw weight, how many warheads it is capable of carrying. We may, then, say that we have better than 95 percent confidence that we know how many ICBMs the Soviets have, but considerably less than 95 percent confidence that we know how many total ICBM warheads they have if they have placed more warheads on their missiles than allowed. For every provision of the treaty there is a similar confidence level for detecting small-, medium-, and large-scale cheating.

The White House people were alarmed that I was planning to tell the Senate just what those confidence numbers were. It was not so much that the numbers would be low as that I would have to disclose that there were many ways in which the Soviets might be able to cheat. The only means I had for calculating whether the Soviets could cheat was to figure out the different ways they might attempt it. I had a team of experts pretend they were malicious, scheming Soviets and think up techniques for cheating. One idea they came up with to hide the construction of new ICBM silos was to build them inside large buildings and plan to fire the missiles through the roofs. I was prepared to say that I had X percent confidence that they could not secretly build more than a hundred missile silos inside buildings without our detecting what was going on, and that our confidence would be X + Y percent by the time they got to two hundred. Some such schemes for cheating were almost impossible to carry out and others would benefit the Soviets very little. Still, there was no way I could give a reliable view of our ability to check on cheating if I didn't study every such possibility thoroughly. What worried David Aaron and others was that the senators might gain the impression that cheating was highly probable because there were so many theoretical opportunities. I could see that that was a risk, but it would be small compared with the risk of undermining the treaty if some opponent of it thought of a way to cheat that I had not addressed and raised with the Congress. The credibility of our whole position on verification could be questioned.

Still another alarm went off in the White House over a distinction I emphasized between "monitoring" and "verifying" the treaty. Monitoring is the gathering and evaluating of information about Soviet military programs related to the treaty, including programs that are forbidden. Verification is our determining whether those Soviet programs comply with the treaty sufficiently for us to consider the treaty intact. Many treaty provisions are not black or white; that is, it is not simply a question of whether or not the Soviets are complying. That's largely because there is often ambiguity in the wording of the agreement (and without those ambiguities we or the Soviets might have rejected the treaty). It is also the case that sometimes there is uncertainty in our measurements. We may, for instance, be able to measure only to plus or minus 10 percent on some values. If, then, we should detect the Soviets "cheating" by 10 percent or less, we may not know whether the discrepancy is theirs or ours. Verification, then, involves judgments about the interpretation of the treaty, about how much we can count on the accuracy of our monitoring systems, and about how serious it would be for the United States if there were cheating at various levels. Let's go back to the example of Soviet cheating by building ICBMs inside buildings. How serious would it be if they added a hundred ICBMs before we could be 95 percent confident of detecting it? That's a question that can be answered only by political leaders, because the answer depends on an assessment of how much advantage the Soviets would get if they could increase the number of their ICBMs by a hundred. And what we could do if we suddenly found they had done that.

Such matters are judgments about what combination of enemy moves and our countermoves will leave our country safe. If, as DCI, I made the judgment that a 95 percent probability of detecting the construction of a hundred ICBMs inside buildings constituted "adequate verification," I would be taking sides on a policy issue. What constitutes security for our country and what warrants our taking some risks in return for the benefits of a treaty are not matters of intelligence. The imperative of keeping intelligence separate from policy ruled out my making such judgments.

In the case of SALT II, President Carter heard from me how well we could monitor the treaty. Then he weighed the risks of possible Soviet cheating against the benefits of the treaty and decided that it was adequately verifiable. If I had supported his judgment in my testimony to the Senate, I could have been suspected of coloring my evaluation of our monitoring capabilities to support the President's policy decision on verifiability. Since verification was the heart of the Senate debate, any doubt about my objectivity in assessing our monitoring capabilities could have doomed the treaty. Thus, although I personally supported the treaty and believed it was adequately verifiable, I could not risk saying so, even in private, lest someone quote me in public.

The White House didn't see it this way at all; hence this meeting of the SCC, a subcommittee of the National Security Council, to review my testimony. At a personal level, it was insulting to an agency head to have his testimony subjected to this kind of advance scrutiny. The excuse was that, though I was the administration's spokesman on verification, others would be questioned on it also, and we should understand each other's views lest avoidable contradictions develop. But the real reason was clearly to get me under control and to push me to testify that the treaty was adequately verifiable.

The treaty was the administration's premier item of foreign policy at this point and the White House was doing everything possible to ensure that it didn't fail. I felt equally strongly that I must not let myself be pressured. I considered it my responsibility to give the Senate just as complete and objective a view of our monitoring capabilities as I had given the President. In our government, both the President and the Senate must decide on whether a treaty is in the national interest. Both needed objective information on whether we could detect Soviet cheating. If I slanted my testimony to help the administration sell SALT II, I would be hurting the ability of Congress to play its proper role.

I weathered the SCC meeting because I had done more extensive homework on monitoring than anyone else in the room and because I stubbornly insisted that the Senate needed my estimates of where the Soviets could cheat. In fact, once the senators had grasped the monitoring data, verification ceased to be the main issue. They understood that there were many uncertainties and that much cheating could go on, undetected. They also understood that no single case of possible undetected cheating could significantly affect the balance of military power. Any form of wholesale cheating that would upset the strategic balance could be detected quite early. Although he never said so directly, I suspected that the President was thoroughly annoyed by my stand on what I would and would not say about verification. His staff had not given him both sides of the story. The ending was happy, though, and when the verification issue had been defused, the President and Vice President both thanked me profusely.

Pressures like this on the DCI to make intelligence support policy are not unusual, but they are almost always blatant. That's because they have to come from someone without authority over the DCI. His only boss is the President. If a President ever pressured a DCI to bias his intelligence reports, the DCI would have no option other than to resign. Pressures on the DCI by outsiders, then, have to be those of persuasion, not threat. In contrast, the chiefs of departmental intelligence agencies, such as the Defense Intelligence Agency, can be pressured by many different individuals. The implied threat is that the boss (that is, the Secretary of Defense or one of his assistants) will take it out on you if you do not fall into line. Policy-makers exert such pressures because they are eager not to have some intelligence report floating around that can be used to torpedo their programs or policies. One way to ensure against analysts giving in to such pressures is to get separate opinions on important subjects, in the hope that a conclusion reached under pressure will stand out like a sore thumb.

One can get several opinions by engaging outside consultants or advisory panels to review analytic work. Or even by having some analytic work duplicated by outside contractors, which may produce a fresh viewpoint. Either kind of outside scrutiny can be very useful, though there are limits. Even though outsiders may be given adequate security clearances, insiders always feel they have a more authoritative view because of their greater intimacy with the fuller range of secrets.

Thus, the principal source of second opinions has always been competitive analysis within the Intelligence Community. That's achieved by having as many of the analytic agencies of the Intelligence Community as have competence on a topic pitted against each other. If the topic is political trends, the State Department's Bureau of Intelligence and Research would probably lead the analytic effort, but the CIA and the DIA would also present views. If the subject is economics, the CIA would have the strongest capabilities and would guide the study, but the Departments of State, Treasury, and Energy would also participate. On military matters the DIA would be in charge, but the CIA would play a major role, and the State Department would join on nontechnical issues. To reap the benefits of such analytic competition, we permit each organization to publish any of its own analyses that it wants. For instance, the CIA, the DIA, and State each publishes a daily report interpreting the latest intelligence reports. In addition, competition in analysis is formalized in intelligence reports that are collaborative efforts of the entire Intelligence Community, the National Intelligence Estimates (NIEs).

NIEs are written jointly by as many of the intelligence agencies as have competence in a given subject. They are coordinated by a modest-sized staff of analysts known as the National Intelligence Council, which is part of the Intelligence Community organization, not of the CIA. The ostensible purpose of this group is to present decision-makers with the Intelligence Community's best view on important topics. Without some such vehicle, a President might find separate pieces of analysis on the same topic arriving on his desk at different times. In a sense, that's competition in analysis, but it needs to be organized. In the NIE process, the Community attempts to resolve its differences before it presents an analysis to the President or whoever else is concerned. When it cannot resolve differences, an NIE at least lays out the differing views in one place.

The number of NIEs published each year varies with the inclination of the DCI and the state of world affairs. A topsy-turvy world may call for more NIEs, though they generally concentrate on long-range problems; interpretation of immediate events is left to departmental reporting. Topics may be the balance of strategic nuclear forces between the United States and the USSR, the conventional military balance in Europe, the prospects for improvement in relations between the Soviet Union and China, the outlook for cohesiveness within the Atlantic Alliance, or the significance of the third world's international debt problems.

The entire Community comments on the drafts as they are produced. Then the heads of all of the analytic agencies meet in what is known as the National Foreign Intelligence Board to discuss each NIE. This is an opportunity for each agency head to try to convince the DCI of his viewpoint when there are differences. In the end the DCI must decide which view the NIE endorses and which dissenting views are also represented. Thus, though the NIE process resembles the work of a committee, the final product is that of the DCI, whose opinion always prevails. It has to, or it would be one of committee compromise, too watered down to be of value.

In fact, the value of NIEs is bound to be limited, because writing them requires so many compromises. There is a natural tendency in any process like this one to attempt to narrow differences and end up with a consensus report. After endless hours of arguing over an idea, or even over a word or two, people tend to compromise simply to get on with the drafting. Compromises, though, can often produce a wrong result. If one group has evidence that a war will start on Monday and another that it will be Friday, a compromise on Wednesday, for which there is no evidence, is almost bound to be wrong. Intelligence analysis heavily flavored by compromise is apt to contain conclusions that are so innocuous that they are of no value to the decision-maker. And the NIE, though an important vehicle for expressing competitive views, is a costly and inefficient one, because so much valuable analytic talent is consumed in negotiating rather than in analyzing. If NIEs are worth the effort, it is because they force healthful interaction within the Intelligence Community, not so much because they produce useful material for policy-makers to read. For instance, in disagreements, the NIE process forces analysts who hold contrary positions to explain them to their peers. Such a process improves not only the NIE in question, but the quality of the long-term analytic effort.

The most valuable NIEs are those which present differences of substance clearly. Alternative views can be presented and evaluated. The one or two key points on which a difference of opinion hinges will, it is hoped, have been identified so that the reader can apply his own judgment. An NIE may state that "the DIA believes we would have X days of warning of a Warsaw Pact surprise attack on NATO with conventional forces, the CIA believes it would be Y days, and the difference between the two is that the DIA is relying on overhead reconnaissance photography to tell us when additional troops move forward, whereas the CIA is counting on informants inside the Eastern bloc." The reader would then weigh his confidence in photography against spies and decide whether he wanted to count on X or Y days of warning, or something in between.

Sometimes such differing views are best presented as part of the text; sometimes as footnotes. Some Presidents, such as President Reagan, I suspect, will want a straightforward conclusion set forth by the DCI with as few dissenting views as possible. In such a situation, the dissenting views are best presented in footnotes. The reader can easily ignore them if he wants, but they are available for those who want to study them. Jimmy Carter wanted to read every detail of each difference and come up with his own conclusion. For someone like him, it is best to include dissenting opinions right in the text of the NIE, alongside the DCI's view. However dissent is presented, it will be useful only if it is directed to the right issues. Unfortunately, it was my experience that many of the differences raised by the agencies of the Defense Department in writing NIEs were ones that affected only Defense's interests, such as whether or not the intelligence report would support or hurt the rationale for buying some piece of military hardware. A debate of that sort may be of little importance to the President, the Secretary of State, or others.

The major weakness of the NIEs, however, derives from the different levels of competence of the analytic agencies, primarily the CIA, the DIA, and the State Department's Bureau of Intelligence and Research (INR). The INR is much smaller than either of its competitors, but in my view it has always done the best political analysis. In part this is because it is close to its customers in the State Department and provides analysis that directly supports their needs. In contrast, the CIA's customers are everywhere in the Washington area except at Langley; that is, they are in the White House, the Departments of State, Defense, and Treasury, and elsewhere. Thus, the CIA's analysis tends to have an academic flavor. Occasionally, because of the proximity to its customers who make policy, the INR has been biased in favor of some State Department policy position, but it is remarkably free of the influence of policy considerations.

A greater problem, I found, was the tendency of the INR to attempt to offset an expected DIA bias. Both the INR and the CIA expected the DIA to exaggerate the Soviet Union's military strength and intentions. I do not mean to imply that the DIA deliberately distorted the facts. But when data about whether the Soviets had a particular military capability were inconclusive, the DIA would always credit them with having it. Or when we knew that the Soviets had a certain capability but did not know how good it was, the DIA would "mirror-image" it; that is, they would assume that the Soviets' capability was just as good as ours. One way or another, just by calling all the shots on the high side, the DIA would usually come up with a more menacing view of Soviet military potential than did the nonmilitary agencies. Both the

CIA and the INR tended to exaggerate in the other direction in order to compensate. Other than that, the INR's only serious weakness was that it did not have sufficient manpower to cover all of the topics on which its views would have been helpful. Even today, it could use more staff to advantage, but wherever it does have the talent to compete, it can play a valuable role.

The CIA has adequate resources to cover all of the topics of NIEs. It does not have an obvious policy bias, since the Agency has no policies to protect, though many people believe there is an institutional bias. James Schlesinger, several years after his brief stint as DCI, stated, "In fact, the [CIA's] intelligence directorate tends to make a particular type of error systematically in close harmony with the prevailing bias in the intellectual community."[1]

Schlesinger was joining with most critics of the CIA's analysis in saying that there is a bias toward the liberal viewpoint or the view in vogue in the academic community. I found that this was the case occasionally in political analysis, but there were about as many instances of bias in the opposite direction. For instance, in military analysis the CIA had a reputation for underestimating enemy strength. It has done that, but more because it knew that the DIA would almost always do the opposite than for any ideological reason. There are also areas of military analysis where I found the CIA inclined to overestimate simply because it had been so criticized for its past underestimations. In short, biases or fixations are bound to develop in an organization like the CIA, but I believe that they are changing biases, based on personalities, on the Agency's past record, and on expected reactions in the DIA, not on a permanent institutional outlook. That, and the capability of the CIA to cover well almost all areas of analysis, make the CIA the key player in the use of competitive analysis. Only in those areas where, as noted earlier, the military and the NSA contrive to exclude the CIA from the necessary data, is the CIA's analysis not likely to be competitive.

The much more serious problem that I saw with competitive analysis was the inability of the DIA to measure up to the competition. There were two reasons for this: an insufficient number of

1. Testimony before the Senate Select Committee on Intelligence, Book I, p. 76, February 2, 1976.

competent people and an inability to withstand Defense Department pressures to support its policies. The DIA was formed from scratch in 1964. The idea was that each of the four intelligence arms of the military services would be reduced in size in order to provide the staff for the DIA. That was done, but the services hung on to as many of their best people as they could and gave the remainder to the DIA. In addition, in less than four years the service intelligence organizations had grown back to at least their former size and were attracting the better people. Military officers, in particular, prefer to be assigned to their service intelligence organization, because that does more for their prospects for promotion. Also, the DIA is a very complex bureaucracy. It works for the Secretary of Defense, the Joint Chiefs of Staff, and the DCI. It is staffed partly by military officers, who rotate in and out and have natural loyalties to their service, and in part by civilians, who have great influence because they have permanent assignments. The DIA is bound to be pushed and pulled by these competing demands and influences. As a result, military intelligence officers find the DIA's internal politics stifling. As long as there are four separate service intelligence organizations that command higher loyalty and are not so bound up in bureaucracy, the better analysts are going to avoid going to the DIA. In my view, only if the service intelligence organizations are disbanded permanently is there hope for measurably improving the DIA's capabilities. There is no serious need for those four separate organizations that the DIA could not fill.

The pressures of policy influence are an even more serious hazard to the DIA's playing a competitive role. In the DIA, the rule of intelligence's independence from policy runs headlong into the more basic rule of the American military, responsiveness to command. The military officer feels free to express his views to his commander, but when the commander has decided, the subordinate stops questioning and supports his superior in every way possible. The military commander has the final word once he has made up his mind. Thus, the military intelligence officer who attempts to interject analyses that run counter to the decisions of his superiors risks being considered disloyal. It is difficult to overstate the amount of pressure the military hierarchy can impose to get its way; it can even pressure military intelligence specialists to abandon the code of clear, unbiased reporting of facts in favor of the military one of loyal support of the commander's decision.[2]

It would hardly be fair not to point out that the budgetary process in our country virtually forces the military to use intelligence to overstate the threats they must be ready to counter. If each military service does not exaggerate the threat, it is almost certain to have its budget cut. The issues of military intelligence estimates, then, are issues of bureaucratic budget politics as well as of intelligence.

Largely as a result of these budget pressures, I found the DIA's participation in the NIE process less than useful. When the DIA disagreed with parts of an NIE, it was almost impossible to get an explanation. I always wanted to place the DIA reasons for dissent right alongside my view in the body of the NIE. What I hoped for in a case like the previous example I cited was something like "The DIA does not agree that we will have Y days of warning of a surprise attack in Europe, because it does not believe the CIA's network of agents can transmit warnings in a sufficiently timely manner. Instead, it believes that we will have to wait until overhead reconnaissance conclusively reveals the movement of forces into forward positions, but that will be only X days from the initiation of hostilities." What I consistently received instead was something like "The DIA disagrees with the conclusion that we will receive Y days of warning and believes we will receive only X."

An actual example of this was a running battle I had with the DIA over estimates of Soviet strategic nuclear forces. It began a few weeks after I took office. I was presenting the CIA's annual briefing on this subject to the Armed Services Committee of the House. I methodically laid out the number of ICBMs of various types that the Soviets and the United States each had, and of

2. An example of this came to light in February 1985, during the testimony in the suit brought by General William C. Westmoreland against CBS TV. As reported on p. 1 of the *Washington Post* on February 18 by Eleanor Randolph, "According to sources close to the case, some of Westmoreland's friends, attorneys and financial backers suggested that he drop the case after testimony last week by retired Army colonel Gains B. Hawkins, who was Westmoreland's chief of Order of Battle estimates. Hawkins said that in 1967 when he told Westmoreland about high enemy-troop estimates, the general called the new numbers 'politically unacceptable.' As a result, Hawkins said, he ordered his intelligence officials to cut their enemy estimates, as the CBS broadcast had said." The case was, in fact, dropped.

bombers, submarines, and so on. An intelligent young congressman from New York, Tom Downey, interrupted. He said that all these numbers weren't very helpful. What he wanted to know was what each side could do with these weapons. He asked if I had studied the formula for measuring the potential destructiveness of any nuclear weapon.

There is a formula for describing what each existing nuclear arsenal could theoretically destroy, in terms of hardened targets that take a lot of power to kill or of cities that almost any nuclear weapon can devastate. Using that formula, we could compare our arsenal and the Soviets' in terms of what each could do if unleashed against hard targets or cities. That was much more useful than a simple statistical comparison of numbers of weapons. We could calculate how much of our nuclear potential would survive if the Soviets conducted a surprise attack on us that destroyed all of our missiles, submarines, and bombers they could locate. Then we could compare what we would have left after absorbing that blow with what the Soviets would have remaining, considering all the weapons they had used in the initial attack on us, again in terms of capability to destroy either hardened targets or cities. This was just what Downey wanted. It showed clearly what sort of advantage each side had under different circumstances. Unfortunately, this kind of analysis did not produce the answers the Pentagon wanted in order to justify its programs, most specifically the MX ICBM. And so a fight began.

For the next three years the DIA argued over and over again that this analytic technique was invalid. They never said why, but one year they did a thorough study of their own to prove their point. Unfortunately for them, the results were nearly identical with the CIA's. When I asked them to put those results in that year's NIE on the strategic balance and compare the differences with the Downey-inspired approach, they declined. They fell back on an old canard: that my preferred form of analysis was a "net assessment," which was beyond the proper role of intelligence.

Net assessment is military jargon for a comparison of the capabilities of some category of U.S. military forces with those of another power. Inside the Pentagon there is a strict rule that intelligence organizations make such comparisons only in numbers of units, not in any other measure of capability. That's because the policy-makers are dominant there. They don't want intelligence people to compare our tanks with those of the Soviet Union in a way that suggests that American tanks are better than the Soviets'. That could lead Congress to conclude that we do not need to buy more tanks, even if we have fewer than the Soviets have. It certainly is outside the proper sphere of intelligence to pass judgment on a policy issue such as how many tanks we need, but it is not helpful to talk only about numbers of tanks when we have many data for comparing the capabilities of ours with those of the Soviets'. Military policy-makers feel safer, though, if intelligence reports are limited to static comparisons of numbers of units or items of equipment, but they do make dynamic comparisons on their own through the use of war games.

A war game not only compares what various forces can do in combat; it uses players on both sides to make decisions and referees aided by computers to judge outcomes. I agree that intelligence organizations should not conduct their own war games in which they decide what tactics our military commanders and their opponents would employ and what the final results may be. But in between war games and static comparisons there is legitimate room for quasi-dynamic comparisons by the Intelligence Community of U.S. and enemy capabilities. For example, there can be a purely static comparison of U.S. and Soviet strategic nuclear forces that counts only numbers and types of weapons on each side. There also can be the quasi-dynamic comparison I described that compares the theoretical capability of both arsenals to destroy hard targets and cities in a surprise attack and after absorbing a surprise attack. Or there can be a war game that hypothesizes a specific war situation and estimates exactly what the Soviets and we would do and what the destruction would be on both sides.

The problem is where to draw the line on intelligence analysis. The more factors a quasi-dynamic analysis takes into account, the more it moves toward being a war game. It is easy for the military to believe they should draw the line so that there is no chance that an intelligence analysis can come to a conclusion that would jeopardize their programs and policies. That's just what they do. They can clearly impose their will on military intelligence. Thus, it was always a struggle to get the military's cooperation if the CIA intended to do more than static comparisons. We made progress as time went by, especially as the result of cooperation from General David Jones, then Chairman of the Joint Chiefs of Staff.

But unless it is directed from the top by someone like Jones, the military will work their will by refusing to give the CIA sufficient data on U.S. forces to allow the Agency to make useful comparisons. The withholding of data on the Soviet Navy I noted previously is a case in point. Another is the case of a study by the CIA of Soviet electronic countermeasure capabilities I once received. My first question was "Do the Soviets have the capability to counter our electronics?" The answer was "We don't know enough about our own electronics capabilities to tell. We only know what the Soviets can do, but not how effective it would be!" That kind of study is not very helpful and shows why the CIA's ability to do military analysis is much less than it should be.

On some military subjects there is no useful competitive analysis, because the DIA's work is vitiated by policy considerations and the CIA's is not much better, owing to a lack of information about U.S. capabilities. The record also shows that inside the military the DIA seldom disputes assessments by the individual services in their areas of specialty. That is to avoid political wrangling. The nation is badly exposed when only the U.S. Navy studies some aspects of the Soviet Navy, or the Air Force the Soviet Air Force.

A new technique of competitive analysis was attempted in 1976. This was the so-called A Team, B Team competition. Two analytic groups were organized to study U.S. and Soviet strategic nuclear capabilities. Team A was the CIA's normal analytic group on this subject. Team B was composed of outsiders with a right-wing ideological bent. The intention was to promote competition by polarizing the teams. It failed. The CIA team, knowing that the outsiders on B would take extreme views, tended to do the same in self-defense. When B felt frustrated over its inability to prevail, one of its members leaked much of the secret material of the proceedings to the press. My reluctance to use this team approach was criticized, but I believe that pitting extremists against one another can only lead to poor results. Instead, extremist views should be permitted to emerge from the analytic effort and be included as a minority view in the report.

TWENTY-TWO

The Reluctant Team

WHEN THE CONGRESS in 1947 decided to centralize intelligence under a DCI, it made no provision for any staff to support him. In fact, the new role was too vaguely conceived for anyone to know what help the DCI would need. The first centralizing effort was the creation of a board comprising the heads of all the agencies involved in intelligence. The demands for stronger control increased, however, as technical collection systems demanded close supervision and as Presidents wanted to be certain that they were getting the best answer available from all the Intelligence Community's resources when they turned to the DCI.

First the board developed committees to coordinate the collection of intelligence. It also developed procedures for debating the different interpretations of the various analytic agencies. And, as a result of the Schlesinger study of 1971, the DCI was given responsibility for putting together the Intelligence Community budget and a committee to advise him. In the beginning of this progression, the DCI was forced to rely heavily on the only staff he controlled, that of the CIA. In early 1962, President Kennedy directed DCI McCone to make a stronger effort to ensure that the Community as a whole was working on the most important intelligence issues. To do this, McCone created a small, separate staff with representatives from all agencies assigned to it on loan.

Then in 1976 President Ford directed that the Intelligence Community staff have its own funding, its own building not far from the White House, an increase in total staff from 163 to 222, and more staff from agencies other than the CIA, including a good number who were hired by the Community staff, not lent to it. The umbilical to the CIA was severed. Thus, when I arrived the stage was set for a clearer distinction between the DCI's role as head of the CIA and his role as coordinator of the Community. A bigger role for the DCI in the Community meant, though, that a power struggle was inevitable. Whatever additional authority the DCI and his Community staff were to assume had to be given up by the agencies themselves. A good example of how little the Community agencies were under the control of the DCI and how they could fight any expansion of the DCI's role was the reaction to my attempt to revise the code word system.

I raised the problem of code words with the Community leadership in August 1978. We were sitting in shirtsleeves in easy chairs around the big, empty fireplace of a rustic cabin not far from Washington. Once every six months or so I gathered the heads of the major intelligence agencies for a day-and-a-half retreat there. Present were Frank Carlucci; John Koehler, the new deputy for the Intelligence Community; Vice Admiral Bobby Inman, Director of the NSA; Air Force Lieutenant General Gene Tighe, Director of the Defense Intelligence Agency; and the people who ran the overhead reconnaissance programs from the Pentagon. We weren't there just to solve specific problems, but to exchange ideas and discuss common concerns.

I raised the topic of code words because of my growing uneasiness with security. In the past year and a half the Boyce-Lee case had confirmed poor security in industry, Kampiles proved the same with the CIA, and a flood of leaks showed how little attention many employees were paying to the security rules. Unscheduled, surprise retesting by polygraph at the CIA had revealed that employees were taking sensitive, classified documents home at night. Although they did so to put in extra hours of work, it was a dangerous and prohibited practice. They were also ignoring prescribed procedures when taking documents out of CIA Headquarters to official meetings; they were constantly breaking the rules about not reproducing documents with certain classifications; and they were not keeping accurate records when highly classified documents were transferred from one person or office to another. In a word, the whole system had become sloppy.

I turned to Inman and asked him under what circumstances we put the code word Bluebird on a document. After a bit of hesitation, he replied, "When the following three conditions have been met," and he listed them.

That's what I had expected him to say. "But, Bobby, when the first two occur, we use code word Lark, and when the third occurs, Robin. Why do we also need Bluebird?"

Inman hesitated a little longer this time. That was unusual. At forty-seven, Inman was a bright and articulate young three-star admiral and a specialist in intelligence. He was as well informed about the U.S. intelligence apparatus as any person I knew. I didn't press him, because it was clear that he didn't know. Although I had asked this detailed question hoping to make just this point, I had expected it to take a lot more burrowing.

I then turned to Gene Tighe, also an intelligence specialist. "Gene, the Navy has code word Raven and the Air Force the code word Heather. As far as I can see they are used when the same conditions exist. What's the reason for two different code words?"

Tighe was a thorough professional. His strength was that he had been in intelligence since World War II and knew all its ins and outs, and he could step back and see the broad aspects of issues. His weakness was that he could be very parochial in supporting Defense Department interests. In this case, though, he was quite straightforward. "Probably none," he replied.

I had started this discussion because, after a year and a half in office, I realized I was not paying much attention to the myriad code words I saw every day on the top of documents. Such code words are over and above the three basic security classification labels of confidential, secret, and top secret. Every classified document must have one of those. What they mean is defined by a presidential order. Code words are not prescribed anywhere. Yet they effectively supersede the President's directive because they impose even more rigorous standards for handling classified materials. An intelligence document that is top secret, but not further restricted by a code word, is considered barely classified. On sensitive documents there were likely to be as many as four or five different code words, like Bluebird or Lark, indicating the particular sensitivity of a document and establishing certain rules for the handling of its contents.

The primary rule of all code words is that you cannot discuss the material in a code word document with anyone who has not also been granted access to material with that code word. At my level I could usually count on my staff to make sure that only people with the proper clearances were involved in my discussions on code word matters. What worried me, though, was that because the system was difficult to understand, others who didn't have the assistance I had might not be observing the rules faithfully. The root of the problem, as I saw it, was that the number of code words had proliferated as rapidly as had the new technical systems. Code words overlapped; even when several code words were originated by the same agency, there was tremendous duplication. In the case I mentioned to Tighe, the Air Force was excluding the Navy from its information in one area, and the Navy, for its part, was doing the same to the Air Force.

It soon became apparent that none of the group understood what material deserved which code word or what the rules were for handling documents with different code words. I suspected that the only people who understood the rules were the secretaries who took out their rubber stamps and decided how to mark up the documents — at least, I hoped they understood.

I suggested that we study the entire code word system. There was little argument, though there was a lot of skepticism that there was any practical way to unscramble this mess. I asked a retired Air Force general, John Vogt, to head a small group to do the job. I knew him as a tough but fair man who got things done. By placing a general in charge I hoped to reassure the military that their interests would be taken into account, since many of the code words originated in agencies of the Department of Defense.

Vogt and his group produced an excellent plan, named Apex, for a whole new system. It was based on two principles: as much information as possible would be downgraded to top secret, secret, confidential, or even unclassified. And the number of code words would be sharply reduced.

Apex would be a simple system, with just five code words instead of something like the fifty that then existed. We hoped that people would comply with a system they could understand. A key point, though, was that under Apex the DCI would control access to all sensitive information. The collection agencies had that authority under the existing system, but they often exercised it in ways that unduly limited distribution to the analysts. There is no question that they were cautious for fear of compromising the sources of their information. Yet information must reach the analysts, and, through them, the policy-makers, if it's to be of any use to the country. Decisions on how to balance these two interests had to be made by someone with an understanding of the need for both security and the use of information. The DCI and his Intelligence Community staff were the only ones who were not part of either a collection or an analytic agency. Hence, they were the ones who could take a broad view of this balance between secrecy and dissemination. In this respect, Apex would have been a significant step forward. It would also have been a significant extension of the DCI's authority.

I knew I had to tread gingerly. In one of our later discussions on this subject, Inman flatly stated that he opposed my taking charge of the code word problem, because he viewed it as exceeding the authority of the DCI. He was wrong. It was right in line with the National Security Act of 1947, which makes the DCI responsible for protecting all intelligence sources and methods of collecting data. Harold Brown gave support to the program, and with Harold on board, I went to the President, who signed a written directive ordering that Apex replace the existing mélange of code words. We then started the immense task of revising manuals, instructing thousands of people in the new system, briefing industrial contractors, and taking dozens of other needed steps.

As it became apparent that Apex was not just an academic exercise, but was actually going into effect, resistance began to grow. The tactic was delay. The many new manuals and directives were to be completed in July 1980. We would then begin phasing in Apex. The NSA simply did not try to meet that goal. It promised delivery in January 1981. It gambled and won. When Jimmy Carter was defeated and I was replaced, Apex died immediately.

The Apex effort was not entirely wasted, however. Anticipating Apex, the agencies in charge of photoreconnaissance shifted a good deal of their product out of code word categories into top secret, secret, and confidential. Wider distribution has meant that more analysts benefit from our expensive overhead reconnaissance systems. The NSA and the CIA's espionage branch, in contrast, gave up very little. Their combined resistance and their ability to defy a written order of the President with which the Secretary of Defense expressly agreed demonstrated graphically how much the Intelligence Community can still be governed by strong partisan feelings. It's only fair to say that the concerns of Apex's opponents for the secrecy of their operations were genuine. They felt more comfortable controlling the distribution of their secrets than trusting the DCI to do it using an untried Apex system. Yet it is also true that protection of bureaucratic turf was an even more important factor.

Interestingly, though, there was not the same bureaucratic resistance to the extension of the DCI's authority into the intelligence budget. The budget question is a complicated one because each intelligence agency's budget request must be included with its parent department's budget: the NSA's money is in the Defense Department's budget; the INR's in the State Department's; and the CIA's budget is hidden by being spread out in a number of departmental budgets. Intelligence budgeting is done that way in part because the departments manage their own intelligence agencies, even though the DCI directs their operations, and in part because it is a way to conceal from our enemies how much we are spending on various areas of intelligence. We know that they could spend commensurate amounts countering the programs we are working hardest on, and we don't want them to have that advantage. Still, someone must set an overall priority for what these individual budgets are to accomplish and ensure that they don't overlap each other more than is reasonable. In the closing minutes of my very first meeting with the President, I had sensed that there was such a need and had made the plea for more authority over the Community budget.

I had not realized it at the time, but it was only in the last half-dozen years that the DCI had been given any say at all in budgetary matters. Jim Schlesinger, in his study of intelligence at the Office of Management and Budget in 1971, had recommended giving the DCI more budgetary authority. Until then the Intelligence Community staff monitored, but did not influence, the individual budget submissions. The Schlesinger study led to the creation of a formal budget committee to review and adjust the budgets. The DCI, as chairman of that committee, at least had a forum in which to persuade the various agencies to adjust their budgets in ways he thought would better serve the nation. In the end, though, he had no authority to impose his views and had to work out the best compromise he could. My first budget was prepared in this manner. It ended up being largely a summation of what the individual agencies had developed on their own.

President Carter lived up to his promise to correct this situation. He abolished the committee and gave the DCI the authority to submit the budget for the entire Community. His Executive Order also provided that a subcommittee of the National Security Council would review the budget before it was submitted to him. That was to assure the various agencies that the DCI could not ride roughshod over their interests. Still, the NSC committee could only comment to the President on the budget, not change it.

My first task was to establish an orderly, fair process for arriving at the budget. I asked John Koehler to leave the Congressional Budget Office and take the helm of the Community staff for that purpose. (John McMahon had left that job to become head of the espionage branch of the CIA.) He established a clear, systematic approach so that everyone knew when decisions were to be made and on what basis. He and his staff took the budget priorities submitted by the different agencies and wove them into a composite budget.

It was much easier to get the Community to accept this budget system than it was to have them agree to Apex, mainly because it did not cut so deeply into the authorities of the agencies. When the NSA, the DIA, the overhead reconnaissance offices, and the military service intelligence agencies formulated their own budgets, they did so within the Defense Department's overall budget. That meant they had to compete with tanks, ships, and aircraft for their slice of the pie. Intelligence often came out second best in competition with these more powerful interests. With the DCI in charge of their budget, they knew that, although they still had to get the approval of the Secretary of Defense for what they submitted to me, they could count on my support. If they didn't get enough money, I would be aware of how the shortfall in their budget might hurt the Community's capabilities and would argue for them with their secretary. In short, though they lost some budgetary authority to the DCI, they gained the support of someone who was more sympathetic to their needs than were their military superiors.

The Congress was also a help in consolidating the DCI's hold on the budget. I established the practice of being the first person to testify on the intelligence budget. I laid out the strategy behind it and showed how the allocations to the various agencies fitted into that strategy. When the agencies' directors testified after me, they might well argue that I had given too low a priority to some of their pet projects. But they knew they were at a disadvantage. I would have made my argument first and with the authority of looking after the good of the entire Community, not just one agency. Hence, they were eager to cooperate in Koehler's construction of the budget so as to resolve issues before they reached Congress.

Finally, committees traditionally produce unsatisfactory compromises. The old intelligence budget committee was no exception, and everyone realized that. It was especially difficult with the committee to establish priorities that took into account preparing for the future. As I've noted, it is hard to get senior officials who are fully consumed with today's problems to concentrate on long-range issues. The budget process is an excellent vehicle for forcing attention on the future. The same people who battled over code words saw that it made sense to give up a little turf here and have a single budgetary authority that could work up a meaningful long-range plan.

The real proof of the pudding came after the Reagan administration took over. Their intelligence transition team arrived in late 1980 with an agenda that included dismantling the DCI's budgetary authority. The Community leaders would have none of it. The system of having the DCI in charge has held. In sum, the Community can rise above partisan interests when the benefits appear great enough.

President Carter also supported expansion of the DCI's authority over the tasking of the collection agencies. My experience in the yam patch case had convinced me that I needed a better way to coordinate the total collection effort of the Community. Two things had gone wrong in that instance. The primary one was that the Intelligence Community staff's three committees to direct collection efforts, one each for photos, electronic intercepts, and espionage, lacked authority. The committee members came from the various collection agencies and tended to protect their parent agencies' interests. Since the committees operated by consensus, any agency representative could frustrate actions he opposed. It was easier to do nothing than to do something. The second problem was that, though the committees attempted to manage the collection effort within their individual collection techniques, there was no system for choosing between them. Someone needed to consider whether to use photos or electronic intercepts in a given situation, for instance, or whether to use both in ways to complement each other rather than overlap. What I had found in the yam patch incident was that there was a good deal of enthusiasm and competition but not much teamwork. We expended much more effort and money than was necessary because we had not coordinated our actions. The results showed it.

The President approved a National Intelligence Tasking Center. The NITC took all the committees and placed them under one man with a small staff. I selected Lieutenant General Frank Camm, U.S. Army (Retired), to head up the NITC. He was my one point of contact with the entire collection effort. With his staff he could make the tradeoffs between collection systems and coordinate the work of the committees. Whenever a new collection requirement came up, I simply called Frank in and asked him to get the most appropriate mix of capabilities.

Unfortunately, resistance to the NITC mounted almost immediately. It was not to be just a committee that operated by consensus, but an organization authorized to command the collection process. That raised the prospect of the DCI's having both the authority to task the collection systems and the mechanism to do so effectively. The old committee could be manipulated or at least thwarted, but perhaps that would not be the case with the NITC. This raised several concerns in military minds.

One was that the military wanted their own systems for collecting tactical intelligence on and around the battlefield. Although these are not under the control of the DCI, there are some fine lines drawn between what is considered battlefield intelligence and what is national intelligence. The more control the military can retain over national collection systems, the more certain they are that their tactical needs will be met.

Another problem was that more and more military intelligence was being collected by large, expensive technical systems. These are termed "national" collection systems because they serve broad national purposes, answering directly the President's needs, not collecting just military or economic or political intelligence that responded to a department's needs. The technical systems themselves were too costly to permit the military, the State Department, the Treasury, and others each to have its own. The only person in a position to allot the use of these systems among the different users was the DCI, but the military were unable to accept that necessity. It made military commanders nervous not to have all the intelligence systems they might need in battle dedicated wholly to their use. They were not equipped psychologically or organizationally to work through a DCI or his NITC to get the intelligence they might require in time of war. Hence, they instinctively resisted any expansion of the DCI's control over such agencies as the NSA or the photoreconnaissance organizations.

The national interest is never exclusively the military's interest, however. The most vital decisions of war are political decisions made by civilian leadership. The military must want those decisions to be as sound as possible; witness the quagmire of Vietnam when they were not. Military intelligence, which so heavily influenced the political decisions on Vietnam, was generally less objective than the CIA. It is in the military's own interest, as well as the nation's, that the final control over the collection of war intelligence from national technical systems be in the hands of someone free of military pressures or biases. And, in the end, the military can always ask the Secretary of Defense to appeal to the President if they feel they are being neglected.

The military's stubborn opposition to the NITC prevailed as soon as the Reagan administration came into office. The NITC was disbanded and its people moved back into the Intelligence Community staff, whence they had come. But all was not lost. The Community had grown accustomed to checking all the collection systems that might gather data in a crisis, and, at the same time, to ensuring that none of them was used more than necessary. At the time of the Soviet combat brigade incident, procedures were in place so that the first clue from one system was passed down the line to other systems, which developed it further. For the Reagan administration not to grasp the importance of keeping the tasking function separate, and not to emphasize its command rather than committee function, was a loss. What counts most is that the procedures function infinitely better than before the NITC experiment. Community partisanship has impeded but not reversed the move we made toward centralizing control of collection.

Having enhanced the DCI's authority over code words, budgets, and tasking, Jimmy Carter walked away from a fourth request I made. Early in my tenure he had twice urged me to be bold in recommending organizational changes to improve intelligence, and I had boldly requested full management and operating authority over all of the agencies operated by the Defense Department for collecting national intelligence, most specifically the NSA. This he would not grant. Other Presidents had also shied away from cutting into the NSA's independence. The reason is simply that Presidents want to have multiple sources of information, and the NSA is a particularly intriguing one. They and their staffs realize that it is easy to become isolated in the White House, knowing only what the various agencies and departments tell them.

Back in the Kennedy days there developed the practice of having almost any agency of the Intelligence Community send reports directly to the White House. It was then that a "Situation Room" was established in the White House basement. The Sit Room is a ready source of operational information about current foreign affairs, including up-to-date intelligence reports fed in directly by almost all the intelligence agencies. The arrangement makes a lot of sense, because the President and his staff need a rapid flow of information during periods of crisis. It has, however, gone too far. The most routine intelligence reporting makes its way into the White House Sit Room through direct pipelines from the collecting agencies. It gets misused. The White House staff become fascinated by raw intelligence. A photo of tanks moving into battle or an intercept of a military commander's signal to commence the attack is immediate and exciting. Such tangible intelligence gives the President the sense of truly being Commander-in-Chief. And, even though staff people often take reports out of context, they want to interpret important reports themselves rather than wait for the analysis of the intelligence experts. Despite these hazards, the practice is too well established to be changed. So Presidents will not let the DCI control the flow of raw intelligence to the degree that he should.

There is an even more fundamental reason why Presidents have resisted giving the DCI complete control over the collection agencies. They do not want any one person to have full control over the way in which special information derived from secret intelligence sources is employed. Only a radical fringe in our country really worries that our intelligence agencies may become another Gestapo, but the record of the CIA, the NSA, and Army intelligence in poking into American lives in the 1950s and 1960s cannot be ignored. If some DCI did abuse the combined powers of those agencies, it could cause untold damage to our citizens — and to our intelligence.

Jimmy Carter had a further reason to exercise control: he was the first President to feel the full impact of having the Congress look over his shoulder in intelligence matters. Whatever expectations his predecessors had had that intelligence errors or abuses might never see the light of day was greatly reduced by the advent of congressional oversight. Presidents now have to be ready to defend what intelligence is doing. Ronald Reagan, for instance, was placed on the defensive in a nationally televised campaign debate in October 1984 because of the error of the CIA in endorsing the manual for Nicaraguan guerrillas that appeared to advocate assassination. This sense of responsibility inclines Presidents to strengthen the DCI sufficiently to be sure that the intelligence agencies are kept on a straight course.

The day-to-day operation of the new technical collection systems also requires more central control. And the fact that American intelligence has shifted away from its post–World War II preoccupation with military matters and pays more attention to political and economic developments means that there is a need for a DCI with central authority to set the balance between military, political, and economic requirements.

These contrary pressures which many Presidents have felt between centralized control over intelligence and independence of the individual agencies is not unexpected. The tension between centralization and decentralization was intentionally built into the structure of U.S. intelligence. It was described in 1975, by a commission appointed by President Ford to review the organization of U.S. intelligence, as "a 'mixed' system, an attempt to combine the best features of decentralization and centralization while avoiding the obvious weaknesses of each."[1] The commission's report went on to point out that "the establishment of 'mixed' systems has given rise to difficulties over the years." How much difficulty or tension there needs to be in our system will vary with the state of oversight. The better the oversight process, the less concern there need be about concentrating too much authority in the hands of the DCI. Still, no matter how confident we are that DCIs will be restrained from abusing the privilege of secrecy, it is unlikely that we will ever want the tensions to be eliminated, that is, to centralize too far. To decide how far we can go, it is important that we understand that the benefits of centralization vary markedly between the two key functions of intelligence, collecting information and analyzing it.

In collection there is far greater need for centralized control than in analysis. That's because good teamwork is essential to operational effectiveness and also because that's where a great deal of money is spent. Careful planning is necessary. The major outstanding issue in the control of collection is the responsiveness of the NSA and the CIA's espionage branch to the DCI. Control over espionage is largely a matter of how firmly the DCI is in control of the CIA. Control over the NSA depends on the definition of those circumstances under which the NSA responds to the DCI and those under which it takes direction from the Secretary of Defense. Presidents Carter and Reagan have clearly defined tasking of the NSA as the province of the DCI. When it comes to the next step, disseminating what is collected as a result of the tasking, there is ambiguity. The authors of the National Security Act of 1947 empowered the DCI to control the dissemination of

1. Report of the Murphy Commission, 1975.

all information collected by all collection agencies. The authors did not want another Pearl Harbor, the result of compartmentation of information about the Japanese plans. But they hedged their bet. They created a tension by stipulating that departmental intelligence agencies would have the right to disseminate "departmental" intelligence. They intended that the departmental organizations, like the NSA, would be free to work on matters of departmental concern and to share their conclusions within their departments. It was not intended that such agencies send their analyses to the White House or anywhere else outside their departments.

What's needed is clarification: Is the dissemination by the collection agencies to be controlled by the DCI or the Secretary of Defense? The presidential Executive Orders empower the Secretary of Defense to "manage" the NSA and other units of Defense that collect intelligence, and the DCI to "task" the same organizations and to formulate their budgets. "Managing" is undefined. Hence, whether controlling dissemination of raw intelligence fits under "tasking" or "managing" is unclear. More often than not, the NSA acts independently; it can usually play off one of its two masters against the other. This kind of tension is not, of course, desirable, and it should be eliminated.

The President should define the DCI's authority so that it includes control over dissemination. The military would probably object to the DCI's having that much control, lest the NSA turn away from its major concentration on military intelligence. They fear that someday the NSA might even have a civilian as director, rather than the admirals or generals it has always had. Because of the necessarily close connection between the NSA and the military's tactical electronic surveillance operations, it would, I believe, be well to stipulate that the director of the NSA always be a military officer. There is, I am aware, a disadvantage. The generals and admirals all look to the Secretary of Defense for their promotions and future assignments, and hence give him far more loyalty than they give the DCI. I would therefore make the selection and tenure of the generals and admirals as Directors of the NSA subject to the concurrence of the DCI, thus helping to ensure their responsiveness to him. A President could set such a rule in an Executive Order on Intelligence.

In analysis we want to encourage competition, freedom to

express iconoclastic views, and independence from the influence of policy. Thus, control over analysis should not be centralized to the extent that a DCI can say what the analytic agencies are to work on or what results they should get. That might lead to the neglect of important departmental concerns or promising but little-noticed lines of exploration. At the same time, there is a need to see that the total analytic effort is utilized efficiently; that is, that some topics are not overlooked and others overdone. One way to reconcile these conflicting needs would be to strengthen the DCI's own analytic organization, the National Intelligence Officers. The number of NIOs should be increased from the twenty-five to thirty people I had to perhaps two hundred. Such a group could then do substantive analytic work to fill gaps left by the agencies. By setting an example, it could prod the analytic agencies into producing work of higher quality. It could make certain that the needs of policy-makers are met by the Community as a whole. This group should be located in downtown Washington so that it is no longer considered an appendage of the CIA and so that the analysts have easier access to the policy-makers whom they attempt to serve.

An enlarged analytic arm could also help to clarify the role of the DCI. At present he has two full-sized jobs: managing the CIA and coordinating the Community. The Community looks on him as a captive of the CIA, biased in its favor. The CIA resents the time he spends on Community affairs and any decisions he makes in his Community role that are not of the CIA's choosing.

Students of American intelligence have examined the idea of separating the two jobs. Until recently, authority over intelligence was not sufficiently centralized to make that practical. The DCI cannot be in the position of wondering whether the various agencies are giving him full information about what is being collected and analyzed. He must know that his authority over the agencies in this area is established and recognized. He also must have an adequate, capable staff, loyal to him. Thus far, his Community staff has not been adequate, and he has had to rely on his CIA staff for much of his preparatory work and for keeping him informed of what takes place throughout the Community. With President Carter's strengthening of the DCI's role and the exercise of the added responsibilities over some years now (even though

DCI Casey has not played as strong a Community role as he could have done), we are approaching the possibility that the DCI can stand on his own as Community leader. An enlarged analytic staff might be just what it takes to keep him abreast of what's going on in the entire Community. It might also give him the ability to produce intelligence reports on his own, if necessary.

There is no question that the two jobs, head of the CIA and Community leader, should be separated, but that can be done only when a DCI feels that his authority as the Community leader has been recognized to an extent that permits him to function independently.

TWENTY-THREE

Agenda for Action

IT WOULD BE EASY for the United States Intelligence Community to become complacent. We have the best intelligence capability in the world and have ample justification for believing so. In comparison with the Soviet Union, the only other nation that has an intelligence capability with global reach, we are about equal in human espionage. They have many more case officers than we do, but their operations are rigid and in many respects represent a shotgun approach to spying that wastes a great deal of effort. Our human effort, on the other hand, is carried out with far fewer people, so we are compelled to be innovative and very precise in our targeting. The advantages of one approach nearly cancel out those of the other, so my assessment is that in human intelligence we and the Soviets have reached something of a draw.

In technical collection, by any measure we are well ahead. If this were not the case, would the Soviets expend so much energy all over the world attempting to steal our technology?

In the interpretation of intelligence data, a society that not only permits but encourages the vigorous exchange of ideas, and does not believe that wisdom necessarily comes from the top, will always have a healthy edge on a society where ideas that do not confirm state wisdom are regarded as treasonous.

We are also fortunate in having allies. The British, French, Israelis, and others have impressive areas of expertise. But as technology moves ahead at an undreamed-of pace, the demands for skilled manpower, extremely expensive new technical equipment, and a commitment to a robust research and development program are outstripping the resources of every country but the United States and the Soviet Union.

There is another aspect to the picture that should remind us that there is plenty for us to do to stay ahead of the Soviet Union. In two areas the Soviets will always have the advantage over us: counterintelligence and protection of state secrets. Their advantage comes not from special capabilities, but from the very nature of their society. The Soviets believe that nothing — like constitutional protection of citizens' rights to privacy — must interfere with the security of the state. Nor should moral or legal constraints inhibit the ferreting out of potential spies. Actual spying, and even the casual leaking of government information such as is tolerated in our country, are capital offenses in the Soviet Union. We clearly do not want to change our societal standards to theirs, but we must recognize that they have this advantage.

In addition to adapting our techniques to stay ahead of the Soviets, we must also adapt to shifts in emphasis on the elements important to our national interests. Today, for instance, the changing nature of worldwide economic competition demands new kinds of economic intelligence; and entirely new problem areas are constantly emerging, like nuclear proliferation and terrorism. My agenda for action is designed to keep us ahead of the Soviets and on top of our own changing needs.

Agenda Action #1. Convince the Intelligence Community that good oversight is essential to effective intelligence.
Although many intelligence "old boys" still view oversight as a ball and chain, the record since World War II proves the opposite. It was the almost total lack of any checks on secret activities in the 1950s and 1960s that resulted in questionable practices, abuses, and dismal failures. The admirable record of first-rate intelligence work that served the country so well from 1945 to 1975 was almost obliterated by a very small number of harebrained enterprises that were eventually brought to light in the 1970s. Because

they did not have to account for their actions, the CIA's espionage experts had to exercise perfect judgment. But, as could be expected, they could not do so, and the result was that all intelligence professionals were subjected to criticism. Moreover, as part of the overreaction, the CIA was directed to cease many of its most useful covert, counterintelligence, and espionage activities, along with the questionable ones, which by that time had been stopped anyway. Caution became the watchword in the CIA. Risks were avoided. Human intelligence activities were few and by 1976 were moving at a very slow pace.

To avoid any repetition of these calamities, President Ford initiated, and President Carter put into practice, a system of White House and congressional oversight. In the period of one administration, through a carefully thought-out and executed strategy of increased but limited openness of intelligence activity to the public and almost complete openness to the Congress, public confidence was largely restored. Unfortunately, over the past four years, the residual skepticism of a segment of the public about the CIA has since been heightened by the Reagan administration's patent disdain for oversight. By the end of President Reagan's first term, the CIA was again being pilloried by the press, largely for covert actions in Nicaragua. The *Washington Post* commented in late 1984, "Controversy surrounding the management of the covert war [in Nicaragua] has brought a renewed sense of vulnerability within the agency after a period of relative calm in which many there felt the CIA had won a hard-fought battle to gain an apolitical and professional image."[1] In addition, the carefully nurtured bipartisan approach to congressional oversight has been shattered. Representative Norman Mineta (D-California) said, "The CIA was rebuilding itself as a credible intelligence-gathering group. But what I see Casey doing is turning it into a paramilitary agency to implement policies."[2]

It is time to acknowledge that secret intelligence faltered badly without some form of accountability. If we want to have good intelligence over the long run, our only option is to make oversight work. The congressional committees on intelligence are in the best position to oversee, responsibly and adequately, what the intelli-

1. Christopher Dickey, *Washington Post,* December 16, 1984, p. A26.
2. Ibid.

gence agencies are doing. Interestingly, almost every major ally is following our early example and moving toward oversight in one form or another.

Agenda Action #2. Improve analysis.
Analysis, especially political analysis, is the Achilles' heel of intelligence. Intelligence analysts have traditionally been seen as secondary to those who run espionage and technical collection operations. There are many small but important ways that the DCI can help to elevate the prestige of analysis and its practitioners.

The DCI can pay personal attention to analysis, value quality more than quantity, and emphasize long-range analyses of trends over short-term news. The Congress, too, can help by providing more funding to train and develop an adequate number of high-quality analysts.

Weakness in analysis is also the fault of the limitations of the four principal analytic agencies. The Defense Intelligence Agency, though it has notable exceptions, has too many mediocre people and is overwhelmed by political pressure to support the Defense Department's programs. The State Department's Bureau of Intelligence and Research does excellent work, but it is so small that its influence is limited to only a few topics. The one analytic organization that belongs to the entire Community, not just to one agency, is the National Intelligence Council; it is also too small. The CIA's analytic branch, in contrast, is so large that it has many of the bureaucratic infirmities that come with size: a tendency to stifle originality, an unwillingness to consider outside criticism, and a proclivity to be more interested in immediate, high-visibility issues than long-range, fundamental ones.

A partial solution would be to increase the size of the National Intelligence Council substantially so that it could do substantive, high-caliber analysis on its own and not merely coordinate the work of others. It could set standards for the rest of the Community and, if it were located in downtown Washington, could react quickly to policy-makers' needs for current intelligence. It could then free the CIA to concentrate more on long-term research, which obviously cannot be postponed until it is needed.

Agenda Action #3. Broaden the analytic effort beyond current events and Soviet military strength.

The larger analytic agencies suffer from inertia. They do not want to shift analysts away from what they've been doing and on to new topics. There is a reasonable fear of losing expertise that has been built up over the years. But unless they can hire enough analysts to handle emerging issues — which they usually cannot do — new issues will end up being covered not very well, if at all. The smaller agencies do not have the resources to undertake new missions. There are at least four areas of growing significance where there was inadequate effort when I left in 1981. The situation is very likely the same today.

a. *What makes the Soviet Union tick?* We do not understand well enough what makes the Soviet Union react the way it does to different kinds of events nor what factors influence change over the mid to long term. Most of our Soviet collection effort is concentrated on discovering what decisions are being made today in the Kremlin, rather than on an understanding of the deeper currents of Soviet society. Just as Russian studies have declined in our universities, so they have in the Intelligence Community. Our struggle with the Soviets is going to be protracted and dangerous, because theirs is a declining society that can compete with us only in military power. We need to understand them much better if we are to win this competition and do so peacefully.

b. *Secondary country analysis.* The Philippines, Pakistan, Indonesia, Nigeria, Saudi Arabia, Argentina, Brazil, Mexico, Morocco, and South Korea are all politically turbulent countries of considerable interest to us. For each of these, the CIA should have a group of analysts, ranging from new to seasoned, who have lived in the country, speak the language, and possess solid academic expertise. People of similar backgrounds are also needed for regional groupings of other third world countries. It will take years to develop this kind of talent. Some will have to come from those presently working on military analyses; the rest from newly hired analysts with these skills.

c. *Economic analysis.* The ability of the United States to compete economically in world markets in peacetime is as vital an element of our national security as having a strong military. Relatively open analyses of economic trends and developments, such as the studies released in 1977–1978 on world energy matters, should be carried out. There is a growing need to discern threatening intentions, subterfuge, and ill will among our competitor nations. We should, then, expand our efforts to collect international economic data, by espionage where necessary.

d. *International threats.* There are a number of issues that threaten our way of life and transcend concerns with single countries or groups of countries. Terrorism, scarcity of food supplies, international traffic in narcotics, and nuclear proliferation are among them. Each presents a challenge for both collectors and analysts. A major effort is needed to develop new collection techniques and more effective analytic methods to provide policymakers with sufficient information to cope with these threats.

Agenda Action #4. Separate the role of DCI from that of head of the CIA.

The two jobs, head of the CIA and head of the Intelligence Community, conflict. One person cannot do justice to both and fulfill the DCI's responsibilities to the President, the Congress, and the public as well. The more the incumbent actively runs the CIA, the more he is seen as the biased head of one of the agencies of the Intelligence Community. He is suspected by the rest of the Community as favoring the CIA on interagency questions, of being biased when arbitrating Community differences. The greater the effort he makes to be seen as unbiased and to act as the leader of the Community, the more he must distance himself from the CIA, the only organization he fully controls and from which he can get exactly what he needs when the chips are down. Without the CIA today, he is powerless. The solution is to have a Director of National Intelligence and a separate Director of the CIA. The former would report to the President and operate out of White House offices. He would have all the authority the DCI presently has over the Intelligence Community and would be the immediate superior of the Director of the CIA.

The limiting factor in separating the two jobs is the time it will take for the DCI's authority over the Community to become strong enough to let him sever his ties with his power base in the CIA. Expanding the National Intelligence Council to give him a substantial analytic staff would help.

With the council physically and organizationally separated from the CIA, its director could become the DCI's deputy for all analytic efforts. He would oversee the DCI's responsibilities for coordinating the analytic efforts of all of the intelligence agencies and would have enough analytic strength at his command to provide the DCI with a good assessment of the quality of work being done by the other, larger analytic organizations.

With a deputy for analysis on one hand, it would be logical for the DCI to re-create a deputy for collection on the other. He would then turn to one individual for advice on all aspects of analysis and another for collection. The division of the DCI's operational responsibilities into these two distinct packages would emphasize the importance of teamwork within both the collection and analytic agencies. It would place responsibility on the two deputies for collection and analysis to ensure that there was clear dialogue between their two groups, because collectors need to know what is expected of them and analysts need to understand roughly the kind and amount of information they can expect to get.

In my opinion the Intelligence Community will not perform anywhere near its capacity until the DCI is its full-time leader and has a strong organization responsible only to him.

Agenda Action #5. Merge the espionage and analytic branches of the CIA.

The division of the CIA into analytic, espionage, and scientific branches is based on the historic evolution of the Agency and administrative convenience rather than on considerations of operational effectiveness. Each branch has its own culture and folklore, its own problems, and its own internal loyalties, which are often stronger than its loyalty to the whole organization. The espionage branch, for instance, must cope with the special problems of people who must remain under cover, who go back and forth overseas, and who depend on each other literally for their lives. The analytic branch's people are for the most part openly employed by the CIA, remain in Washington much of the time, and lead lives not unlike other civil servants.

From the point of view of the end product that the branches jointly produce, though, it would make more sense to merge the collectors and the analysts into units organized by world geographical regions. The logic is obvious. Both the espionage and analytic branches are already subdivided geographically, and merging those subdivisions (and a few operational units of the scientific branch) would bring together people working on the same parts of the world. A combination of the analytic and espionage subunits on Africa, for instance, could be a branch in itself. With a reorganization along these lines, the resulting new branches would have to work together continually. Now they do so primarily by means of ad hoc action teams when crises arise, and such temporary mergings are made only with difficulty. The new arrangement would promote teamwork, efficiency, and far better communication between the collector and the people he is collecting for.

In addition, I believe this is the only way to ensure that the espionage branch becomes a team player and updates its procedures to meet today's and tomorrow's requirements. As long as that branch is independent, it will remain predominant in the CIA and will never play the role it should in supporting the analysts. Merging it with the analysts in a group of geographical branches would make cooperation inevitable.

Some of the new geographical branches would be headed by espionage officers and some by analytic officers. Although there would be immediate objections from the espionage professionals that outsiders cannot make judgments on espionage operations, that simply is not true. It is not that difficult to understand the basics of espionage. There also would be objections on the grounds of security, but there are ample ways to protect the necessary information about agents and espionage techniques. Espionage must be solidly linked with analysis, because it exists only to provide support to the analysts.

Agenda Action #6. Strengthen the DCI's authority over the National Security Agency.
Teamwork in both collection and analysis is impeded today by the NSA's insistence on doing analysis, which is neither its mission nor its forte, and by its penchant for withholding information from the rest of the Community so as to be able to give it directly to the President or the National Security Council. Scooping the

rest of the Community is the game; the NSA plays it well and the overall intelligence effort suffers. The NSA can get away with this in part because there is ambiguity as to whether the DCI or the Secretary of Defense has jurisdiction over these aspects of its work. The President can eliminate that ambiguity by stating in an Executive Order that the DCI has the authority to control the dissemination of the NSA's product and to limit the NSA's analytic efforts to what is necessary for the effectiveness of its collection efforts.

Agenda Action #7. Help the Defense Intelligence Agency improve its analysis.

The DIA's analytic product is well below the caliber of the rest of the Intelligence Community's. Correcting this will be painful and will involve many steps, some small, some large, but all badly needed.

a. The Secretary of Defense should disestablish the four intelligence organizations of the military services. Only when they are gone will the better qualified military and civilian intelligence personnel seek assignments in the DIA. The services should rely on the DIA.

b. The Congress should give the director of the DIA authority to dismiss or retire unproductive civil servants. They clog the DIA's upper echelons today and inhibit the prospects for bright young analysts, who too often leave for greener pastures.

c. The Secretary of Defense should launch a program of exchanges of analysts between the DIA and the other analytic organizations to stimulate the DIA's analysts and enlarge their horizons.

Agenda Action #8. Take more effective precautions against leaks of intelligence information.

The increase of classified information within the entire government has diminished respect for it and encouraged carelessness in handling it. Steps to correct the situation will be difficult, but they must be taken.

a. The two intelligence committees of the Congress should be fused into one Joint Intelligence Committee, with limitations on the size of its staff.

b. A new, simplified, and understandable system of code words should be created to protect highly sensitive materials. The system created under President Carter, stonewalled by segments of the Intelligence Community, and rejected by President Reagan, is but one approach to the problem. Resistance to change will recur, but the security of the nation demands that something be done soon.

c. The open publication of all materials that can be declassified should be encouraged. This would reduce what really must be kept secret.

d. The President must take seriously the need to discipline senior members of his administration who are guilty of indiscreet handling of secrets, especially within the White House. An example or two at that level would do wonders.

e. Many more scrambler telephones should be installed, and officials with high security clearances should be required to use them as a matter of course, almost regardless of the topic of conversation.

f. Provision should be made for random, surprise use of the polygraph for those holding code word clearance. To avoid abuse, congressional monitoring must be a concomitant.

Agenda Action #9. Enact a charter for the Intelligence Community.
The principal legislation governing the organization and responsibilities of the Intelligence Community is thirty-five years old. It is hopelessly inadequate for today's needs and does not reflect the procedures and organizational arrangements actually in effect. For instance, it does not even mention covert action; it assigns to the CIA functions that are actually performed today by the DCI in his Community capacity; and there is little guidance for intelligence professionals on what they are expected to do or prohibited from doing.

During the Carter years, efforts to secure congressional approval of a charter were stymied by extremists on both sides. Some, who were little interested in what intelligence should accomplish, concentrated on tying down the CIA securely with such a list of prohibitions that the Agency would have ended up being ineffective. Others, who wanted the best intelligence possible, insisted that the Saltonstall approach — having Congress know as little as possible — was the right one. Today the former group has had ample opportunity to see that oversight works, even if not perfectly, and that detailed controls are not needed. The other group has seen, especially in the recent experience with covert action in Nicaragua, that some oversight is needed. A more balanced view of intelligence is emerging, one that should make possible a consensus on a new charter.

Agenda Action #10. Reduce the emphasis on covert action.
Covert action should be brought back from the Reagan administration's excesses to the limits prescribed by law. The congressional committees must agree on the meaning of "important to the national security" and insist on adherence to that provision of law. They should also outline in the new charter the limits of what can be done in the name of covert action. In addition, everyone involved should be required to read the history of covert action to be reminded of how little it can actually accomplish on its own.

Agenda Action #11. Depoliticize the role of the DCI.
DCIs George Bush and William Casey and nominee Ted Sorensen were bad choices, not because they lacked competence but because they were too close to partisan politics. Most successful DCIs were not political: civilians like James Schlesinger; military officers like General Walter Bedell Smith; and professional intelligence officers like Allen Dulles and William Colby. In recognition that the President is best served by a DCI who is politically neutral, there have been suggestions recently that only a professional military or civilian intelligence officer be the DCI. But that would be unwise. The President's freedom to select an adviser with whom he has good rapport and in whom he has confidence should not be restricted. It would also be unwise to limit the post of DCI to an intelligence professional, because the CIA and the rest of the Intelligence Community are extremely resistant to change. There are times in the life of almost every bureaucracy when change is important, and frequently it can be brought about only by an outsider. Insiders are often either too close to the problems or too circumscribed by their affiliations within the organization.

With the accomplishment of these agenda items, plus the adoption of a few other suggestions for improvement mentioned throughout this book, American intelligence should be more than capable of supporting our national interests well into the future. Promoting the national interest has, quite understandably and properly, long been considered the sole reason for having a strong intelligence arm. But perhaps the time has come to consider whether the American intelligence establishment should not also support even broader interests, in the belief that they too are in our national interest.

Since World War II, for instance, the United States has increasingly accepted new international responsibilities. This began with our efforts in the founding of the United Nations and our willingness to provide the largest share of funding for its activities. It has grown well beyond the United Nations, though, in recent years, and as it has we have often turned to the Intelligence Community for help. For over ten years following the 1967 Arab-Israeli war, we provided special intelligence services to Egypt and Israel in the form of aerial photographs taken monthly of the Sinai. These reports on the location and numbers of military forces in that area gave assurance to both sides that the provisions of their cease-fire agreement were being followed. We have led the free world's financial institutions in trying to find solutions to the growing problem of third world debt. To act as the world's banker and to do it well takes good economic intelligence. Today we are fighting worldwide terrorism and drug-trafficking through exchanges of intelligence and other cooperative measures.

To what extent should we utilize our national intelligence capabilities in support of such broader responsibilities? Interestingly, it was President Eisenhower who proposed a plan to reduce the probability of war between the United States and the Soviet Union based on an exchange of intelligence data. In 1955 at a Four Power conference he suggested that we and the Soviets agree to an Open Skies plan. It called for an exchange of blueprints of the military establishments of the two countries and the right of aerial inspection of their respective territories. As a former military man, Eisenhower knew how often the miscalculations of a potential enemy's military strength and intentions had influenced nations' decisions to go to war. His Open Skies plan at least would have reduced that possibility with respect to the United States and the Soviet Union. The Open Skies idea was not even considered seriously by the Russians back then, but a seed was planted.

In 1978 France expanded on Eisenhower's concept by proposing that the United Nations establish an international satellite agency. France at the time did not have her own photographic satellites; she was using information from our LandSat satellites, operated by the Commerce Department to acquire economic data. It was obvious to the French that such data from satellites, even those as elementary as LandSat, could provide invaluable help in solving a variety of economic problems all around the world. France's idea was that the United States or the Soviet Union would give the United Nations the necessary satellites, and the UN would operate them and provide the world with the gathered information.

We and the Russians both rejected this updated version of Eisenhower's Open Skies plan. I agreed with our decision, but I believe now that it was a mistake. We made that mistake because of an excessive concern about protecting our revolutionary technical collection capabilities. We wanted exclusive control over the data we could gather and France and others could not. Today, though, the French, the Indians, Japanese, and a Western European consortium all have satellite programs in existence or under development. While our capabilities have advanced and will be much better than any of these programs, a lot of our older satellite technology could be shared without risk. Besides, it will not be long before we reach a point where all satellite photography will be so good that the differences between various models of satellites will be insignificant.

Despite ours and the Soviets' rejection, the United Nations conducted a study of the French proposal from 1978 to 1982 and drew up a detailed plan on how to form and operate what was called an International Satellite Management Agency. Although the UN has not been able to proceed with this plan because of U.S. and Soviet objections, pressures to do something like this will be kept up, because the potential benefits are so considerable. The question for us today is whether we will continue to resist sharing those benefits with the rest of the world or whether we will promote such use of satellites. The two principal areas of benefit would be in reducing the risk of unnecessary and unwanted wars and in helping to improve the standard of living and quality of life in the many less fortunate nations of the world.

The danger of unwanted wars brought on by misunderstanding and miscalculation could be mitigated by:

a. Providing international notification of any sizable buildup of conventional military power in position for attack. The knowledge that achieving surprise, and thus a decisive first blow, was out of the question might alone deter some aggressors.

b. Detecting and publicizing border violations. Ambiguous border situations could be mapped and adjudicated.

c. Monitoring cease-fire agreements, peace-keeping arrangements, demilitarized zones, and confidence-building measures. Violations, such as the movement of more forces into an area than agreed on, might be resolved peaceably if they were disclosed early.

d. Focusing the type of systems we now have to warn of a nuclear attack by the Soviet Union on all nuclear powers or suspected nuclear powers. If, then, there were a nuclear explosion anywhere in the world, we should be able to identify the source almost instantly and inform all interested parties. While the damage might already have been done, there is the chance that identifying the country that did it could avoid an escalation brought about in the confusion of the moment, perhaps resulting in retaliation against the wrong party.

e. Disclosing the efforts by nonnuclear nations to develop nuclear weapons. Such disclosures could permit international pressure to be brought to bear on them at an early stage in weapons development. This might cause them to stop or at least slow down, and it might discourage others from cooperating with them. It also might bring about more vigorous action by the world community to discourage proliferation in general.

We could assist in improving the global standard of living and quality of life by:

f. Forecasting the world's food supply on a continuous basis. Food surpluses and shortages could be better managed on a world scale. Famines could be anticipated so that effective actions could be taken well before any nation's population found itself facing starvation.

g. Helping to increase food production by measuring soil moisture, identifying land resources and the acreage under cultivation, locating fish shoals and other resources of the sea, and inventorying reserves of water in snow layers to warn of floods or conserve water resources.

h. Identifying areas where drug-producing crops are being grown. Although there would be no guarantee of eradication by national authorities, publicity might cause the governments to act against the growers.

i. Helping out when natural disasters like earthquakes, forest fires, tidal waves, or typhoons strike. Photoreconnaissance could aid rescuers in concentrating their resources more efficiently.

We have the capability to supply the information needed in all of these categories by deploying satellite-based reconnaissance systems, which, along with other intelligence techniques, will permit us to detect any substantial activity anywhere on the globe with reasonable regularity. While those systems are presently designed to support only our national requirements and would be overtaxed by added requirements, their capacity could easily be expanded sufficiently to provide this kind of support to the world without impinging on our national interests. National requirements would always come first, but that need not prevent our helping others.

There would, of course, be objections to our doing this, both at home and abroad. The most serious would focus on the potential risk to the necessary secrecy of our intelligence. We could not afford to reveal so much about any advanced technical collection system that the Soviets and others might be able to take defensive actions. We also would be reluctant to release information that, because we alone hold it, gives us an important advantage. There are ways, however, to circumvent these problems.

The place to start would be the creation of a separate intelligence agency that would be our liaison with other nations. I will call it the Open Skies Agency. Although only the OSA would release information to the world at large, we could control what information the OSA received if it was necessary to protect a certain technical collection system. We might, for instance, give the OSA access only to intelligence collected by systems so old that they were no longer a mystery to the Soviets. If there were instances where it was necessary to use a more modern system, we could limit the data that the OSA received from it to no more than an equivalent Soviet system could provide. The OSA would not employ some of the more sophisticated techniques our analysts have developed for interpreting photos and other intelligence data. What the OSA would have to rely on primarily would be data not requiring extensive interpretation and data from collection systems that are well known to the Soviets. This would limit any possible loss of secrecy about our collection systems themselves but would still provide most other nations with much useful information.

With one limitation, we could also keep to a minimum any losses of information that might benefit us solely because we held it exclusively. That limitation is that for an OSA to be credible, we would have to agree that it would release certain types of information on a regular basis, regardless of whose actions it revealed. That is, we would want to reassure other nations that they could count on receiving such information as warnings of impending military attacks and predictions of harvests. If we were selective about which wars we predicted or whose harvests we forecast, the OSA would quickly be viewed as a political tool of the United States. All of its reporting then would be suspect.

Thus, the OSA's operations could place us in a position of disclosing something we would prefer to keep secret. If we detected one of our allies preparing to attack its neighbor, we might want to remain silent. If we calculated that there was going to be a large surplus of grain in the world in a given year, we might prefer to withhold that information until our farmers had sold as much of their crop on the world market as possible. These would certainly be losses that we would have to accept in order to make an OSA workable. I believe they are not really very great losses, however, compared with the loss of secrecy to the world's troublemakers and the potential benefits to enormous numbers of people who are just barely surviving today.

Obviously, many governments and some individuals would not want to have certain of their activities revealed. From a larger, more humanitarian point of view, though, it must be viewed as an advantage, not a disadvantage, to open all the skies for the good of mankind.

I think it could be expected that the nations objecting most strenuously to an OSA would be the communist and totalitarian ones. Concealing much of what their governments do, even from their own people, is a dogma to many of them. Some nations, like the Soviet Union, are also paranoid about others prying into their homelands; witness the Soviets' tragic overreaction to the Korean Air Lines flight 007 in September 1983. If we proceeded with an OSA, the Soviets might even retaliate by releasing information on the United States that they thought would embarrass us before the world, such as photos of demonstrations or riots or of military activities they might claim were threatening. In fact, because we are so open already, there is not much chance for embarrassing us. As far as true secrets are concerned, such as the configuration of U.S. military systems, if the Soviets can discern them, it seldom would make much difference to us whether they disclosed them to the rest of the world. Only, perhaps, if they discovered our preparations for a surprise military action, like that in Grenada in October 1983, would we be at a disadvantage. But there is little reason to think that the Russians would not make such a disclosure even today.

Civil libertarians at home and abroad might also object to the potential of an OSA to invade individual privacy, even inadvertently. There is no way to gainsay such a possibility, but there are many other more egregious means of intrusion today, which we all must live with, and do. There might also be legitimate objections that the information an OSA would disclose could be abused. One commercial enterprise might use OSA data to spy on another, or one country might use the information to uncover another's military weakness and take advantage of it. These are distinct possibilities. Although precautions can be taken against them, they are a price that will have to be weighed against the benefits in considering whether or not to proceed in this direction.

In fact I believe the benefits are so attractive that some move in this direction is inevitable. Since 1972 our Department of Commerce has been selling pictures from its civilian LandSat satellites to any nation or citizen that wants them. Some eleven countries have already built stations to receive LandSat signals directly from our satellites. In 1981, the Commerce Department filled 173,357 requests for $100 worth or more of LandSat data from individuals or government agencies in eighty-nine countries. While LandSat does not reveal anything like the detail that military satellites do, it is still useful for agriculture, cartography, geology, hydrology, and oceanography and can identify such things as roads, railway tracks, airports, and depots. The world is moving inexorably into an era of openness. We have the choice of being pushed into this new era or of leading the rest of the world into it.

Not only is it inherently the right thing to do because of the benefits to mankind, but it fits perfectly with our strengths in the basic struggle between our free way of life and the Soviets' closed society. The strongest weapon we have to offset Soviet aggressiveness is our vibrant ideology. A major part of our advantage is the openness of our government to its citizens. If we truly believe in the principles by which our country has stood and prospered all these years, we should have the courage to lead the world into an era in which international peace and prosperity are fostered by international openness. The magnificent capabilities of American intelligence can be employed as an important offensive weapon in our struggle for peace and security. We must, though, be willing to move with the boldness and vision that befits our heritage.

Our intelligence capabilities are suited to this special role on behalf of our own security and the welfare of all mankind, because we have reconciled the necessary secrecy of intelligence to the democratic processes on which our government is founded. In bringing secret intelligence under democratic control, we have opened vast new opportunities to demonstrate the superiority of our democratic system through the employment of our intelligence capabilities to serve not only our nation, but the rest of the world and all mankind.

Appendix: A Word on Censorship

All CIA employees agree to submit whatever they write after leaving the CIA to that agency for review as to whether it includes any classified material. I fully support the requirements for such review. In fact, it was I who urged Attorney General Griffin Bell in 1978 to prosecute an ex-CIA employee, Frank Snepp. Snepp, after promising me that he would fulfill his contractual obligation to submit a book he was writing for security review, proceeded to publish it surreptitiously. The government won its case against Snepp for violating his contract. My problem was just the opposite, I scrupulously submitted every draft before it left my control. What I object to is the way the present administration conducts its reviews. There are two problems: timeliness and arbitrariness.

The delay in the CIA's handling of my book was not, in my opinion, the fault of the actual reviewers. Paul Schilling, Chuck Wilson, and Marlene Bozan, with whom I dealt, could not have been more accommodating. The problem was that, as more and more former employees have taken to writing, the CIA has not assigned enough people to the review process. Normally a single chapter would take three weeks for an initial review and three or four more for an adjudication of differences. In one case the clearance and adjudication process lasted more than five months. Since every chapter was processed three or four times, the delays were terribly costly to me.

Arbitrariness stemmed from an administration policy of drawing the line of secrecy on the overcautious side. Though that may seem to be the safest course for the country, it actually endangers secrets by making a mockery of the secret label. Having been responsible for protecting the nation's intelligence secrets for four years, I am well

288 / SECRECY AND DEMOCRACY

aware what the release of some kinds of information could mean to our national security. In the review of my book, more than one hundred deletions were made by the CIA. These ranged from borderline issues to the ridiculous. I appealed many of these questionable deletions to the higher levels of the CIA and obtained only three minor concessions.

The extreme arbitrariness of the review process was vividly illustrated in the last appeal I made. I had given in on most of the deletions demanded by the CIA, but two requests were particularly egregious and unnecessary. Anthony Lapham, on my behalf, sent the CIA a letter stating that unless they either (1) provided me with a convincing reason for their position, or (2) obtained a court injunction against my publishing the information, I would proceed to do so. The CIA, after consulting with the White House and the Department of Justice, chose to do neither. Instead, they replied that I should do whatever I deemed to be "appropriate," but that the CIA reserved "the right to take whatever action it deemed appropriate."

This was the most irresponsible position they could possibly have taken. The supposed "secrets" were clearly of no importance to them, since they left it to my discretion whether or not to publish them. The threat to take me to court after the fact could not have retrieved the secrets. It could only have exacted retribution, if the government won. Clearly the administration knew that a court would not have upheld a petition for an injunction. Their only other recourse was to threaten me.

They resorted to this tactic because they were upset with the book's highly critical view of the Reagan administration's mishandling of our intelligence activities, especially its indifference to any oversight of the CIA. The administration does not believe that anyone should check on whether even simple decisions of the CIA, such as what authors are permitted to say, are fair and in the public interest. Yet our entire constitutional system is built on checks and balances between the Executive, Legislative, and Judicial branches of our government. Anthony Lapham's and my objective in suggesting that the government enjoin publication was to gain the intercession of a third party to arbitrate the dispute, namely the court. The administration's devious response was a deliberate effort to avoid any such check on the arbitrariness of the CIA's decisions. Clearly the Reagan administration does not understand that oversight of intelligence in our society includes constructive criticism from outsiders like me.

The administration's response left me in a difficult position. I wanted neither to release secrets nor to appear to be releasing them, since even the appearance that a responsible former official has defied the security system could encourage less responsible individuals to be cavalier about releasing secret information. Accordingly, I decided not to include the material that the CIA objected to.

I made that decision in February 1985. Just eight months later the CIA sent one of its deputy directors, Evan Hineman, to court to testify in an espionage case. In an effort to gain a conviction against Samuel Loring Morison, the CIA and the National Security Council approved Evan Hineman's breeching the restrictions that had been placed on me. This was a change of policy.

This change involved one of the two points that Anthony Lapham had appealed for me in February. What had been so very secret at that time was now declassified. Setting aside whether that indicated that the original classification was unnecessary, I next found that the CIA could be even more arbitrary than before. I immediately submitted a request for permission to insert into this edition of the book those items which Evan Hineman had disclosed publicly in court. That request was denied pending a review by the National Security Council of the basic policy. In short, although a new policy had been developed for Hineman's public testimony, that policy was not made available to anyone else.

Three months later, as this book went to press, the new policy had still not been resolved. I was, in effect, denied permission to say the same things the CIA was having said in public. The citizens of our country deserve better assurance that their interests are truly being served by the CIA's review process.

As long as there is almost no check on the arbitrariness of the CIA, it is likely that there will be further abuses of the public's right to knowledge about its government. I believe corrective actions are in order. First, the CIA must assign more people to its review staff. Second, the congressional committees on intelligence should play a role in the process. They and the CIA could select a standing panel of arbitrators and give each author the option of selecting one of the arbitrators and of submitting his differences with the CIA to binding arbitration. It would also be useful for the committees to require the

CIA to have an explicit, written explanation of each deletion of material it demands. Periodic sampling of these statements could do much to curb the arbitrariness that has often manifested itself in the review process in the last few years. Finally, Congress should establish the period during which former employees must submit their writings for clearance.

The happy ending is that, although I was greatly inconvenienced, the message of the book has not been vitiated by the CIA. Because it could have been, however, the process of CIA security review needs review itself. Needless to say, the CIA's review does not constitute CIA authentication of any material in the book, nor does it imply CIA endorsement of my views.

Glossary of Acronyms

CIA	Central Intelligence Agency
CJCS	Chairman, Joint Chiefs of Staff
CNO	Chief of Naval Operations
DCI	Director of Central Intelligence
DDCI	Deputy Director of Central Intelligence
DDO	Deputy Director of Operations, CIA (espionage branch)
DIA	Defense Intelligence Agency
FBI	Federal Bureau of Investigation
GCHQ	Government Communications Headquarters (Great Britain)
GRU	Soviet military intelligence
HPSCI	House Permanent Select Committee on Intelligence
IC	Intelligence Community
INR	Bureau of Intelligence and Research (State Department)
JCS	Joint Chiefs of Staff
KGB	Soviet intelligence agency
MI-5	British counterintelligence agency
NATO	North Atlantic Treaty Organization
NITC	National Intelligence Tasking Center

NSA	National Security Agency
NSC	National Security Council
OSA	Open Skies Agency
SCC	Special Coordinating Committee of the National Security Council
SSCI	Senate Select Committee on Intelligence

Index

Aaron, David, 237, 239
academia: as source of information for CIA, 100, 105-8
aerial photography, 94; *see also* photography; satellites
Afghanistan, 87, 92, 130, 230, 232
Africa, 130
Agee, Philip, 62-63
agents: assessment of, 48, 53; clearance of sensitive operations by, 144-46, 148; code names for, 101n; communications with case officers, 49, 52-53; definition of, 48; double, *see* moles; exposure and arrest of, 50-52; identity of, and congressional oversight, 147; need for secrecy, 45-46, 51-52; personal relations with case officers, 216-17; placement of, difficulties in, 207-8; polygraph testing of, 70; recruitment of, 48-49; risk-taking by, 216; Soviet recruitment of American, 66-67; *see also* espionage; espionage branch of CIA; human intelligence
aircraft carrier, 10
Allen, Lt. Gen. Lew, 24

Allende, Salvador, 79-81
Amherst College, 105, 158
analysis, 47, 113-27, 237-51; analysts as managers, 189; British, 34; of Central America, 121-22; centralization of, 265-66; competitive, 237-51; computers, use of, in, 136-37; declassification of information, 114-18; by DIA, need to improve, 276; economic, need for, 272-73, 279; forecasting, 117, 124-25; improvement of, need for, 271-73; independence of interpretation as strength, 121; by INR, 242, 245; of Iran crisis, 114-18, 124, 125, 126; of Korea, 122; "net assessment," 249-50; NIOs, 266; NSA involvement in, 235-36; and policy-making, 121-24, 133-34, 241-51; and presidential briefings, 130; and "processing," 235; publication of declassified information, 117-20; role of DCI in, 266-67; of secondary countries, need for, 272; of Soviet strategic nuclear strength, 248-50; status reports, 117; warnings, 117; *see also* analytic branch of CIA

About the Author

A native of Highland Park, Illinois, Stansfield Turner entered Amherst College in 1941 and was graduated from the United States Naval Academy in 1946. As a Rhodes Scholar he received a Master's Degree in philosophy, politics, and economics from Oxford University in 1950.

Admiral Turner has commanded a mine sweeper, a destroyer, a guided-missile cruiser, a carrier task group, and a fleet; and he has served as President of the Naval War College. His last naval assignment was as Commander in Chief of NATO's Southern Flank. In 1977 President Jimmy Carter selected him to be the Director of Central Intelligence, where he served until January 1981.

Stansfield Turner is currently a lecturer, writer, and TV commentator, and serves on the Board of Directors of several American corporations.